DUST TO DUST

THE GOLDSTEIN-GOREN SERIES IN AMERICAN JEWISH HISTORY

General editor: Hasia R. Diner

We Remember with Reverence and Love: American Jews and the Myth of Silence after the Holocaust, 1945–1962
Hasia R. Diner

Is Diss a System? A Milt Gross Comic Reader
Edited by Ari Y. Kelman

All Together Different: Yiddish Socialists, Garment Workers, and the Labor Roots of Multiculturalism
Daniel Katz

Jews and Booze: Becoming American in the Age of Prohibition
Marni Davis

Jewish Radicals: A Documentary History
Tony Michels

1929: Mapping the Jewish World
Edited by Hasia R. Diner and Gennady Estraikh

An Unusual Relationship: Evangelical Christians and Jews
Yaakov Ariel

Unclean Lips: Obscenity, Jews, and American Culture
Josh Lambert

Hanukkah in America: A History
Dianne Ashton

The Rag Race: How Jews Sewed Their Way to Success in America and the British Empire
Adam Mendelsohn

Hollywood's Spies: Jewish Surveillance of Nazi Groups in Los Angeles, 1933–1941
Laura Rosenzweig

Jewish Radical Feminism: Voices from the Women's Liberation Movement
Joyce Antler

Dust to Dust: A History of Jewish Death and Burial in New York
Allan Amanik

Dust to Dust

A History of Jewish Death and Burial in New York

Allan Amanik

NEW YORK UNIVERSITY PRESS
New York

NEW YORK UNIVERSITY PRESS
New York
www.nyupress.org

References to internet websites (URLs) were accurate at the time of writing. Neither the author nor New York University Press is responsible for URLs that may have expired or changed since the manuscript was prepared.

Library of Congress Cataloging-in-Publication Data

Names: Amanik, Allan, author.
Title: Dust to dust : a history of Jewish death and burial in New York / Allan Amanik.
Description: New York : New York University Press, [2019] | Series: The Goldstein-Goren series in American Jewish history | Includes bibliographical references and index.
Identifiers: LCCN 2019012056 | ISBN 9781479800803 (cl : alk. paper)
Subjects: LCSH: Jewish funeral rites and ceremonies—New York (State)—New York—History. | Jews—New York (State)—New York—Social conditions. | Jews—New York (State)—New York—Death. | Burial—New York (State)—New York—History. | New York (N.Y.)—Social conditions.
Classification: LCC F128.9.J5 A527 2019 | DDC 974.7/004924—dc23
LC record available at https://lccn.loc.gov/2019012056

New York University Press books are printed on acid-free paper, and their binding materials are chosen for strength and durability. We strive to use environmentally responsible suppliers and materials to the greatest extent possible in publishing our books.

Manufactured in the United States of America

10 9 8 7 6 5 4 3 2 1

Also available as an e-book

For my grandparents,
who taught me why history and family matter

CONTENTS

Introduction

Ashes to Ashes, Dust to Deeds

One can only wonder if Joseph Myers (1802–62), who was raised by his grandmother and uncle in Richmond, Virginia, ever visited his father's grave in Lower Manhattan. If Joseph did make that pilgrimage before 1821, he would have found Samson Myers isolated from most of the graveyard's other interments. Any comfort from paying respects to the father he had never known may have battled with the knowledge that his own birth—to a Christian mother and possibly out of wedlock—had led synagogue elders to separate his Jewish father's grave.[1] This assumes, of course, that Myers was aware of his family's recent past and understood the ways that synagogue authority over Jewish cemeteries in early New York could deny access or differentiate the graves of those who did not adhere to Jewish customs as well as their family members. More than a century later, New York synagogues still tied Jewish burial to family and tradition, but having lost much of their power, their tone was markedly different, as they encouraged burial within the congregation. "May you live until one hundred and twenty," a Brooklyn Jewish Center promotion dutifully wished its readers, but a chorus of sobering pragmatism tempered that hope: "And yet—and yet—it is not given to all men and women to remain on this earth for as many years as were granted to Moses. . . . And that is why we, today . . . do not consider it amiss to urge upon each and every member of the Brooklyn Jewish Center the advisability of purchasing, *Now*, family plots in the cemetery acquired by this institution." In 1961, that campaign headlined a guidebook by the United Synagogue of America on cemeteries and fundraising. Its bottom line, "to encourage members to purchase plots before the need arises," contrasted family duty with the consequences of failure to plan for death in advance.[2] That pitch echoed across New York and the nation, as

1

most midcentury synagogues found it an effective strategy to boost their cemetery real estate.

Selling cemeteries through family loyalty and just the right amount of guilt became a common approach to preparing for death among twentieth-century synagogues, but it marked a significant departure from the monopolies that their forebears had enjoyed hundreds of years earlier. From the time Jews first settled in North America until well into the nineteenth century, synagogue elders wielded immense control over local Jewish graveyards. And as with Samson Myers, they commonly leveraged access to Jewish burial in their aim to regulate communal behavior. In matters like dues payment, marriage within the community, warding off conversion, enforcing circumcision, Sabbath observance, or maintenance of Jewish dietary laws, synagogues across the Caribbean, British North America, and even the new republic all threatened to deny burial or to stigmatize the placement of graves in order to promote communal bonds and traditional religious practice.[3] Yet steadily emerging priorities around the emotional and economic security of affiliated households ultimately undercut synagogues' authority. In fact, Jewish end-of-life planning came to focus so centrally on the family by the nineteenth and twentieth centuries that rank-and-file women and men continually gained more influence over Jewish communal institutions and social structures due to the sway they came to hold in the burial enterprise. Despite the legacy of funeral authority among select synagogue elites for most of early American Jewish history, the balance had shifted so starkly by the middle of the twentieth century that synagogues had to resort to marketing strategies like those of the Brooklyn Jewish Center above, evoking anxiety and family obligations just to entice their members to bury among the congregation.

This book traces how family and financial concerns when dealing with death gained equal importance to communal cohesion and other traditional priorities as the city's Jewish funeral industry developed over the centuries. At least three changes overtaking the nation and its approaches to death shaped that evolution. These included the increased reality of death-related poverty in American industrial society (augmented by wage-labor and deficiencies in emerging social welfare), the broader commodification of kin and rituals in America's developing funeral economy, and an emphasis on the family and marriage as the central institutions for social and economic security. All conferred new value to American households in general and afforded them more power in the funeral realm specifically. Additionally, New York and other cities' thriving markets of cemetery real estate and private funeral parlors allowed Jews and others an unprecedented ability to organize collectively through the acquisition of excess commercial cemetery land and the ability to hire funeral professionals rather than depend on communal circles or congregations when death arose. With a new stake in end-of-life provisions and new commercial avenues to free themselves of older communal norms, Jewish women and men gained the capacity and, over time, the sense of consumer entitlement to challenge centuries-old synagogue power structures linked to funerary concerns.

This volume explores those evolving Jewish strategies to plan for death and burial in New York City between the seventeenth and the twentieth centuries. Through a survey of Jewish cemeteries—including their changing governing policies and managing institutions—it charts a remarkable reciprocity among Jewish funerary provisions and the workings of family and communal life. This book describes how and why financial and family concerns about death came to equal (if not almost outpace) long-standing priorities that elevated tradition and communal bonds. At the same time, it shows how emerging emotional and commercial approaches to death and dying afforded average Jewish households the ability—and the prerogative—to advocate for greater funerary protections and material entitlements, such as widows' benefits, individual ownership of cemetery real estate, and other forms of family coverage and funeral insurance, to name just a few. That process inevitably reshaped the contours of communal and domestic social structures among the living. Ultimately, this book argues that planning for the end of life has shaped broader social systems within religion, community, marital patterns, and ideas about family ideals in ways that frequently go unrecognized.

The examination begins in the 1650s, just after Jewish settlers first arrived on Manhattan Island. Among their first official acts, these newcomers requested a separate Jewish graveyard. As the Dutch put it, "They did not wish to bury their dead . . . in the [colony's] common burying ground."[4] By the 1960s, sprawling Jewish cemeteries covered the Brooklyn-Queens border, and the metropolitan area was filled with private parlors selling only the most trusted names in New York Jewish funeral services. Family lots and adjoining spousal graves filled those cemeteries' rows. They had all been purchased in advance and tied to intricate financial mechanisms, like lump-sum death endowments that Jewish burial societies paid to surviving beneficiaries or growing fees for cemetery upkeep and burial privileges. As marriage and nuclear-family norms defined interment rights and endowment claims, the complex financial ties among societies and affiliated households decidedly grew as benefits evolved. The city's Jewish funeral industry developed simultaneously, and professionals marketed directly to loved ones, equating a family's sense of care and satisfaction to respectable services for the dead. Not to be supplanted as they competed for communal loyalty, synagogues and waning benefit societies retooled their funeral provisions to please affiliated members. They geared new coverage and protections in death that could not easily be purchased from a Jewish funeral parlor alone toward the social and economic well-being of households. In the process, however, they helped elevate a sense of consumer entitlement among the wider public they served. All these developments stood as monuments to evolving Jewish deathways in New York over three hundred years, and all paved the way for Jewish families to drive communal change through their newfound control of cemeteries and expectations of funeral entitlements.

Death and burial have always played a central role in New York Jewish communal structures, especially because the majority of Jews have chosen to maintain the tradition to self-segregate in death. Most Jewish New Yorkers have perpetuated in remarkable consistency a longstanding practice to keep to themselves in death due to Jewish laws prohibiting burial among different religious groups or those at variance in their levels of observance, requirements to bury in land owned by other Jews (at minimum physically separating Jewish and non-Jewish cemetery holdings), or simply deep sensitivities to turning over the dead to outsider care.[5] Even nonobservant New York Jews or those far less committed or familiar with the particulars of Jewish law have nonetheless internalized its spirit over time. Death has offered a line they are highly unlikely to cross. In valuing those funerary boundaries, Jews have not differed from most ethnic, racial, and religious groups in America. Unlike some of their counterparts, however, New York Jews have largely chosen for themselves to segregate their burying places and to perpetuate a distinct funeral industry.[6] Rarely, if ever, did external hostilities force the creation of separate sprawling Jewish cemeteries in New York, nor did fear of non-Jewish professionals' refusal to handle their bodies inspire the city's thriving twentieth-century market of private Jewish undertakers. Even in the earliest chapter of New Amsterdam's Jewish history, mutual unwillingness to bury together arose both from Jewish settlers' efforts to establish an alternative to the colony's common burying ground and from Dutch reluctance for Jews to lay down the foundations of a permanent community. Over the coming decades and despite their comfort and prestige, as New York Jewish elites established new burying places, they still took pains to purchase land beyond the city and away from existing churchyards. These Jews, however, did not face official laws or church prescriptions like those forcing enslaved or Christian Africans to be interred in an isolated ground from at least 1712 to 1795. Similarly, no Jew in New York City who converted to Christianity found her or his remains banned from churchyard interment, unlike any black Anglican after 1774.[7] And when early Jews formed close-knit burial societies or commonly expressed a wish in their late eighteenth-century wills—"My body to The Earth to be buried in the Jews Burying Ground according To the Jewish Custom"—they did so not for fear of racial or nativist animosity that might dishonor or desecrate their remains but for respect of their own traditions that called for separate burial in communal soil.[8] A century later in 1888, when the Hebrew Free Burial Society began its work to ensure that the Jewish poor would always receive a proper burial, it was not motivated by worries that the city's general potter's field would exclude their Jewish bodies. On the contrary, the charity believed that all Jews—regardless of their wealth or access to fellowship—deserved the dignity that their traditions invested in timely and nonanonymous burial, with all accompanying rituals performed by Jewish hands and in Jewish land. That the organization has grown into the largest of its kind outside of the State of Israel and laid more than sixty-five thousand Jews to rest speaks to the persistence of that ideal and its value among the wider Jewish public.[9] Likewise, when the secular Workmen's Circle overwhelmingly hired Jewish undertakers and purchased lots in Jewish cemeteries, it quietly honored similar inclinations and plainly acknowledged an inability to disregard entrenched Jewish taboos.[10]

As that drive to separate in death continued throughout the nineteenth century, it fueled the beginnings of New York's thriving Jewish funeral economy. Alongside Protestant peers, midcentury synagogues and early Jewish fraternities engaged in land speculation, buying up old Brooklyn farmland to establish separate rural cemeteries for exclusive Jewish use. In the 1850s, when one of the city's earliest Jewish undertakers began to advertise his services, he noted specifically that Jews prepared all his shrouds and caskets and that even his carriages would "be driven by a Jew."[11] Twentieth-century counterparts bandied similar claims, with one in the 1920s even marketing himself as "the only Jewish undertaker who does not make Christian funerals."[12] From the 1840s to the 1940s, countless Jewish burial and benefit societies filled certificates of incorporation, constitutions, and anniversary journals with aspirations and satisfaction at securing proper Jewish cemetery land. Over long spates of time and at nearly all levels, most Jews in New York City continued to highly value and prioritize separation in death and burial. That impulse not only rendered end-of-life planning and institutions providing Jewish funerals as incredibly important in their own right but also cast them as highly potent arenas to drive communal change or to accept the status quo within and beyond Jewish cemeteries.

Scholars of Jews in America have long addressed the importance of separate burial and the power that came with controlling it. They have also especially focused on the earliest phases of American Jewish development, when small boards of synagogue elites enjoyed hefty social influence over their communities through graveyard monopolies. As sociologist Nathan Glazer and many others have reaffirmed, because "they controlled the cemeteries, and almost all Jews wished to be buried in hallowed ground . . . heads of the Jewish community could in turn make certain demands on Jews. They could insist that their members obey the dietary laws, be married by the 'minister' of the congregation, attend services, and so on. And they actually secured some measure of obedience."[13] Others have afforded equal importance to funeral provisions among American Jews, such as a tendency of local histories to find communal origins in the foundation of a Jewish cemetery.[14]

Consistent importance did not mean static practice, though. Nor did early models of communal sway by controlling the graveyard mean that Jewish burying places and funeral institutions could only serve as sites of top-down authority. Indeed, precisely because most American Jews from the seventeenth century to the twentieth continued to prioritize separate burial and funeral needs, evolving Jewish institutions and strategies to plan for death offered ripe sites for Jewish women and men to challenge communal systems that did not meet their needs. And because funeral provisions remained so central to Jewish communal life, changes in death and the death benefits that synagogues and burial societies built around it inevitably impacted wider social structures. Such transitions played out as the United States underwent massive industrial, urban, and commercial change and as New York developed into one of the largest Jewish centers in the nation and the world.

Those forces alone would have impacted Jewish death practices, but they reshaped them all the more given the state's long delay in taking up social welfare measures and the ways in which popular and market responses excelled at filling in some of the gaps. In the absence of meaningful public aid, Americans favored grassroots communal efforts to guard families from poverty and the shame of a pauper's funeral. Although ritual boundaries that most Jews would not compromise already led them to seek communal support when planning for life's end, external pressures only reinforced their inclination to address death collectively. Jewish New Yorkers not only continued to organize around funerary needs but folded in larger ideals as the nation enshrined the family, male wage-earning, and marriage as pillars of economic stability. Beyond ensuring proper funeral rites at Jewish hands and in Jewish spaces, *hevrot kadisha* (traditional burial societies; singular, *hevra kadisha*) and later Jewish fraternities and *landsmanshaftn* (immigrant mutual aid associations) provided monetary aid to surviving beneficiaries, as the cost of dying and related poverty grew during the nineteenth century. Additionally, as urban sprawl, rising hygienic concerns, and tight apartment spaces made transporting and treating the dead ever more complicated, an eager class of professionals stepped in at the family's service. Jewish undertakers offered dignity to departed loved ones and devised new funerary accoutrements backed by medical and emotional assurances to justify the charges. Each phenomenon only raised the stakes for Jewish households when they planned for death and burial. With communal policies around death directly impacting their personal lives and a crowded field of communal and commercial providers devising new ways to compete for Jewish business and loyalty, an expanding sense of consumer entitlement among local households empowered average Jewish women and men at each stage of the funeral industry's development. They could perpetuate practices and social structures that satisfied them, but they could also reshape those that they felt did not align with monetary needs and consumer desire. In New York City especially, where a wealth of Jewish residents produced an excess of cemeteries, synagogues, and burial societies and developed the core of America's Jewish funeral industry, the wider Jewish public created not only one of the most dynamic Jewish funeral economies in the nation, if not the world, but one poised to exercise outsized influence over the living.

This book charts the ways in which funerary provisions served as an engine of changing communal life, as family, financial security, and consumerism grew in importance in shaping Jewish approaches to death and burial over time. Chapter 1 pits early Jewish New Yorkers' drive to validate family interests against the Jewish elites who placed communal ties over bonds of kin. In addition to regulating dues payment, marriage, or religious observance through threats to deny a member or his dependents a grave, the synagogue also refused families the ability to bury loved ones alongside one another until the nineteenth century. Despite members' increasing protests for that right, synagogue elders felt that rows of chronological graves organized by date of death were a more fitting monument to the long Jewish communal ties and history in New York. The city's sole synagogue in this early period managed its few Jewish burying places for more than a century and through them promoted religious and communal cohesion. Yet families innovated new commercial avenues to protest interment policies that they felt had outlived their use. These efforts forged an early funeral alliance between families and the market, asserting through the graveyard congregants' rights to self-determination. They also began charting a path to contest authority from above through debates over burial that would only continue over the next several hundred years.

Nineteenth-century industrial change further validated those family and pragmatic concerns, as mounting anxiety over death-related poverty inspired the proliferation of Jewish burial and benevolent societies to supplement synagogue charity. Chapter 2 follows Jewish New Yorkers as they embraced American-style fraternalism and applied it to emerging funerary institutions. Grassroots Jewish burial societies were some of the first groups to incorporate more democratic models of Jewish governance and mutual regard. They paved the way for alternative forms of Jewish social welfare in New York by breaking up the synagogue's monopoly over charity and communal organization. They also introduced broader mechanisms of preemptive aid to affiliated families through regular sick pay, funeral costs, and early pensions to surviving dependents. The republicanism that inspired these groups bolstered the ideals of collective responsibility already circulating among New York Jews after the Revolution, but the associated gravity of proper funeral rites through which wider swaths of the Jewish public engaged those principles further validated specifically Jewish expressions of early American fraternalism. These groups laid some of the foundations for New York's (and the nation's) first Jewish fraternal orders, which would multiply later in the century. In their mission to decipher and disseminate Jewish funeral law and to educate family members on their active roles at times of loss, early Jewish burial societies also set new attention on the family and its spiritual and emotional well-being. Alongside innovations of monetary aid to surviving dependents, the period ushered in new holistic attention to individual Jewish households as they planned for the end of life.

The urban and commercial growth that propelled New York City throughout the nineteenth century also shaped Jewish funeral priorities, especially as Jewish cemeteries finally introduced family lots in which spouses and other family members could be buried side by side. Chapter 3 discusses the Rural Cemetery Movement as it took Jewish New Yorkers by storm. Lush landscapes and ornate cemetery holdings would have attracted Jews on their own, but the decision among synagogues to finally allow their congregants to purchase family holdings became its own Jewish cultural phenomenon. As city laws banned Manhattan burial and new park and roadway construction tore up old communal burying places, synagogues established new cemeteries across the East River. Inspired by the open space and pent-up congregant demand, they laid out unprecedented Jewish cemeteries with dedicated sections for family lots and mausoleums. As a result, waves of consumerism and contests over property rights infused the city's emerging Jewish cemetery economy.

Within congregations, controversies raged among religious leaders and households seeking to disinter loved ones from Manhattan yards to reunite departed kin in newly acquired family holdings. More broadly, a glut of easily purchased cemetery land fueled communal autonomy as Jewish burial societies and fledgling fraternal lodges found new self-determination in their ability to buy cemeteries independently from synagogues and their demanding rules. Each trend empowered Jewish households, as the city's figurative Jewish communal landscape adjusted to the physical changes around it. The new Jewish cemeteries offered a prime site for a family and market alliance that had wide-ranging implications for decades to come.

Spurred on by mass migration and widely available cemetery land, Jewish fraternities and burial lodges flourished between the nineteenth and twentieth centuries. Building on the need for grassroots aid in America, these groups also incorporated pensions and large lump-sum death benefits to members' surviving beneficiaries. Chapter 4 traces an unexpected trajectory in that system of communal relief as rapid industrial change and innovations in Jewish cemetery real estate inverted priorities once centered on widows and their economic security. Although all groups continued to pay widows over that period, the increasing vulnerability of the Jewish working class in New York led societies to add and inflate benefits to male members. Whether sick pay or compensation for unemployment, new payments were an important addition to supplement men's ability to provide for their families. To balance those expenses, in part, burial societies slowly introduced new charges around the cemetery and burial privileges that widows and their children had previously received for free. Groups withheld some costs from death endowments directly before paying them out while subsuming others in new widows' dues and added fees folded in over time. The result led to a complex system that retrieved and redistributed widows' aid through new charges for cemetery privileges. At the same time, ever-more-complicated policies came to govern marriage, remarriage, widows' and children's interment rights, adjoining double graves for spouses, and widows' rapidly changing institutional standing. Although all beneficiaries could be impacted by these policies, wives and widows in particular bore the brunt of these shifts, since their institutional status was linked so closely to their husbands' membership and the cemetery and endowment transactions between themselves and the benefit societies. The new system may have initially developed in an effort to offer aid to workingmen and widows simultaneously, but mounting institutional costs and the complexities of cemetery policy triggered a fundamental inversion of widows from recipients of society money to contributors in their own right by the middle of the twentieth century.

Chapter 5 follows these developments to their mid-twentieth-century climax as commercial Jewish funeral chapels, burial societies, aid groups, and synagogues all competed for Jewish business and loyalty. Family interests truly gave these campaigns their meaning so that, by the 1960s, immense purchasing power through the funeral realm and cemetery holdings recast old communal dynamics among Jewish members and their traditional communal providers. Still, midcentury synagogues and their rabbis found powerful foils in Jewish funeral directors and the rancor against their supposed profiteering at the expense of bereaved families. Little ritual oversight in a market long left to its own devices offered another substantial argument for congregations to motivate and sustain Jewish membership. Without religious guidance, nearly all denominations claimed, Jewish families could not reasonably navigate the industry on their own. Still, whether appealing to a family's sense of comfort by caring funeral directors or championing the family's protection when at its most emotionally vulnerable, all parties centered family well-being as their selling point for public trust. Although slightly new formulations appeared in the twentieth century, these shifts only punctuated the material and family priorities that had been threading Jewish approaches to death in New York since they first broke ground for burial three hundred years earlier.

For as much as we can learn about Jewish life through this story of evolving Jewish deathways, those ties to the living can also tell us a bit more about the workings of death in America. Classic scholarship, after all, took a very different perspective, occupied as it was with the distance that Americans put between themselves and their dead.[15] Many pursued that question by digging into the nation's thriving funeral business, seeing the drive to soften loss through consumerism as a cause and an effect.[16] But beyond solving the puzzle of America's difficult relationship to dying, recent works have tried to restore death to the foreground as an engine of history in its own right. Studies have applied once poorly explored categories like gender, race, ethnicity, and regional variation and thoroughly challenged the idea that any *one* way of dying ever existed in the United States.[17] Scholars have conceived of death as a site of power, useful in exploring topics like early Atlantic encounters and charting through attitudes around death various instances of cultural continuity, the exercise of power, and even cross-cultural conquest and exchange.[18] Others have questioned the societal impact of moments of large-scale loss and trauma. Studying the unprecedented death tolls of the Civil War has thrown into powerful focus the prewar idealism of noble sacrifice that set such devastation into motion.[19] Conversely, the aftermath of that "staggering human cost" forced a reordering of culture, to say nothing of the political and social impact going forward regarding the national narratives that justified it.[20] Economics of death have also revealed powerful stories, such as the political and financial capital that African American funeral directors were able to find in a segregated industry, allowing an amassing of resources to fight for modern civil rights.[21] And returning to an older line of inquiry, a reexamination of American anxiety over dying as it relates to modern medicine has revealed to those looking closely a drive to cure disease rather than comfort or alleviate the incurable.[22] The give-and-take in Jewish graveyards that rippled across faith, family, and funeral parlors tells a story all its own about the workings of death and its often unnoticed impact on the living in American society.

Far from stilted or static concerns, Jewish funeral priorities evolved over time, responding directly to key forces and values shaping the nation writ large. In that sense, the long history of Jewish burial in and around New York City tells a broader story of life in America. It frames the power of death and the strategies to manage it as integral forces that influenced larger social systems and experiences beyond the cemetery gates. So too the story of New York Jewish efforts to plan for life's end over a long period of time highlights the crucial role that death played in shaping lived experience.

The cemetery remained of utmost importance to Jews, not only for ritual concerns to separate their dead but also because it served as a site through which to order and organize the world all around them. The rise and fall of those groups that Jews formed and joined to access burial and its evolving considerations form part of that story. Another element rests in the interactions among members and policy makers of those Jewish institutions, playing out through funerary regulations, benefits packages, forms of funeral coverage, and action on the city's Jewish cemetery spaces themselves. At times, elites of Jewish institutions leveraged control over burial grounds and funeral provisions to promote religious, collective, or institutional ideals. Other times, rank-and-file members challenged and responded to that dynamic through the graves they purchased or the funerary and financial needs they expected to have met. In this way, Jews at all levels who affiliated with burial-providing institutions exercised and underscored shared influence through the funeral realm, especially as it placed a greater priority on family, material, and consumer concerns. As a result, individual women and men gained the ability and a sense of authority to perpetuate or alter long-standing hierarchies shaping their broader social reality. Debates around the graveyard thus truly mattered in that process—not only at moments of loss but also well beyond them.

1

Toward a Market and Family Alliance

Community, Kin, and Social Control in
New York's Early Jewish Graveyards, 1656–1830

It was an odd scene at the Jews' graveyard when Henry Phillips, alone, laid his son to rest. No procession, no ceremony, and no gathering of local Jews accompanied him. Phillips acted quickly, just three hours after telling synagogue leaders of the boy's death. He buried his son on his own because trustees would have refused him otherwise. Phillips had strong convictions and a history of challenging authority. Had he predicted his son's death, he may have paid his synagogue dues, already £4.17 in arrears. Without that contribution, however, he had forfeited interment rights for himself and his family. Trustees agreed to the burial only if they could settle all debts after interment. Torn between independence and duty to his son, Phillips chose a third route. Alone, he carried the boy to the yard, dug a grave by hand alongside its fence, and gave up his child without surrendering to communal elites.[1]

Henry Phillips's dilemma took place in 1795, but the Jews' burying place by the Fresh Water Pond had long served as a site of social protest or control among congregants and trustees. The yard remained New York's only consecrated Jewish burying ground for more than a century. In the absence of any alternative, and as it was one of the few exclusively Jewish spaces that most New York Jews would not yet willingly forfeit, synagogue leaders who controlled the yard enjoyed significant leverage over their community. Although the Phillips case hinged on communal contribution, family debt represented just one question defining New York's early Jewish burial enterprise. Who met leaders' standards of moral or physical purity? Whose body required ritual or social exclusion from the burial ground? How should the community treat the intermarried or their children? What about the poor, the stranger, suicides, or victims of disease? How best to organize the dead, highlighting deviance among those who transgressed communal expectations while erasing social and economic difference among those who had not? Finally, and perhaps of greatest consequence, could trustees abandon an old and strict commitment to chronological burial so that families might gather their loved ones together? Between the early eighteenth century and the middle of the next, Jewish New Yorkers engaged these questions every time the need arose to lay a Jew to rest. The decisions they made, the tensions they raised, and the responses they inspired among synagogue elders and affiliated families revealed the inner workings and worries of early New York Jewry. But as the synagogue's small cohort of leaders attempted to enforce traditional norms by control of the graveyard, congregants pushed back on that authority. In the process, they tested the limits of individualism, popular will, and evolving ideals around the family in early American society. Family will especially resonated, since most burial policies, whether intentionally or not, elevated collectivism and communal cohesion over family sentiment and the interment rights of members and their dependents. That dynamic positioned the graveyard as a key site to reinforce old social structures or to work out communal debates that would ultimately drive change among New York Jewry.

New civic and social freedoms that Jews enjoyed in North America only further influenced that process—perhaps nowhere more than in early New York. While a separate Jewish burial enterprise took root when Jews first arrived to New Amsterdam, the shift to English rule made that bastion of particularity all the more consequential. English pragmatism only expanded civic and social opportunity. Eighteenth-century Jewish and Christian New Yorkers forged rich ties of leisure, trade, and in some instances, even marriage. New fluidity challenged cohesive communal bonds in nearly unprecedented ways. If social and political limits in Europe had encouraged greater deference to communal authority, opportunities in New York made Jewish exclusivity far more voluntary. Synagogue leaders struggled to temper blurring boundaries within an ever-porous social setting. Demographics also mattered, as the small and still-developing Jewish center depended on peripatetic Jewish merchants for its size, infrastructure, and future. Those circumstances limited the kind of continuity that Jewish leaders would have preferred.

In this context, New York's early Jewish graveyards represented natural strongholds with which to foster communal bonds while strengthening social and religious boundaries among the living. By emphasizing ties between interment rights and religious observance, endogamous marriage, or financial contributions, elders hoped to limit expanding avenues that might lead local Jews too far beyond the communal fold.

That strategy met its limit, though, by challenging family interests. Inasmuch as elders stressed community in death, their privileging of the collective failed time and again to honor family concerns. When they conditioned burial on the settlement of unpaid fees, they jeopardized a surviving member's grave as much as the fate of his loved ones' remains. When they denied burial due to a marriage out of the community, they denied whole families the security of a grave awaiting them, thus encouraging Christian spouses to raise their children in their own church congregations, which would not deny them pivotal life-cycle rites if baptized. Finally, and most far-reaching, when the synagogue insisted on organizing its burying place sequentially by the order of decease, it denied members' growing desire to bury among families so that loved ones might rest alongside one another or take comfort in a symbolic reunion sometime in the future. New York Jews accepted most of these policies over the eighteenth century, but by the decades surrounding the American Revolution, they challenged them in greater numbers. On the one hand, they drew on changing conceptions of the family and popular will emerging in the early republic. On the other, they acted on their own sentimentality and frustrations with overseas trade that rendered the long-term separation of spouses, siblings, parents, and children a normative Jewish experience.

Although congregants invoked family sympathy and obligation more frequently into the early nineteenth century, trustees still resisted any formal or far-reaching concession. The give-and-take that played out in these debates reflected an ongoing legacy of family and community as the key pillars in the city's Jewish burial system. At the same time, the financial solutions that members devised to circumvent these policies—whether offering extra payments to the synagogue to bury family together or making creative use of city fines to bury in outlawed areas of New York that already contained loved ones' graves of past generations—laid the foundation for market forces to shape Jewish burial in the city for decades to come. Those strategies allowed congregants to sidestep restrictive policies and win, at least in part, the privilege of family burial. These innovations also marked an early alliance between family and finances in New York Jewish burial. They also provided households with new avenues to gain some say over synagogue policies and one of the most important provisions sustaining affiliation. Because community and kin proved to be contentious issues when planning for death during much of the eighteenth century, the graveyard became a natural site for that rivalry to play out. By extension, the unraveling of that system by the century's end set the stage for the first great infusion of monetary considerations in New York's Jewish funerary sphere, which in turn has shaped developments into the present day.

"Inasmuch as They Did Not Wish to Bury Their Dead . . . in the Common Burying Ground"

That the city's Jewish graveyard assumed any of these outsized influences rested in the fact that Jews and their earliest Christian counterparts refused to bury together. Indeed, a separate Jewish burial system was established on Manhattan Island in 1656, just two years after a now-famous handful of Jewish refugees first arrived there following Dutch Brazil's surrender back to Portuguese control. Although most did not stay long, subsequent Jewish contemporaries saw potential in New Amsterdam. Dutch Caribbean trade, ruled by the Dutch West India Company, which oversaw American and African colonial interests, grew in the 1650s, and an increasing network of Sephardic (Spanish Portuguese) Jewish merchants underwrote its expansion by settling across West India Company colonies.[2] Even though New Amsterdam's leadership initially attempted to reject the Jewish newcomers, the appeals of influential Jewish shareholders in the Dutch West India Company allowed them to remain, and the colony's director general, Peter Stuyvesant, grudgingly granted them rights of residence and trade.[3] As Jews of increasing stature followed, they pressed to uphold and expand those privileges. Beyond day-to-day protections, however, they understood too that for any long-term settlement, Jews would also have to secure a separate place to bury.

Although neither Christian Dutch nor Jewish colonists would have imagined burying together, the creation of a separate Jewish burying place happened only after strained negotiations. In July 1655, a trio of prominent merchants, Abraham de Lucena, Salvador D'andrada, and Jacob Cohen Henriques, petitioned New Amsterdam's council for the right "to purchase a burying place for their nation."[4] No Jewish settler had died when they made that request, but they acted in advance since they had few other options. At the time, the colony maintained only one common burying ground, which served Christian Europeans. Jews, however, could not bury there since religious law forbade them to mix the dead across faiths. Likely hoping to discourage permanent settlement, Stuyvesant and colonial authorities simply postponed any decision to grant a Jewish graveyard.[5] The council only recorded it "inasmuch as they did not wish to bury their dead (of which as yet there was no need) in the common burying ground." Gambling that the Jews might depart before a death occurred, the council ruled that "when the need and occasion therefor arose," they would grant the fledgling community "some place elsewhere of the free land belonging to the Company." The Dutch lost that wager in February 1656. Likely facing the first Jewish death, the trio returned, and the council finally conceded "a little hook of land situated outside of this city for a burial place."[6] Though officials initially rejected several early Jewish petitions, such as rights to militia service, property holding, and expanded trade, authorities ultimately granted piecemeal protections fairly quickly. A dedicated Jewish graveyard not only represented the first communal and public space that Jews created in North America but counted among several legal, social, and religious privileges that paved the way for long-term settlement in the colony. It also set an important precedent that—perhaps even more than with other philanthropic needs—early Jews would depend on communal elites and collective maneuvering to fulfill basic funerary needs.

That situation spoke to the complex status of Jewish colonists as social and religious outsiders in a church-centered society. Indeed, Jewish separation after death stood out under Dutch rule as a rare and perhaps the only case of a European group not burying in the common ground. In 1628, shortly after Dutch settlers arrived on the island, they established a common yard for burial on Heerestraet, land later bound between

Exchange Place and Morris Street west of Broadway.[7] Most other Europeans buried there, since they were not allowed to establish their own churches or churchyards. That ban was part of a broader strategy to foster a uniform Calvinist society by preventing religious competition and forcing European colonists to affiliate with the Reformed Church. Indeed, until New Amsterdam came under English control in 1664, the Dutch Reformed Church remained the only option for public worship or performance of life-cycle rites. Church leaders welcomed any to pray, marry, or baptize without requiring Dutch descent. They hoped to promote Reformed doctrine and forge new ties among Europeans of diverse national backgrounds.[8] French Protestants, for instance, engaged the church early on in their tenure. After Stuyvesant repeatedly thwarted Lutherans of mixed European origin from bringing a minister or holding meetings for private services, they too looked to the colony's existing church infrastructure. They "reluctantly attended worship on occasion and brought their children there to be baptized by Reformed clergymen and educated by Reformed schoolmasters."[9] Even English settlers had no alternative, marrying and baptizing through the church even though most never became members.

Without independent congregations or surrounding churchyards, the colony's European Christians buried in its common ground. Most may have preferred to set up their own communal burying places, but they only did so only after the transition to English rule. With that shift, congregations could establish independent churches and, on acquiring communal property, quickly and commonly set aside land for burial.[10] In Dutch New Amsterdam, however, interment either took place beneath the floorboards of the Reformed Church, an honor for the well-to-do, outside with those of limited standing, or within the common yard. Local authorities even appointed churchwardens to care for the graveyard. The court also designated sextons and precentors as gravediggers and *aansprekers* (those spreading news of recent deaths) to tend to funeral needs. Even after New Netherland transitioned to English rule, Dutch authorities still maintained some say over Christian funerals.[11] In all, the system centered on and served Protestant communities in the hopes of rendering death, like other life-cycle needs, a tool to transcend denominational or cultural differences dividing European settlers.

Despite regional or linguistic diversity among English-, French-, Dutch-, or German-speaking Protestants, at least theologically, Anglicans, Huguenots, Calvinists, and Lutherans had far more in common with one another than their Jewish counterparts in their laws or traditions governing burying spaces. Indeed, until the 1680s, when these communities could establish independent churches and burying grounds, they felt few ritual misgivings about burying their dead side by side. In some cases, they even exchanged cemetery land when they began establishing independent churchyards. Portions of the old common yard, for instance, passed among Lutherans and Anglicans in the 1670s and 1680s. Lutherans set up a church and churchyard in close proximity to it, and the English settlers who founded Trinity Parish also buried there beginning in 1682. The Lutheran church even sold some of its property to Trinity in 1697 when the latter received its charter, including some extra land in exchange for the "liberty of burying their dead in the [Episcopal] church yard."[12] Even by the early 1780s, since New York City had still not consecrated a Catholic church or burying place, Trinity buried Catholic and Irish individuals alongside Dutch and English Protestants.[13]

Jewish settlers, of course, could ill fit into that system. In the absence of conversion, which few Jews would have imagined, the Dutch could no more bury a Jew in the colony's common ground than most Jews would have desired to rest in consecrated Christian space. The symbolism of a Jewish yard on the colony's physical and social landscape not only signaled a pragmatic difference but also reflected Jews' complex status under Dutch rule. A devout Calvinist, Stuyvesant sought to elevate the Dutch Reformed Church, particularly by avoiding competition among other Protestant denominations. As Joyce Goodfriend has argued, given the population's heterogeneity, he also sought to fold in those groups that he considered ethnically, linguistically, and religiously prime candidates to bolster the colony's meager Dutch numbers.[14] Although the West India Company forced Stuyvesant's hand in allowing Jews to settle, he did succeed in relegating most of their religious life to private and unseen spheres. That earliest Jewish graveyard, nestled just beyond the colony's physical border, embodied their marginality. It also foreshadowed the distinct foundations they would carve for Jewish life and spaces over the coming centuries, negotiating communal provisions in a church-centered colonial society.

"My Body to the Earth to Be Decently Buried among the Jews"

The colony's next Jewish burying place was established in 1682 when New York's most renowned Jewish resident, Joseph Bueno de Mesquita, purchased land in trust "for a Jew Burying Place, with free Liberty of a passage from the Highway thereto to carry their Dead."[15] By then, the colony extended beyond the land a mile and a half from Manhattan's southern tip that the Dutch had occupied. As New York became an important port of English exchange among the mainland and Caribbean colonies, new Jewish traders arrived and established new communal structures. By the 1680s, with nearly one hundred Jews residing in the colony, they began to gather for private worship.[16] Not coincidentally, they also sought new land for burial. New York's growth since the 1650s had likely eclipsed the earliest Jewish yard, leading the fledgling community to seek a new site in which to bury. Bueno's stature rendered him a communal leader until his death in 1708, but it also allowed him to oversee the initiative to purchase a lot for Jewish interment beyond the colony's new boundary. After Bueno purchased land from William Merret and his wife, Margery, perhaps appropriately, his brother, Benjamin Bueno de Mesquita, received the first grave. His headstone, reading in part "Wait for thy God who revives, The dead of His people in mercy, To live eternally without end, 5444 (1683)," remains the oldest stone still extant in those grounds.[17]

Like that first Jewish yard purchased from the Dutch, this one not only enabled long-term settlement but also reinforced another Jewish legacy for the colonial period: dependence on communal elites for burial needs. This was especially the case in the late seventeenth century, when only a handful of Jewish merchants like Bueno had yet won letters of denization or the rights of freemen necessary to acquire property.[18] Lacking the funds or widespread legal ability to buy and maintain a Jewish yard on their own, Jews' interment options remained not only limited but also contingent on wealthy peers to purchase land on their behalf. Like the trio before him or the subsequent prominent merchants who would expand the graveyard by buying surrounding lots in trust,

Bueno deployed his social and commercial status on behalf of the community. He and others secured that important institution of a graveyard because the social status and recognition that these men commanded in wider circles empowered them to purchase and win official recognition of Jewish spaces at variance with those of their Christian peers.

That lot formed the basis of the Jews' yard by the Fresh Water Pond, later to become Chatham Square, New York's oldest surviving Jewish graveyard and the only one serving Jewish residents in the early nineteenth century. That longevity reflected the inability of average households to address interment on their own, given the limited communal funds and legal restrictions over congregational affairs, especially as a small non-Protestant minority. When the yard reached capacity in 1728, New York's wealthiest Jewish residents again secured additional land. In fact, they did so twice after a temporary mortgage setback prevented initial efforts to purchase adjoining lots. Although at least twenty-nine Jewish households donated small sums to the effort, the largest shares, totaling half of the entire purchase, came from members of New York's two wealthiest Jewish families. A widow like Simcha de Torres could take pride in an offering of ten shillings toward the hallowed need, but without the personal wealth and estates of the Gomez and Levy-Franks families, the multiple initiatives to expand the graveyard would have ended in failure.[19]

The inability to formally incorporate a Jewish congregation until 1784 also limited the average Jew's ability to act independently. In that year, New York passed a Religious Corporation Act that enabled any church or synagogue to receive an official charter, but until then colonial authorities had only formally recognized the Dutch and Anglican churches. The limit was a vestige of appeasement following English acquisition of the colony and the transition from Dutch rule. Without corporate status, no other religious communities could officially purchase collective real estate in the name of their congregations. Individual members, however, commonly purchased land in trust for wider communal use in order to sidestep that limitation. Although New York's Jewish residents differed in many other practices from Christians around them, they too employed this strategy. As a result, when need arose to expand the graveyard in 1728, Moses Gomez, then president of the Jews' congregation, Shearith Israel, and a freeman since 1705, bought each new lot in trust for the broader Jewish public. In fact, the deed and title for that purchase remained in the family's name until 1828, when a descendant finally turned it over to the congregation.[20] Jewish households of meager means depended on their wealthy counterparts for the majority of funds to secure a place to bury, and the civic and commercial privileges that these men had already accumulated proved invaluable for larger communal initiatives as well.

That dependence on elites for funerary provisions continued for more than a century, especially since few Jews took the need for Jewish burial lightly. Many even commonly suggested a belief in their wills that acceptance of their soul directly correlated to proper interment in consecrated Jewish ground and all of the associated ceremonies. In 1704, for instance, merchant Joseph Tores Nunez reflected a common sentiment when he requested "my Soule to God that gave it me & my body to the earth there to be decently buried in hopes of a glorious resurrecion at the last day." Later testators made similar associations. Joshua Isaacs spoke for many in his 1744 request: "I humbly Recommend My Soul, unto [God's] holly hands & Care & desire my body may be buryed In Our Jews burying Ground in said New York among my relations & friends." In 1750, Mordecai Gomez similarly proclaimed, "I commit my Precious and immortal Soul into The hands of God who gave it To me and my body to The Earth to be buried in the Jews Burying Ground according To the Jewish Custom."[21] It was no wonder that when congregation leaders sought Common Council permission to consecrate a new burying place in 1728, they stressed it would "be and remain forever hereafter for a burying place for the inhabitants of the city of New York, being of the Jewish religion, and to and for no other use, intent or purpose whatsoever."[22] As a result, ownership of the graveyard, the ability to include or exclude congregants, and even the determination over their graves' location in the yard represented an important source of leverage to influence communal behavior and sensibilities.

The lack of alternative Jewish yards for much of the eighteenth and nineteenth centuries only further augmented that power. From 1682 until 1812, only one dedicated Jewish burying place served New York's fledgling Jewish community. Even with the gradual establishment of two additional yards by the 1820s, the city's one synagogue, Shearith Israel, still controlled them exclusively until a second congregation, B'nai

Jeshurun, finally broke away in 1825. Had Jews made up a larger share of the population, they may have enjoyed the numbers or resources to create earlier alternatives. With roughly one hundred Jews residing in New York by 1695 and transient mercantile families settling for a time before moving on to other ports, however, their numbers had only increased to a figure between about 242 or 350 a century later. Out of a larger population of 33,000 on the eve of the Revolution, Jews still only represented about 1 percent of New York's population.[23]

Interment also remained one of the few religious matters that Jewish families could not deal with on their own. Knowledge of ritual slaughter, for instance, remained fairly widespread, enabling Jews to sidestep the synagogue's desired monopoly of providing kosher meat. In other instances, some families, particularly those beyond the city, even performed circumcisions independently.[24] Burial, however, remained the domain of the synagogue. Although those versed in procedures to wash the dead did offer voluntary services before a permanent burial society emerged in the nineteenth century, the earth to receive those bodies remained ever beyond their control. Congregation leaders not only maintained tight symbolic control of the Jews' burying place but also locked its gates when not in use and resolved that the key "be always lodged" with the synagogue's president.[25] With that dearth of alternatives—and, of course, few if any Jews willing to repose in a neighboring churchyard—access to the burying place by the Freshwater Pond promised significant influence in earthly matters as much as those of the hereafter.

Although scholars in recent decades have offered a more nuanced perspective on the limited authority that early American synagogues enjoyed over congregants' lives, the very real monopoly that New York Jewish elders maintained over the graveyard played an important part in that dynamic. Congregants' irregular financial support or attendance at services frustrated communal elders, to say nothing of some members' marital choices and other religious observances. Funeral provisions, however, remained well within the synagogue's oversight and beyond domestic confines. In that sense, Shearith Israel's control over burial complemented incessant edicts or a panoply of fines regulating communal life and religious practice that only grew in frequency over much of the eighteenth century. All these tactics likely reflected the elders' frustration with their inability to adequately drive social change more than their belief in the effectiveness of these tools to exercise authority.[26] Nonetheless, policies defining exclusion or inclusion in the grounds continually threaded these efforts, and even if it was not wholly effective, the monopoly over burial offered an arena to refine communal influence. Long-term matters of affiliation and collectivism became especially ripe for edicts surrounding the graveyard. Although Shearith Israel's leaders never took lightly the need for Jews to rest in Jewish ground, by tightly controlling the one local graveyard, they hoped to foster communal cohesion and promote religious conformity—issues, as the century wore on, that were rapidly evading their control.

"And When Dead Will Not Be Buried According to the Manner of Our Brethren"

The colony's physical growth challenged Jewish communal ties in more ways than one. Until the mid-eighteenth century, most New Yorkers had been concentrated below Wall Street, but development over the coming decades led homes and businesses to spread north of the port along the East River. Many even began settling in Harlemtown or Greenwich Village. Some Jews followed that trend, though it meant increasing the distance from the Dock Ward and East Ward where they had settled since the late seventeenth century. They dispersed from not only early Jewish enclaves but also Shearith Israel's first synagogue structure on Mill Street. Communal leaders chafed at this residential dispersion. First, it weakened communal oversight because, as Holly Snyder points out, "the move inland necessarily meant escape from the constraints of life in an urban Jewish quarter and in particular removal from the supervisory gaze of one's neighbors and synagogue elders."[27] Second, declining attendance or recourse to the congregation to provide religious needs could only precipitate declining contributions.

In matters material and spiritual, synagogue elders used the graveyard to reinforce communal bonds. In the summer of 1737, for instance, they introduced a new annual fee of forty shillings because, they claimed, "we are not able to defray the charge of the Congregation without the help & assistance of our brethren dwelling in the Country." Ten years later, they instituted another quarterly tax on any "leving either in town or countery." In both instances, they warned that refusal to pay would sacrifice not only synagogue honors but also membership and all associated services.[28] If burial was implicit in those pronouncements, subsequent edicts addressed it even more directly, this time tied to religious deviance. In 1752, elders "unanimously" agreed that to prevent "all manner of discord & Division . . . on the demise of any person, that in his life time absented himself from the Sinagogue, or was no ways a benefactor to the Congregation, His Corps or the Corps of his wife or children under thirteen years of age shall not be laid & Burried within the walls of our Burrying Ground." In 1757, they escalated even further on rumors that "severall of our Brethren, that reside in the Country have and do dayly violate the principles our holy religion, such as Trading on the Sabath, Eating of forbidden Meats & other Henious Crimes." In response, elders charged that any "act[ing] contrary to our Holy Law . . . will not be deem'd a member of our Congregation, have none of the Mitzote [honors] of the Sinagoge Confered on him & when Dead will not be buried according to the manner of our brethren."[29] These dramatic resolutions proved more theater than practice, for within six months, the elders walked back these threats, claiming the message well received. Perhaps more importantly, though, they realized the ineffectiveness of regulating temporal or day-to-day observance with end-of-life punishments.[30]

Despite those limitations, synagogue elites did not abandon the graveyard as a source of communal authority. Instead, they shifted their focus to more long-term concerns challenging communal cohesion and deployed interment rights to reinforce collective bonds. Punitive measures by the second half of the eighteenth century reflected that approach as threats to deny burial rights focused far more on enduring challenges like contributions to the congregation, conversion, or intermarriage. Even nonpunitive policies governing interment—like the practices of assigning graves by chronological order of decease or burying nonresident Jews who died while passing through town in separate areas—highlighted the efforts to stress communal belonging and conformity through the burial place. As noted earlier, however, this evolving approach to death inadvertently pitted family interests against those of the larger collective. This resulted in an important by-product—a stand-off between community and kin in matters of New York Jewish burial by the decades surrounding the Revolution.

Conversion, Intermarriage, and Communal Contribution

Conversion represented the easiest issue for Shearith Israel or other early synagogues to use to deny graves. In fact, the congregation rarely had to struggle with independent Jewish conversions to Christianity, since churches would bury parishioners even if they had once professed Judaism. When Moise Mendes Seixas died in 1817, for instance, his 1794 Episcopal conversion after arriving to New York from Bordeaux ensured that a grave awaited him in St. Paul's Churchyard.[31] Similarly, despite Judah Monis's earlier service as a religious leader for Shearith Israel during his residence in New York, he too came to rest in a churchyard in Northborough, Massachusetts, in 1764. Distinguished as North America's first instructor of Hebrew at Harvard College, Monis converted to Christianity in 1722 to assume that position.

Marriages between Christians and Jews proved far more complicated because they triggered several sensitivities surrounding conversions. For one thing, no rabbis formally trained and ordained in recognized European seminaries settled in America until the 1840s. In their absence, early American Jewish communities lacked the necessary tribunal to perform ritually valid conversions and therefore remained reluctant to convert even desiring Christian spouses. To be sure, they did so in a handful of cases like Frances Isaacs or Jane Nathan, members' wives whom the congregation would later bury without any distinction. However, examples like those were not the norm. Most synagogue leaders also worried about the appearance of active proselytizing. Few wished to undermine a seemingly probationary standing in a world that had still only recently allowed Jewish resettlement. In an unforeseen consequence, though, limits on converting Christian spouses raised additional questions for children of interfaith unions. Initially unsure how to classify these children, most synagogues would not recognize them as Jews. Although that decision hoped to discourage subsequent intermarriages, in cases where they had already occurred, it led those families to baptize and rear their children in a Christian spouse's church. Although no uniform policy had emerged in the nineteenth century, this phenomenon became a self-fulfilling mechanism to stigmatize these families in death.

In its edicts and attitudes, the congregation maintained a strong opposition to intermarriage and conversion over the second half of the eighteenth century. In 1763, for instance, Shearith Israel's leadership passed a law against "making proselytes, or performing the marriage of any Jew to a proselyte."[32] In 1782, while still taking refuge in Philadelphia during the Revolution, New York transplants debated and ultimately rejected Jacob I. Cohen's request to marry the widow Esther Mordecai (once Elizabeth Whitlock) because of her previous marriage and conversion. When Cohen disregarded their wishes, they also forbade any member from attending the couple's wedding or mentioning their names in the synagogue.[33] In 1784, after returning to New York, trustees also refused a request by Benjamin I. Jacobs to convert his fiancée, who was "desirous to live as a Jewess . . . that she may be married according to the manners and customs of the Jews."[34] Shearith Israel even turned away James Foster in 1788, who simply hoped to convert to Judaism for admiration of the religion.[35] In its new 1790 bylaws, the congregation reiterated that "any person hereafter marrying a [non-Jewish woman], or otherways contrary to our custom . . . shall forfit the right of [membership], and shall not be considered or hereafter admitted as a member of the society."[36]

These stipulations stood out since the earliest 1728 constitution made no reference to intermarriage.[37] That emerging focus by the latter half of the eighteenth century was likely a response to several prominent marriages between Christians and Jews that occurred in quick succession in New York and Philadelphia at midcentury. Phila Franks and Oliver Delancey, for instance, children of two of New York's most noted commercial dynasties, eloped in 1742, keeping their marriage a secret for six months before briefly moving outside of town due to the Franks family's disapproval.[38] A year later in 1743, Phila's brother, David, wed Episcopalian Margaret Evans, whom he had come to know after settling in Philadelphia. Although David never converted and contributed over the years to Mikve Israel, Philadelphia's congregation, and Shearith Israel in his native New York, he and Margaret baptized all their children and raised them in the church.[39] Similarly, when Phila and Oliver Delancey resettled in England, stigmas there led them to favor the Christian high society in which they raised their children. Some years later, David and Phila's half-uncle, Samson Levy, left New York for Philadelphia to join the family trade and there married a widow, Martha Lampley Thompson, in Old Swedes' Church in 1752. Although Samson had his first son circumcised in 1754, he and Martha baptized the rest of their children in Christ Church.[40] Although the synagogues' initial unwillingness to accept children of interfaith families arguably only predisposed their baptism, concerns over continuity still fueled a reluctance to accommodate conversions or intermarriage by the century's end.

Despite these policies, however, early American Jews and Christians who desired to marry found other means to do so. If the synagogue would not recognize or perform their marriages, they either lived together or married through a spouse's church or civil ceremony. Trinity Parish, for instance, married Asher Levy and Mary Thompson in 1782. Jacob Hays, who served as New York's constable for almost fifty years, married Christian women at least twice—Catherine Conroy in 1798[?] and Mary Post in the 1820s.[41] In Philadelphia, Moses Nathans approached Mikve Israel in 1793 to convert a former servant, Betty Hart, even though the two already had three children after living together and maintaining a common-law marriage since 1790. In New York, Bernard Hart pursued a similar short-lived marriage with Catherine Brett in 1799.[42]

Although outliers, cases like these were frequent enough to frustrate synagogue elders with their perceived lack of social control. In an effort to discourage further intermarriage and wrestling with very real ritual complications, congregations ultimately stigmatized these and similar families in death. It was, after all, one of the few realms they still controlled that deeply resonated among the public, particularly as state oversight greatly neutered older forms of excommunication. Philadelphia Jews stressed that point in a query to Amsterdam's rabbinic authority as they struggled with two contemporary intermarriages. One case involved young Judith Levy and James Pettigrew, a Revolutionary soldier. The congregation had to decide whether to overlook their initial church wedding that a chaplain had performed, given a second ceremony that had been officiated by Mikve Israel's Mordecai Mordecai. The other centered on a heated debate upon Benjamin Moses Clava's death in 1785. Since Clava had married a Christian woman in a church, most favored denying his body the ritual shrouds and washing and relegating his grave to a corner by the graveyard fence. Seeking advice or validation, the Philadelphians sought the counsel of their European counterparts and vented their exasperation at the ways in which the voluntary nature of early American society completely inverted a congregation's traditional authority: "The matter touches the very roots of our faith, particularly in this country where each [individual] acts according to his own desire. . . . The congregation here has no power to discipline anyone . . . therefore, the duty and the need are great to make an impression on the public in a matter where the congregation has jurisdiction, and to close the breach as much as possible."[43]

New York elders shared those sentiments, as did most early American synagogues. They refused to bury Christian spouses because they simply could not include them in consecrated ground, and they easily refused converted Jews or their children if they had been baptized. Accordingly, Samson Levy (1781) and his entire family came to rest in St. Peter's Episcopal Churchyard, just as David Franks interred his second daughter, Polly, in Christ Church's burying ground after her death of illness in 1774.[44] Franks himself ultimately came to rest there too after his death in 1793.[45] Although he never converted and continued to observe Jewish rites and contribute to New York and Philadelphia synagogues, Jewish peers could not reconcile his weekly attendance at Christ Church with wife, Margaret, or their children's baptisms. Conversely, contemporaries likely had an easier time burying Jacob Hays in New York City's Marble Cemetery in 1850 since he had converted long before and reared his children as Christians.[46] Although in 1803 Shearith Israel buried Samson Myers, whose story opened this study, trustees set the young man's grave far apart from the regular row because a year earlier, he had fathered a child with a Christian woman. Although Myers's mother moved the boy to Richmond, where she and an uncle could raise him away from communal judgment, Samson's isolated grave on the outskirts of the yard kept his actions fresh in the community's collective memory for at least twenty years until a lack of space forced the graveyard to fill in around it.[47]

By the turn of the century, trustees may have realized that their rigid rejections of Jewish and Christian marriages only encouraged communal detachment or the baptism of subsequent offspring. As a result, even as synagogues refined their policies on mixed-faith marriages, they still deployed their burial monopoly to encourage communal ties. Trustees often justified the performance of funeral rites and a Jewish spouse's burial (even if marginalized) on continued synagogue participation and whether a minister had performed the couple's marriage. In New York and Philadelphia, perhaps the majority of Jews who married Christians by the nineteenth century did so in civil ceremonies in order to maintain affiliation over the course of their lives so that they could receive proper rites when dead. New York even saw a brief period of openness when Shearith Israel's 1805 constitution removed explicit prohibitions against intermarriage and allowed Jews who had married Christians to rent seats and become electors.[48] In those rare instances where synagogues recognized formerly Christian wives who had converted to Judaism, they also laid them to rest after years of affiliation. As mentioned above, New York leaders buried Jane (or Jean) Nathan in the regular row when she died in 1823, since she had converted and upheld synagogue ties for decades after her husband's death in 1798.[49] Shearith Israel even grudgingly accepted Benjamin Seixas's marriage to Mary Jessup in the 1830s after her conversion by another synagogue when the former refused. Despite that disapproval, years later in 1869, Shearith Israel still buried Mary in congregational grounds.[50] Perhaps reflecting a greater number of occurrences than in New York, Mikve Israel's leaders recognized the conversions of members' wives even more frequently and laid them to rest in its graveyard throughout the early nineteenth century.[51]

Similarly, trustees focused on children's rites when making the difficult decision of how (and if at all) to bury them while underage. They considered whether the daughters and sons had been baptized and, in the case of boys, whether they had received circumcision.[52] Into the nineteenth century, Shearith Israel and New York's emerging congregations looked near and far in their struggle to find a uniform policy. Their efforts reflected a tension between the demands of Jewish law and their sense of obligation to these children whom they did not wish to abandon. In 1826, for instance, I. B. Kursheedt, who assumed a role of religious guidance at B'nai Jeshurun, ruled counter to regular principles of matrilineal descent that "a daughter of a Jewish father but a non-Jewish mother could be buried on consecrated ground." In a similar case in 1838, authorities deviated by ruling that such a child should be buried to the side and out of the regular row. Clearly still struggling, Shearith Israel sought advice from London's chief rabbi, Solomon Hirschel, who directed that in all cases except a high priest's intermarriage, the faith of a child's mother determined his or her religious identity. Even after the arrival of America's first rabbis holding European ordination, Shearith Israel still sought clarification years later. In 1847, it petitioned Max Lilienthal, then serving the congregation Shaare Zedek; Abraham Rice, presiding in Baltimore; and another visiting rabbi, Moses Noah. Although responses do not survive, the congregation wrestled with questions over if and how it should bury uncircumcised children under thirteen and separate scenarios in which these children had Jewish fathers and Christian mothers or the reverse.[53]

To an extent, these policies succeeded, but they also played some role in a much larger trend of nonmarriage by early American Jews in this period. Indeed, while rates of intermarriage did increase by the early nineteenth century, Jews who married Christians remained a minority, as most early Jewish Americans and New Yorkers either married other Jews or, in strikingly large numbers, simply did not marry at all. From the colonial period to 1840, just 16 percent of Jews married Christians.[54] Conversely, about half of all Jewish men and women of marriageable age remained single between the 1770s and 1820s.[55] In New York specifically, about 45 percent of Jewish men and 41 percent of Jewish women still had not married by the age of fifty.[56] That reality became so common at Shearith Israel that trustees even passed a motion in 1800 to reserve the front row of the women's balcony for single women over forty.[57] Although the bulk of the elders' attention clearly focused on Jews marrying across religious lines, those Jews who did not marry at all had equal if not greater influence on communal continuity as well. Take, for example, children of the Judah family. Although three sons did marry, the bulk of the Judah children did not. Daughters Amelia (1761–1849), Rebecca (1765–1846), Bella (1770–1847), Fanny (1771–1833), and Rachel (1772–1836), along with another son, Cary Jekuthiel (1766–1837), all died single.[58] Although larger trends like imbalanced gender ratios certainly contributed to widespread rates of Jewish nonmarriage, the structures and taboos that synagogues built between burial and family life also played a part. Adding to early Jews' awareness of the social and ritual consequences facing interfaith families in life, the risk of a grave for themselves or their children after death may have further dissuaded some from marrying beyond their community or marrying at all, and so might the prospect of trading a life with a Christian partner for the comfort of lying thereafter among loved ones and friends.

Drawing on similar impulses, the effort to encourage regular dues payments by threatening to deny interment rights to delinquent congregants or their dependents paralleled the issue of intermarriage in at least two respects. On the one hand, wielding the cudgel of the graveyard aimed to preempt financial insolvency and lackluster participation. Those two realities more than others continued as persistent threats to the synagogue's long-term stability, particularly at the turn of the nineteenth century. On the other, even though the congregation almost always allowed retroactive payments for burial provision, the momentary crises that the policy forced on families in arrears similarly set individual household interests against those of the broader collective. Recall the case of Henry Phillips burying his son independently in 1795 because of lapsed dues. Despite that act of nonconformity, a court case that the congregation brought against him did force payment of the debts he had promised. A formal resolution followed soon after in 1796, declaring that for anyone age twenty-one years or above who received a benefit from the congregation but failed to contribute an annual twenty shillings, "any of his, or her, family dying, Shall not be permitted to be buried, in our Burial Ground." That edict drew on long-standing policy in New York but perhaps also mirrored the recent example of Mikve Israel, which in 1793 refused to bury a member's son until he paid two years' worth of fees toward the ritual slaughterer and the child's circumcision.[59] Shearith Israel also issued another edict in 1800 reiterating "in the case of death of such delinquent, or any of his Family, he or they, shall not be intered in the Burial Ground belonging to this Congregation, untill a Settlement be previously made, to the Satisfaction of the Trustees."[60] The congregation recorded at least thirteen cases between 1816 and 1836 of charging families who did not belong to the congregation but wished to bury in its grounds.[61] Whether interacting with members or unaffiliated local Jews, trustees once more found an effective source of leverage in their control over Jewish interment to promote extended communal ties. By the early nineteenth century, these policies laid the ground for an increasingly contentious relationship between family and communal concerns in death.

"As It Shall Please God in His Own Good Time to Call Us to Himself"[62]

If punitive burials aimed to promote social and religious conformity, trustees' regular approach to the graveyard also privileged the collective. This manifested especially in the commitment to bury in chronological rows, reflecting the order in which members died. Chronology, the elders believed, would affirm a long chain of New York Jewish history or communal bonds tracing back at least as early as Benjamin Bueno in 1682. As later proponents also argued, "the Row" ensured equality so that only the order of death determined a member's physical place in the yard rather than one's prestige or personal accomplishments. For trustees and members who supported those ideals, sequential burial took on its own informal sanctity.

Exceptions to that practice affirmed those principles, particularly the burial of Jewish foreigners with no immediate links to the community in separate areas of the graveyard that did not correspond to the overall order of communal death. Although Shearith Israel still ensured that nonnative Jews who died while in the city received traditional burial in consecrated ground, trustees and members did not feel that these individuals merited the same symbolic honor of inclusion in the regular rows. Between 1806 and 1809, for instance, the synagogue deviated from chronology at least three separate times to cluster the graves of nonlocal Jews. They chose a section removed from the rows then actively in use, leaving the next regular graves open for Jewish New Yorkers who died shortly after.[63] Three decades later, in a new graveyard that Shearith Israel had established on Twenty-First Street, the congregation still buried Jewish "strangers" apart. In one instance, it even interred a stranger who had drowned among several suicides in that yard's corner.[64] Conversely, despite the fact that Miriam Lopez Levy had died in Wilmington, North Carolina, in 1812, Shearith Israel assigned her the grave that would have gone at that point to any local when lack of family in Wilmington led northern kin to transfer her grave to New York in 1819. Her inclusion

within regular chronology attested to the contributions of her prominent father, Aaron Lopez, and grandfather, Jacob Rodriguez Rivera, who
had both initially lived in New York and been involved in Shearith Israel's growth before achieving acclaim as two of Rhode Island's wealthiest
Jewish merchants. The family retained close ties to New York's Gomez
clan, and those relationships—and the fact that Miriam's siblings already
rested in New York's old Jewish yard—all assured her normative treatment.[65] In excluding foreigners with few or no ties from the graveyard's
regular rows, trustees not only marked them as nonlocals but further
reinforced the communal symbolism that they invested in chronological burial.

The importance that most New York Jews invested in those normative rows came at the expense of household interests. It especially chafed
against a growing desire at the turn of the century to bury loved ones
together or to reserve individual or several graves for relatives to lie side
by side, no matter how many years separated their deaths. As proponents and protestors of the Row traded barbs into the 1830s, their arguments brought new attention to the family in New York Jewish burial.
The strategies that some devised to circumvent chronology also foreshadowed an alliance between the market and family will that would
totally reshape New York's budding Jewish cemetery economy.

A series of epidemics at the turn of the century unexpectedly added
to these spatial hierarchies in death. They not only drove debates about
creating additional Jewish graveyards but added the pressing question of
where to bury victims of disease and whether or not their inclusion
was appropriate in the old hallowed yard. When yellow fever raged in
the city between 1795 and 1803, the outbreak claimed a total of 2,806
New Yorkers. At least 10 Jews died between August and early October
1798.[66] Although Shearith Israel did not abandon chronology in the
throes of the epidemic, the experience led the congregation to consider
separate burial for future victims of disease. The move came during a
period when city leaders also considered limiting urban interment in
cases of contagion. Within two years, the synagogue began its search
for another place to bury "in case of any pestilential disorder should
prevail, whereby we might be prevented from using the present Burial
Ground."[67] In 1800, Shearith Israel first approached the city to buy a portion of the potter's field to fence off for future Jewish deaths of illness.

Although that plan never came to fruition, in a few years, the synagogue did dedicate a new ground, initially intended for any subsequent epidemic victims.

Whether the stigma of contagion initially associated with new Jewish burying places or the old yard's weighted history, a marked preference soon emerged among the multiple burying places that Shearith Israel accumulated in the nineteenth century. Members of prominent and long-present families tried with greater frequency to claim exclusive rights to bury their kin in the old yard, limiting Jewish peers with shorter ties to New York to the yards that the congregation had more recently purchased. When Shearith Israel dedicated its new ground on Eleventh Street,[68] the leaders initially intended its use for victims of disease. However, by 1812, it increasingly came to serve as a burial ground for strangers and, even more significantly, "newcomers who had no family ties with and sentimental attachment to the older ground on Chatham Square." That practice reflected a motion floated by leading members Aaron Levy and Benjamin Seixas as early as the new yard's purchase in 1805. They suggested that only "all persons Natives their wives and Children and Relatives who may become Electors at the time of the adoption of the Congregational Bye Laws" should merit burial in the original graveyard. Otherwise, the motion relegated to the new grounds "every person who may hereafter come among us that shall not come under the above Title."[69] While the motion never passed, spatial and communal hierarchy within and across the yards ultimately reigned in practice.

Nevertheless, the emphases on family ties spoke to a deeper desire to elevate kinship as a principle to organize the graveyard as well. Although congregants accepted sequential burial for most of the eighteenth century, they challenged the synagogue's inherent ban on family interment with greater frequency in the decades surrounding the Revolution. Widow Deborah Gomez made the first successful request in 1770. Roughly a month after the death of her husband, Isaac, she petitioned that the congregation leave a grave open beside him for whenever her time came.[70] Minutes do not expressly state why leaders granted that request, but the family's standing and Isaac's own recent terms as parnas (president) clearly influenced the deviation.[71] The fact that the Gomez family still retained the title to the burying ground purchased in trust for the congregation in 1728 clearly also mattered. Emboldened by those developments, the Gomezes made two similar petitions fairly quickly in 1774 and 1794.[72] This time, they hoped to reserve vacant lots in the yard to bury wives and children together. Although never granted, the appeals inspired other families. Isaac Moses, another frequent parnas and a man of means himself, asked first for a portion of the yard for "the exclusive use of [his] family" following the death of his young son Israel Ariel in 1801, who died at just sixteen. Upon rejection, Moses petitioned that a grave at least be left open for him to rest beside his beloved child. Other families hoped to carve out vacant space in the yard for protofamily plots in 1829 and 1836. And, of course, all these individual requests came against the backdrop of the failed 1805 motion to designate the old yard for the use of New York's oldest Jewish families.

Although trustees rejected the bulk of these petitions, their growing frequency and sentimentality demonstrated an evolving view of the family among Jewish New Yorkers in the early republic. Isaac Moses, for instance, framed his request after his son's death as a matter of comfort through family burial. "It is Inherent with our nature (if practicable)," he argued, "to have our Families together when ever it pleased the Allmighty God to take us from this Transitory Life."[73] If Moses considered family a principle just as natural to organize the graveyard as chronology, his contemporaries did not agree. In fact, they countered that it threatened the very communal ideal that sequential burial so closely guarded. Trustees' refusal reinforced larger collective priorities and underscored their added intention to regulate through placement. They remained uneasy about distinguishing in burial "except where persons were at variance or did not adhere to our profession." They also refused to set a precedent that might put individual families at odds with the larger community, claiming that if they granted Moses a section for his family, other members would feel "equally entitled to the same privileges and thereby our Beth Haim [traditional name for the graveyard] would be divided among a few families to the exclusion of others who already have some Relations interred there."[74] In this context, the rhetoric of the 1805 motion to entitle only legacy families to interment in the old yard played off of those limitations. If trustees would not allow individual families to cluster their loved ones, at least they could limit the old grounds to families with long ties to the city and the congregation.

In light of that rejection, others waited almost three decades to peti-tion again for individual family graves. The tone and conditions that they suggested in their next request showed not only greater emphasis on the family but also a new receptivity to larger consumer forces as an incentive to counter trustees' refusal. In 1829, ten members requested "the privilege" of purchasing one to five graves together "in case that the Calamaties of death should visit them or their families." They even offered additional payment above regular dues for the option. Antici-pating a counterargument that reservation fees would favor wealthier families, petitioners also suggested capping the payment at $25 "that it may enable all to avail themselves of it who wishes—the poor as well as the sick." They assured leaders that "the object for it is not distinction but a mere matter of feeling and Altogether Voluntary to be adopted or not by those who may be affected."[75] The rhetoric and drive in these requests highlighted early Jewish New Yorkers' internalization of broader new thinking around the family. The additional payments that they offered to validate family graves marked a realization too that the introduction of market forces might also prove to be a new means to counter traditional strictures that trustees would not otherwise compromise.

The emphasis on family graves illustrated broader American senti-ment making its way into early New York Jewish circles. During the pe-riod between the 1770s and the 1830s, European Americans developed new views of the family, infused with greater sentimentality and affection and different from the functionalism that defined family life in Europe or earlier colonial society. White northeasterners especially began to soften an older corporate view of the family by the mid-eighteenth cen-tury. Greater prosperity and less precarious social conditions recast the functions and expectations of various members of the household as well. Population growth and the move away from an agricultural society or in-home production also reshaped these dynamics. Parents assumed more caregiving roles, and their authority eased, as did their ties to land in-heritance. Broad changes even recast marriage as an institution based on love alongside pragmatism and property. By the time the Revolution upended colonial hierarchies even more, white Americans' family sys-tems emerged equally reformed. Egalitarianism offered new recognition for wives and children, and early American siblings enjoyed new social space to express their support and the importance of fraternal bonds.[76]

As early American Jews embraced these changing ideals, the evolution of their own internal commercial and family rhythms also elevated the value that they placed on ties of kin or the permanent comfort of proximity in death. For New York's peripatetic Jewish merchant community, arriving to trade, learn local markets, or establish business ties for a period, family members often separated to work in the Caribbean or other mainland colonies or returned to larger European centers.[77] Children especially embarked for far-off ports to apprentice, marry into other merchant families, or broaden a trading house's reach. Their likelihood of returning remained a function of their distance. One letter between Abigaill Franks and her London-based son, Naphtali, reflected the matriarch's sad resignation of that reality in her twilight years:

> I wish but for the happyness of Seeing you wich I begin to fear I never Shall. . . . If parents would Give themselves Leave to Consider the many Difficulties that attends the bringing up of Childeren, there would not be Such Imoderate Joy att there birth. I don't mean the Care of there infancy—thats the Least—but its affter they are grown Up and behave in Such a maner As to Give Satisfaction, then to be bereaved of them in the Decline of Life, when the injoying of them would be Our Greatest happyness, for the Cares of giting a Living Disperses Them Up and Down the world, and the Only Pleassure wee injoy (and that's intermixt with Anxiety) is to hear they doe well, Wich is A pleasure I hope to have.[78]

Although Abigaill spoke from the reality that the bulk of her adult children had left home at early ages and she would never see them again, similar sentiments echoed among many of her early American Jewish peers. Given the strain of family distance, it is little wonder that Jewish New Yorkers staked so strong a claim on overdue eternal proximity among their loved ones in the graveyard when there was a steady decline in commercial dispersion by early nineteenth century.

That elevation of the family and the strategies to promote it through material avenues, such as a willingness to pay extra fees, foreshadowed an eventual turn to family lots and the new commercial dimensions fostered by the 1850s. In the 1820s, however, the prospect of innovating the city's Jewish funeral sphere and disturbing so many traditions and social structures tied to it still fueled an uproar among other members.

Shearith Israel's board postponed a decision on the matter for three days to the protest of thirty-five other congregants. The dissenters claimed to have "heard with much concern" the application to reserve space for a fee in the old yard and charged that "the many objections to such a plan are so obvious that it is a matter of surprise that the Trustees would give it a serious consideration." Opponents claimed that the request was an affront to the divine and democratic benefits of chronological burial. "Each person should be Buried in the Row," they insisted, "as it shall please God in his own good time to call us to himself—for whatever destinction exists in Life, there is none in Death." The plan's commercial dimension also created much anxiety. Protestors argued against advanced payment because of the inequities it would create based on a family's means. "To give to the opulent a preference over the pious and religious poor might tend to cause to them feelings which in no manner could be compensated and which we shall on all occasions avoid," they argued. "We pray the Board to take this into their serious Consideration, and direct that each person shall be interred regularly in the Row, without any Space being left but next to the last Grave."[79] The fight for and against chronology clearly intersected larger sensitivities regarding the family, faith, the community, and the ability of market intervention to undermine long-standing tradition. By the episode's conclusion, leaders deferred again to the status quo, declaring it still "inexpedient to grant the reservation of ground for any grave or graves."[80] Despite clear discomfort over change or an unwillingness to compromise within the congregation, proponents of family burial continued their efforts into the 1830s, both as individual households and together as larger family coalitions. The actions signaled new value for member households in their own right over a broader collective ideal.

The bulk of these requests reflected a genuine comfort in burying among family. One isolated 1830 case showed the power of sentimentality, both for Joshua Moses, who made the appeal, and for trustees who ultimately granted it. That year marked the start of city plans to begin constructing Eleventh Street amid the larger project to lay a grid on Manhattan's street plan. The placement of Eleventh Street threatened the Jewish grounds on Milligan Street because it rested directly in the project's path. Trustees feared they would have to move eighty to one hundred graves and began planning to disinter any disturbed remains for reburial in a safer area of the same yard. Amid that crisis, Joshua Moses called on synagogue sympathies, unsettled by the prospect of his family's disinterment. Moses also drew on recent debates over a larger turn to family burial and echoed his own father's earlier plea for a grave alongside his brother, Israel Ariel. In otherwise unnerving conditions, he found great comfort in the idea of a family grave. "As it will soon be necessary to remove the precious remains of my Wife & Child," he wrote, "I have to solicit permission to have them reinterred in the Beth Haim [graveyard] as they now rest side by side & in addition One adjoining grave left Vacant for myself when it pleases the Almighty to issue his summons." Likely sympathetic to the urgency that drove this request, trustees granted a rare agreement to the appeal.[81]

By 1836, the board faced yet another petition that built on those before it. Now twelve families asked for the privilege of burying their loved ones together—a wish, they prefaced, "not for any distinction, but for the earnest and ardent desire of being near to those in death, we loved most to be near in life." They pointed out that when compared to old and recent Jewish communities in the Americas and abroad, "all but our congregation enjoy this right or privilege, also in Europe and the West Indies. Why should it be denied or withheld from us?"[82] While New York remained one of the only Jewish centers that did not allow family burial, that norm may have developed from the fact that from the start, New York Jewish burial stemmed from collective efforts. In other early Jewish communities, collective Jewish grounds often grew as an extension of land that one family had originally purchased for its use and then turned over to the rest of the community.[83] In these cases, prominent families enjoyed private and dedicated lots for their kin, predating the innovation in New York by decades.[84] New York churches, as far back as the seventeenth century, had also long offered parishioners the option of free burial in the churchyard or to pay extra for family vaults.[85]

For members petitioning Shearith Israel in the 1830s, though, justification for family burial not only rested in the fact that other communities enjoyed the option near and far but also stemmed from deep family will. With that passion, they also suggested that continued denial might force them to invoke unprecedented costs. "Such feeling is sanctioned by natural affection," petitioners argued, "by all moral, religious and civil institutions. . . . Our forefathers made it one of their first and urgent objects to secure such right, there is no religious obstacle to the contrary, and there should be no other. No man's right is invaded, no ground lost, the best feelings of our nature demand it, the harmony and welfare of our congregation call for it."[86] Despite that appeal, trustees fell back on their standard policy. They cast such requests as "improper, inexpedient and partial in their operation, and as conferring privileges that cannot be enjoyed equally by all members of the congregation: and the present board being of the same opinion, and having moreover recently decided that all interments should be made in rows it is therefore, RESOLVED that this board cannot comply with the request."[87] Even amid popular dissent, collective priorities still defined official policy.

Although trustees still refused to grant the majority family burial, members would not so easily give up their demands. Certain families, especially those of means, ultimately found ways to sidestep the prohibition by employing the old yard as a kind of larger family lot by proxy. They did so by taking advantage of city laws that intended to discourage urban burial and, in the process, demonstrated the power of the purse to circumvent leaders' policies.

After a particularly severe yellow fever outbreak in 1823, city officials issued the first in a series of fines to limit legal burial areas in Manhattan. In March of that year, they outlawed all burial below Canal Street and charged a $250 fine for any who disobeyed. As the old graveyard at Chatham Square fell within that zone, the policy ended the ground's use for the bulk of Jewish burials. Initially, the yard on what became Eleventh Street replaced it, but by 1830, once the congregation interred more than one hundred members, that newer ground also neared capacity. Moreover, the city's creation of the impending roadway ended its viability, as the expansion of Eleventh Street cut through the burial place. In 1829, the synagogue purchased its third active ground on Twenty-First Street, leading one member, Grace Nathan, warmly to imagine in a dedicatory poem that the new yard, "where yet no spade has rudely turned a sod . . . the soul of the just be deposited there."[88]

Despite an official move away from the old yard, many wealthier families still arranged for burial in that historic site at Chatham Square. Well into the 1830s, they paid the city fine for that privilege because they preferred to have their loved ones rest together in the same yard with other family, either recently buried or laid to rest in the distant past.

When the widow Brandly Isaacs died in 1825, her family paid the $250 fee so that she could repose among three grandchildren as well as her husband, Joshua, who had been interred exactly fifteen years earlier to the day.[89] When Moses Gomez died in 1826 and Benjamin Gomez in 1828, their prominent family also paid the fine for burial there so they might rest among kin dating to the eighteenth century.[90] Even Grace Nathan, despite her poetic ode to the new Twenty-First Street cemetery just years before, received a grave at Chatham Square in 1831. Her son, Seixas Nathan, preferred that she rest in the old yard among her prominent brothers, Benjamin and Gershom Mendes Seixas, and her husband, Simon Nathan, as well as other extended relations.[91] Between 1823 and 1831, the congregation buried at least twelve members in the old yard, most of them because their families paid extra fees for that privilege. Some, like the Gomez or Nathan families, valued a sense of legacy and historic ties within the yard's walls that they felt was lacking in the new grounds established only years before. Others simply sought the comfort of burying among their kin, especially in moments of tragedy. When Lavinia Brandon died in childbirth in 1828, only four years after her marriage, her husband, Isaac Lopez Brandon, paid the fine so his wife could lie in proximity to her parents as well as his. For Lavinia, sharing common space had an added meaning, especially given the strong desire of her father, Isaac Moses, when he made one of the first attempts to secure a family lot not even thirty years prior. When Lavinia's daughter, Lavinia Reyna Brandon, died of scarlet fever two years later, Isaac Brandon paid the fine again so that his daughter could rest with her mother and so many other generations of the family.[92]

Even if their loved ones' graves were scattered among the old yard's sequential rows, Jewish families that could afford the extra fine found solace in their dead sharing common earth. By paying the city fee, certain members worked the system, inverting the old yard into a makeshift family lot despite its long service as a symbol of community set high above the family. The spirit of those last interments at Chatham Square marked another gesture to family ties and their growing prominence in Jewish burial. The fact that they took place because certain families could afford that privilege also foreshadowed how purchasing power would soon offer members new influence over the funeral sphere. With it, they could promote greater popular will and, in coming decades, legitimize family burial as never before. Only in the 1850s would proper family lots became a viable option for the majority of congregants at Shearith Israel and other New York synagogues to purchase if they so desired. That option would revolutionize the city's Jewish cemetery economy as much as the basic structures of communal organization. In the interim, family priorities only continued to rise.

From a deeply communal endeavor centered on ritual and collective priorities in the mid-1650s, New York Jewish burial began to find more room for family interests two hundred years later. The seeds that early congregants and trustees had planted in their debates around the graveyard went a long way in that process. From their very first efforts to acquire and consecrate a Jewish burying place under Dutch rule, Jewish elites in New York continued to privilege community and tradition in their burial policies well into the nineteenth century. They realized that as American society allowed Jews greater self-determination and voluntary affiliation, burial provision remained the best safeguard to temper new challenges to Jewish cohesion. Despite that focus on community, congregation trustees weakened their own authority as their graveyard monopoly drew much of its power at the expense of family will. Time and again, as the synagogue conditioned burial on broader communal ideals, it triggered family vulnerability that led members to acquiesce or, eventually, to challenge the status quo. For more than a century, deep tensions between community and kin defined Jewish burial in New York.

Family loyalty and obligations could only stretch so far. Jewish New Yorkers accepted most of these policies during the early years of communal development because they had not yet built sufficient infrastructure or alternatives to communal support, particularly in death. If they wanted traditional burial in limited Jewish ground, the city's one congregation remained their only outlet. That situation changed by the early nineteenth century, however, as internal and external shifts forever altered the city and the new republic's Jewish social landscape. Although the synagogue could invoke Jewish law to deny burial for transgressions or social taboos, its denial of an increasingly valued comfort to bury among loved ones simply rang hollow. In changing the very assumptions around communal authority and the family in death, early Jewish congregants gained new footing to challenge at least one source of elders' long-standing control. Their openness to pay for that power would also usher in important changes.

Family well-being in funerary provisions was not limited to interment, though. Within a few decades, new grassroots Jewish burial societies—charged to pursue egalitarianism and the family's emotional and economic security—proliferated across the city and the nation to further those concerns. Trustees may long have maintained authority through the gravity of death and burial, but lay members began to realize that those concerns could also be harnessed for their own self-determination. As a result, emerging Jewish burial societies that promoted collective responsibility and new financial aid to affiliated families facing sickness and death raised new attention to the needs of individual households when planning for death and burial. At the same time, they fostered change from below that would ripple out for much of the nineteenth century.

2

Acts of True Kindness

To Tend the Dead, to Foster Fraternalism, 1785–1850

Few New York Jews would have imagined that a funeral procession "wending its way toward the potter's field" could help reshape their experience of dying for decades to come. They also may not have believed it could promote fraternalism in local Jewish life, a trend that was already in process since the American Revolution, recasting well-worn communal structures. Yet one early procession did amplify those changes when Gershom Mendes Seixas, Ephraim Hart, and Naphtali Phillips happened on it unwittingly in the summer of 1802. After stopping the funeral party to ask about the departed, they paled to hear that the stranger was "only a poor Jew" unknown to the community. The stigma of a pauper's grave collided with the knowledge that one of their own, even if only an itinerant, had come so close to spending eternity not surrounded by other Jews. Taking charge of body and burial, these men ended the ceremony at once. Determined that a similar situation should never happen again, they founded the Hebra Hased Va-Amet, a "society for true kindness" for the Jewish deceased. Its members pledged to sit with the sick, watch over the dying, lay the dead to rest, and pray among the mourning. Most importantly, it guaranteed that from death's onset to interment, Jews dying in New York and the loved ones they left behind would always benefit from the service of well-meaning contemporaries.[1]

As a part of their larger mission, the *hebra* founders also hoped to promote a Jewish variant of American fraternalism through the mutual regard and collective responsibility underlying those promises. While Jewish New Yorkers had already affiliated with groups like the Freemasons and the General Mechanics Society, they had not yet established distinctively Jewish aid associations similar to those begun by other Europeans who were also new to America.[2] For most of the eighteenth century, Jews in New York and other mainland colonies organized philanthropy and early social service needs through their synagogues. While their congregations served as centers of religious worship, they also dispensed relief in times of sickness, death, or monetary need. In New York City especially, Shearith Israel, the sole synagogue for roughly a century and a half, closely guarded oversight of those activities until the turn of the nineteenth century, when financial insolvency and a growing Jewish population simply rendered its monopoly untenable. Although lay members tried on occasion to found dedicated societies to offer needy Jews additional support, synagogue trustees curtailed most efforts or limited these groups' ability to operate alongside the congregation. Those that did survive would not function independently until the 1820s and 1830s.

As Shearith Israel's control finally fragmented, Jewish burial and benevolent societies flourished in direct correlation. In the process, they reshaped a long legacy of centralized communal organization and laid the ground for more egalitarian governing structures, grassroots forms of organization, and preemptive aid mechanisms to enter subsequent Jewish institutions. Jewish burial societies in particular embraced those ideals. They built on a legacy forged by the city's first short-lived, semi-independent burial order, the Hebra Gemilut Hasadim (roughly 1785–90), but their ubiquity decades later helped spread fraternalism among a far wider array of Jewish residents. In so doing, the proliferation of burial societies shifted New York's Jewish institutional framework closer to a prevailing model of multiple lodges, congregations, and friendly societies coexisting within American ethnic or religious communities. Since dedicated burial societies like these played an important early part in the evolution of Jewish social welfare, that interplay also raised new concerns about the family and its economic security when facing death. Similar groups proliferated by the 1850s, many of which soon detached from parent synagogues or formed through independent action. In under a decade, they spawned some of New York and America's first Jewish benefit societies and national Jewish fraternities. By the end of the nineteenth century, Jewish lodges, burial societies, and fraternal orders became so pervasive and integral to Jewish communal life and end-of-life planning that affiliation to these groups wholly outpaced synagogue membership.

The spirit of the American Revolution in which the city's first semi-autonomous Jewish burial societies took shape enabled some of that influence. Inspired by new forms of republicanism, these groups offered members more avenues of direct participation in the life and governance of their societies, and the collectivism and mutual regard that they promoted created an outlet for specifically Jewish expressions of early American fraternal culture. Most importantly, the financial relief and collective support that members provided to one another and their dependents offered Jewish households popular alternatives to the goodwill and deep pockets of the synagogue elites on which the wider public had depended for so long until then. Increasing Jewish migration into the nineteenth century only continued that revolution. For one thing, Jewish need simply outpaced the resources that any one synagogue could provide. For another, Jewish immigrants transplanted brotherhoods geared toward relieving the sick and dying or looked to the model of *Vereine* (voluntary associations), which were popular among their German-speaking neighbors in Manhattan's immigrant quarter. In greater numbers, they also joined many popular American fraternal orders or founded wholly new Jewish variants like the B'nai B'rith and the Independent Order Free Sons of Israel.

Whether they were inspired by early democratic impulses or the need for communal support among a growing cohort of working-class Jewish immigrants, burial societies again offered natural conduits for these forces to permeate Jewish social structures. Even if native-born Jews or recent arrivals looked to America's inviting fraternal culture for social and financial benefits, the long-standing Jewish priority to keep death within tight-knit circles ensured they would not stray too far. Whether infusing their hevrot kadisha with American fraternal ideals or building American Jewish fraternities to tend to burials, these forces remained closely linked in New York Jewish life. Likewise, as the city's Jewish population grew and fragmented, players in a crowded field of synagogues, lodges, and benevolent societies understood that ownership of Jewish graveyards assured communal autonomy. If the city's early synagogue had resisted the egalitarianism and self-determination circulating during the waning years of its social monopoly, the innate fraternalism of its first burial hebrot offered a ready platform for those ideals to flourish in the social landscape that succeeded them. Evolving Jewish approaches to death and burial altered Jewish social welfare and communal life in nineteenth-century New York, but once more, the alliance between family and financial well-being drove much of that change from below.

Dispensers of Kindness: Recognizing Unseen Funeral Labor

Although burial remained a central concern of nineteenth-century New York Jewish communal life, the public Jewish emphasis on death and dying underwent a marked change with the development of the city's first formal Jewish burial societies. Groups like the Hebra Gemilut Hasadim (Society for Dispensing Acts of Kindness, ca. 1785–90) or its more durable successor, the Hebra Hased Va-Amet (Society for Acts of True Kindness, 1802–present), altered New York Jewish approaches to death by formally institutionalizing societies to guide the dying through their last hours and perform the necessary rituals to prepare their bodies for their return to the earth. These groups also strove to bring as many Jews as possible into that work. In the decades after the Hebra Hased Va-Amet's creation, for instance, leaders not only compiled instructional materials to spread knowledge of Jewish funeral law and labor but worked with Jewish women to organize a formally recognized women's burial society. Few, if any, earlier synagogue records suggest similar efforts to engage the wider public. That absence stands out, in contrast to a wealth of edicts and resolutions regarding the graveyard and its disciplinary power. Unlike so many public pronouncements leveraging death and burial, members and managers of the city's new Jewish burial societies focused on the intimacies of the deathbed and compassion shown in the houses of mourning. Through these efforts, the work of aiding the sick, comforting the bereaved, and carefully performing rituals over the dead received new public recognition and participation.

Little evidence survives detailing funeral labor before those burial societies, but all traces suggest that synagogue leaders, any family members present, and perhaps knowledgeable congregants willing to volunteer their services likely carried out that work.[3] Jewish New Yorkers do not seem to have organized any long-term burial society until the establishment of the Hebra Gemilut Hasadim sometime in the late eighteenth century. In that sense, they may have mirrored their counterparts in Philadelphia, where most responsibilities associated with a hevra kadisha—funeral arrangements, prayer over the dead, or services during the week-long period of mourning—still "remained in the hands of the congregation's *adjunta* [governing board], who also acted as overseers of the cemetery."[4] Little wonder that Abigaill Franks marveled in 1737 at the news that her young son Naphtali had risen to the task of participating in these activities during his uncle's death in London and "had the Satisfaction of imploying y[ou]r Indefatigable Endeavours in discharg[in]g Your Last dutys to him in Such a manner As procoured you ye commendations of all his friends."[5] As Erik Seeman speculates in his study of death and dying in early America, her perspective in New York may have only elevated her pride given colonial Jews' dependence on far less organized networks to administer the last rites.[6]

Of course, the emotional weight of the deathbed likely impelled relatives to similar action. Even when American Jewish burial societies grew far more common in the nineteenth century, widow Catherine Solomons (1768–1852), who outlived her husband and four of her five children over the course of her eighty-four years, cataloged her role at many of those losses. Her son Lucius, she wrote in 1830, "was Sencible to the last" when she arrived in time to witness his final breath and recite the Shema, the traditional prayer accompanying death. At the passing of her youngest son, Levy, two years later, she wrote, "Miriam Judah [a cousin], with myself Said the Shamong [*sic*] at his last moment."[7] Similarly, one can easily imagine many contemporaneous Jewish death scenes in New York, echoing one that Rebecca Gratz described in 1826 of a young niece's recent death. In resolute anguish, Gratz wrote, "Her mother never quitted her bedside, was able to perform the last duties—to embrace the cold remains and give directions about the . . . scene."[8]

Although synagogue officials and family members may have shared enough commitment to serve as attendants at death, early North American Jewish communities stood out in their lack of well-developed formal burial societies for most of their formative years. In Europe, distinct Jewish brotherhoods and hevrot kadisha that oversaw the last offices and offered mourners some monetary assistance had existed for several hundred years by the eighteenth century. In larger Caribbean centers like Curaçao, where Jews began settling in the 1650s, a separate burial society formed between 1686 and 1692.[9] New York's comparatively small

Jewish population accounted for the delay, but so did Shearith Israel's drive to centralize communal services, particularly given its sensitivity to the authority vested in funerary provision.

The complicated relationship between the synagogue and the short-lived Hebra Gemilut Hasadim demonstrated that anxiety over institutional competition. On the one hand, the hebra foreshadowed later cooperation between Shearith Israel and nineteenth-century semi-autonomous philanthropic groups, but during this society's eighteenth-century tenure, its existence created more tension than collaboration. The congregation leaders especially chafed at the possibility of diverting communal funds or jeopardizing their control of burial. This is not to say that membership did not overlap. Several men listed as hebra members in 1788, for instance, also occupied key positions in their lifetimes as Shearith Israel presidents, elders, or trustees.[10] Similarly, although Jacob Mordecai served in 1785 as the hebra's *gabay* (chairman of its board of four managers), it did not prevent him from acting as a member of the synagogue *adjunta* the following year. It did perhaps make his input more colorful when the hebra repeatedly petitioned the congregation for permission to solicit funds during services and synagogue gatherings.

Despite basic cooperation, synagogue elders remained cautious, clearly fearing that a hebra with too much independence might allow congregants to circumvent the synagogue in death. At first, the congregation jealously guarded funerary tools and reaffirmed through edicts its exclusive control of the graveyard. In one of the earliest extant exchanges in April 1785, hebra representatives had to make several requests before the synagogue board finally agreed to repair and turn over the communal hearse to the society's care. Elders did so only after underscoring that it would remain "for the use of the Congregation Shearith Israel, & to be at the Disposal of the Trustees."[11] Just months later, in June of that year, they reaffirmed their symbolic and literal control by resolving that a key to the graveyard's gate "be always lodged with the Acting Parnas & that Places for Interment be Alotted" only by him and trustees.[12] Although the board did soften its stance in October the following year, promising to supply a new "Bier & Mautar [purifying] Board" and to turn over "the Cloths, Towels, Spades, & Pick Axes," to the hebra, that agreement still came just a month after a resolution "that no person, presume to Break Ground, or put up any Tomb Stone in the Beth A Haim, without Liberty first Obtained from the Trustees."[13] Shearith Israel may have facilitated the hebra's sanctified labor, but it still jealously guarded access to the graveyard and the influence that came with it.

Competition for communal revenue also concerned Shearith Israel's trustees. For one thing, the synagogue struggled to maintain its budget during rebuilding efforts following the Revolution and the city's broader economic crisis. For another, its newly constituted board of trustees had not yet developed a strategy to share power with the older group of elders that would slowly disband over the same period. For the remainder of their tenure, elders took on spiritual matters with the fiction that trustees oversaw the synagogue's fiscal health. As a result, the two bodies ultimately carried out extended debates in 1785 over the hebra's request to set up a separate collection box at funerals and synagogue services to supplement its dues. While the president and elders agreed with some conditions, trustees refused and rescinded the privilege.[14]

It is perhaps unsurprising that the Hebra Gemilut Hasadim disbanded within five years and turned over its assets to Shearith Israel in 1790. No records explain why the group dissolved, but its growing financial independence likely sounded its death knell. By 1789, the hebra gained sufficient means to rent a piece of land from the synagogue in its burying ground and to pay for construction of a shed there to keep its tools. In the most significant departure from earlier debates over funding and fixing instruments, the society even amassed a treasury large enough to loan the congregation fifty pounds. Trustees forgave that sum when they absorbed the hebra's assets the following year.[15]

The fear of divided communal loyalty only heightened those budgetary battles, particularly as the Hebra Gemilut Hasadim also took up philanthropic aid, which had once been Shearith Israel's exclusive domain. Few society records survive, but one nineteenth-century overview described that the hebra relieved "the needy by donations in money and fuel, and when sick, it provided them with proper medical assistance."[16] The group also paid a local doctor for his services and made provisions among members to nurse each other in illness. In the event of a death, the society even innovated monetary benefits that echoed broader fraternal models that had not yet fully permeated Jewish social welfare in New York. Drawing from dues paid, the hebra guaranteed "Abel [bereavement] money" of £1.4.0, likely paid to compensate for earnings lost during shiva, the week of mourning. Members also enjoyed the guarantee that others in the society would pray at their houses during that period to ensure mourners' ability to recite the requisite prayers for their dead.[17]

In these efforts, the hebra introduced a more collective model of aid, and its financial, social, and medical assistance gestured at a far more preemptive and comprehensive approach to need than anything Shearith Israel had practiced until then. Although the synagogue offered significant charity to impoverished Jews and their families, those gifts took the form of limited stipends, paid passage to other ports, food, fuel, occasional loans, medical and funeral expenses, and in limited cases, pensions to widows or the infirm until they secured long-term care from family members. In most cases, however, that aid went to transients or members after they had fallen into poverty rather than doling out guaranteed funds to prevent extended need. The synagogue's power to give also remained squarely among its elites, with the president and his advisors ultimately making those decisions. By founding and joining that first hebra, Jewish New Yorkers created an alternative source of Jewish philanthropy, and as members who paid dues for predictable services, they also secured more control among themselves and their peers in the use and receipt of society funds. Perhaps ironically, although the congregation may have understood the hebra as a group potentially supplanting it, its members actually created an institution to supplement gaps in synagogue aid. By addressing deficiencies in the synagogue's reactive approach to charity, a group like the Hebra Gemilut Hasadim stood poised to assist households in need of assistance but not quite so imperiled as to have fallen into the ranks of the poor.

That spirit of focused and grassroots mutualism closely paralleled other ethnic communal efforts in eighteenth-century America, particularly coexisting churches and nationally oriented benevolent societies. Although colonial congregations had long overseen charity, that work did not preclude other immigrants from founding parallel societies based on place of origin. Boston's Scots Charitable Society (1657) represented one of the earliest examples, and its poor, sick, and funeral relief succeeded in "reducing the number of public dependents at a time when official agencies were heavily burdened."[18] The group served as a model for countless others across early America, and New York was no

exception. By the mid-eighteenth century especially, when increased immigration and epidemics caused severe need, poverty grew so prevalent
by 1752 that New York poor-law officials drew £150 against the next year's
tax revenues just to lighten the load. Churches and religious groups collected for needy members, but several other ethnic or fraternal societies
formed to supplement those efforts. Two such groups, the city's German
Society and the French Benevolent Society, were formed in the late 1760s.
English residents founded the St. George Society in 1770 for countrymen
in need.[19] It is not very surprising then that some of the earliest extant
signs of a robust Jewish effort at mutual aid beyond the synagogue dated
to this period too.

The Limits of Synagogue-Centered Social Welfare

Despite its short-lived tenure, the Hebra Gemilut Hasadim and several
benevolent and burial societies founded soon after its dissolution created three important legacies that complicated New York's model of
Jewish social service in the nineteenth century. First, they recognized
the limits of Shearith Israel's approach to need, especially regarding
death or death-related poverty. Second, vocal efforts to fill those gaps
demonstrated the role for distinct and specialized Jewish philanthropies,
putting to rest the insistence that one congregation could reasonably,
or responsibly, provide for all the city's Jews. Finally, the Hebra Gemilut Hasadim and its successor, the Hebra Hased Va-Amet, served as
important initial conduits for American forms of fraternalism to enter
New York Jewish communal life. As Daniel Soyer has argued for the
second half of the nineteenth century, Jews modeled mutual aid associations on widespread American fraternities or joined existing orders
themselves in greater numbers.[20] Early Jewish burial societies like the
Hebra Gemilut Hasadim, the Hebra Hased Va-Amet, and others following their example in the early nineteenth century served as important
transitional institutions in that longer process among the city's rapidly
fracturing synagogues. They gave credence to the effort to decentralize
synagogue aid and nurtured early seeds of American fraternal interests
in specifically Jewish communal expressions. The pull of death and
burial exposed those ideals to wider swaths of the Jewish public, and the
gravity of the matter at hand added to their legitimacy. If the colonial

synagogue—itself a transplanted legacy of Jews' corporate status in European society—had resisted those forms, the city's first semiautonomous Jewish burial societies emerged in a far different context. Whether for their guaranteed monetary benefits in sickness and death or the egalitarianism shaping their governing structures and the style of the funeral rites performed (discussed in more detail below), these groups took on dual functions. Outwardly traditional hevrot kadisha, they also constituted early Jewish gestures at fraternities like the Freemasons, the Tammany Society, or the St. George and General Mechanics Societies to which their Jewish founders already belonged. The sensibilities that these groups instilled among Jewish members offered powerful models for New York's Jewish communal framework, especially in that sacred work over the dead.

Shearith Israel's inadequate responses to increasing crises of death, disease, and poverty enabled that transition. The Hebra Gemilut Hasadim's disbanding made the absence of popular Jewish aid groups seem all the more egregious. The city's 1798 yellow fever outbreak, for instance, offered a ripe incentive for new leadership and institution building, especially as most synagogue leaders had fled the epidemic to safer areas outside of town. Filling that void, those remaining behind assumed communal reins. Young Walter Judah, for instance, then completing his studies at Columbia College's medical school, committed at just twenty-one to stay in the city and see patients every day until he too contracted and died of the disease. "Old in wisdom, tender in years," his ornate and lengthy tombstone recalls, "skilled he was in . . . the labor of healing. . . . He gave money from his own purse to buy for them beneficent medicines / But the good that he did was the cause of his death."[21] Others, like Shearith Israel's spiritual leader, Gershom Mendes Seixas, compensated for the synagogue's absence by founding an impromptu charitable institution called Kalfe Sedaka Mattan Besether, a society to distribute charity and "undisclosed gifts" to Jewish epidemic victims and survivors. Concern for the city's most vulnerable Jews drove that effort, especially since trustees' flight inhibited congregation action, since they remained the only leaders authorized to dole out synagogue funds. Jewish residents too poor to flee not only faced medical turmoil but required assistance to regain their footing after the scourge due to their limited means. Through the society Mattan Besether, Seixas created an important institutional mechanism to harness giving among the public at large. In the long run, he also created a way to gather funds independent of the congregation, particularly through annual efforts to make the group a mainstay of New York Jewish charity.[22] "Our contributions were small," he admitted in one 1805 drive, but "still they were found to be of great service to our distressed friends."[23] Days later, he and others revised the group's bylaws to expand charitable efforts that they claimed "have heretofore been considerable, but applied in such manner, as to have been productive of a limited effect." Population growth, they claimed, and the need for new strategies to assist Jewish New Yorkers into the future demanded "that the foundation of a permanent charitable institution should be laid."[24]

Drawing on frontline experiences of tending to the Jewish dead during the outbreak, several men involved in that society began a parallel effort to reestablish a hevra kadisha for New York in 1802. Bookended by epidemics visiting Gotham between 1798 and 1823, the period saw a sharp increase in Jewish mortality. That reality only further strained a centralized approach to death. Although a voluntary system may have sufficed while New York Jewry remained fairly small over the previous century, the increasing number of Jewish deaths that the synagogue registered demanded a formally organized burial society. After all, by the 1790s, the congregation had buried fourteen Jewish New Yorkers, the majority yellow fever victims, and most of them had been concentrated between 1796 and 1799. Thereafter, a high of twenty-seven Jewish deaths marked the decade between 1801 and 1810 alone.[25] While a Jewish stranger's near burial in the potter's field in 1802 may have culminated in the establishment of the Hebra Hased Va-Amet, longer trends set the stage and receptivity for its founding. Little wonder that although Shearith Israel had never before listed a burial society in its constitution, by 1805, leaders embraced the hebra and the very real need it filled in a new constitution.[26] In an even more striking act of recognition, by early 1812, trustees even gave the hebra a key to the gate of the graveyard.[27]

A handful of groups specializing in death or death-related poverty in this period also supplemented the synagogue, foreshadowing the wave of Jewish fraternal lodges with origins in Jewish burial societies that emerged in New York by midcentury. The Female Hebrew Benevolent Society, for instance, founded in 1820 under Shearith Israel's auspices, specifically offered aid to "'indigent females' and their families."[28] As a core portion of the Jewish poor, widows benefited most from their efforts. Although Shearith Israel offered pensions to its employees' widows, few if any Jewish institutions provided regular aid to deceased members' wives. That basic entitlement only came several decades later through autonomous burial societies, fraternities, and lodges not attached to any synagogue. Along those lines, B'nai Jeshurun's burial society, which later became the Hebrew Mutual Benefit Society, reintroduced monetary awards to members and their families during illness and loss. Former Ashkenazic (central European) members of Shearith Israel established the group in 1826, just after they seceded from the first synagogue. It not only paid members for up to four weeks of sickness and regular shiva money during the week of mourning, but by 1855, with a $5,000 gift from philanthropist Judah Touro, the group also set aside a fund to address the needs of widows and orphans.[29] Alongside the significant work of administering the last offices, "it soon became a real mutual benefit society and forerunner of the multitude of mutual benefit hebrot that grew up in New York."[30] These and other societies marked an important new stage in New York's Jewish approach to social welfare. Their legitimacy during Shearith Israel's waning social monopoly not only validated a cooperative system between synagogues and Jewish fraternities but laid important foundations for more effective monetary relief to families in sickness and death. They also allowed average Jewish households far greater access and self-determination over those resources, independent of congregation treasuries and elites.

Fraternalism through Funeral Rites

In addition to mutual aid and collective organization, the city's early Jewish burial societies did much to promote egalitarianism and collective responsibility among the wider Jewish community in the early republic. The Hebra Hased Va-Amet especially nurtured that synergy through democratic governance and efforts at reciprocity involving as many city Jews as possible. It also subtly reinterpreted Jewish funeral rituals in favor of universal deference to be applied to all recipients, regardless of status. That hebra leaders imbued their project with these ideals spoke to broader sensibilities they had developed in the decades surrounding American independence and the inspiration they drew as new Jewish citizens with access to non-Jewish social circles.

Most hebra founders and longtime leaders, after all, remained passionate republicans for most of their lives. Gershom Seixas, for instance, almost single-handedly sustained groups like the Society Mattan Besether until his death in 1816 and was deeply committed to the Hebra Hased Va-Amet in its formative years. From Seixas's early activism fighting religious disabilities in Pennsylvania's state constitution during his self-imposed exile to Philadelphia when the British occupied New York during the war to his discomfort with Federalist deference and hierarchy, he used his pulpit and the weight of his communal example to promote collectivism and a sense of mutual responsibility among Jewish New Yorkers upon his return. As one of Shearith Israel's most well-regarded ministers in that period, Seixas not only lived as a committed Jeffersonian but also offered "a model for Jews in New York who strove to be Jewish citizens of the new republic."[31] His contemporary, Naphtali Phillips (1773–1870), shared a similar outlook and committed his long life to local and national politics. At just three years old, he was also whisked with his family to Philadelphia during the British occupation and, as an adolescent, became an ardent supporter of Washington. Returning to New York in 1801, just a year before founding the Hebra Hased Va-Amet, Phillips became proprietor of the city's premier newspaper, the *National Advocate*. Along with his fourteen terms of service as Shearith Israel's president, he gained prominence in democratic politics during a seventy-five-year membership to the Tammany Society.[32]

Similar pedigrees graced two of the hebra's early managers, ardent republican printer Naphtali Judah and Bernard Hart. Before his 1804 term as manager, Judah also played a prominent role in the Tammany Society and earned some distinction as one of New York's first Jews to belong to the Freemasons and the General Mechanics Society in 1796. Little wonder that he later applied that organizational sensibility to Jewish philanthropic experiments like the Society Kalfe Mattan Besether.[33] Likewise, Bernard Hart drew on his membership to New York's St. George Society in 1792, where he was "said to have been very active in aiding the sick and dying among his fellow members."[34] Cutting their teeth on these early American fraternities, the founders of the city's first viable semiautonomous Jewish charities applied those models to Jewish social welfare beyond the synagogue. The social fluidity that allowed them as Jews to step beyond the confines of community and confession cast them as cultural brokers, bridging and introducing fraternal constructs into specifically Jewish forms.

The egalitarianism that these early hebra leaders learned in those societies influenced the policies that they introduced in their new Jewish burial society, from mutual responsibility to decision-making. The group's 1812 constitution promised affiliates "all the services of the Hebra usually practiced, both in the last minutes of life, and to the tahara [purification] and kvura [interment] with every other ritual duty of the members."[35] In addition to affiliation, those entitlements hinged on expectations that members would reciprocate whenever called on to assist others in the society who arrived at their times of need. The group's president, treasurer, and secretary formed a special board of managers with specific power to assign members "to attend our brethren in their last moments and . . . to perform the rites and ceremonies practiced among Jews as it respects the dead."[36] A series of fines for refusal to sit with the sick or dying or failure to participate in purification and prayers further attested to the gravity of those obligations. The group also leveled even heavier charges against members who neglected duties that they had promised to fulfill.[37]

The hebra's democratic approach to governance reinforced mutual regard. In matters ranging from new applicants' admission to constitutional amendments, the group required a two-thirds majority of all members from the start. Aspiring applicants had to submit a formal written application, and the matter did not receive attention until a ballot at the next stated meeting. This differed from some European counterparts in which wealth, prestige, and unanimous consent that often veered toward nepotism could define admission to the society.[38] The group demanded a similar two-thirds majority for any change to its constitution and policies.[39] In its inclination toward collective authority, the hebra likely reacted against the synagogue's parallel reversal of power to elites. Although Shearith Israel had adopted more democratic features just after the Revolution, its board of trustees steadily reconsolidated power over subsequent decades. By 1805, Shearith Israel's new constitution departed in striking form from the one penned in the 1790s by men like committed Whig Solomon Simson. Although that earlier document

had invoked popular will and members' freedom "in a state happily constituted upon the principles of equal liberty, civil and religious," to enter
a compact of self-government, the revised version fifteen years later
lacked a bill of rights and embraced a governing structure tied to the
board and parnas, who held strict control over synagogue philanthropy,
employees, and its school.[40] Trustees also enjoyed the power to impose
heavy fines on disruptive members during prayer and to demand $10
from unaffiliated Jews in New York seeking services.[41] The hebra's commitment to democratic governance when precisely the opposite trend
resurfaced in the synagogue highlighted the burial society as an alternative communal force, fusing Jewish brotherhood in New York with early
republican ideals.

Efforts to promote mass participation expanded that drive. In its most
enduring legacy, the hebra spread knowledge of funeral rites by compil-
ing a handbook in 1827 called the *Compendium of the Order of the Burial
Service and Rules for the Mournings*.[42] The guide served as an equalizing
tool, presenting centuries-old religious law in an easy-to-use English
gloss. Its writers even incorporated ritual questions that had come up
in New York or nearby communities over the last few decades. In so
doing, they removed old barriers of elite control over funeral knowledge that stood at the heart of the synagogue's dominance of the funeral
realm. Before the manual's publication, Jewish New Yorkers often simply
deferred to communal elders in difficult or time-sensitive burial decisions. For even basic ritual questions, Jews would have needed literacy
in rabbinic Hebrew or an understanding of legal precedent to consult
the standard sixteenth-century reference text, Joseph Caro's *Shulhan
Aruch* (Code of Jewish Law). The average Jewish New Yorker had little
access to that discourse, to say nothing of complex questions for which
even knowledgeable synagogue officials wrote and deferred to rabbinic
counsel overseas. With the compendium, any Jew at least literate in English had a basis to engage in funeral debates or to understand his or her
obligations at times of personal or communal loss.

The work also democratized performance of Jewish funeral rites by
scripting procedures and prayers when washing the dead as well as those
called for at the deathbed and funeral. Until then, although Jewish New
Yorkers could find prayers for the sick facing their final moments or
the service for interments at the back of daily prayer books, they would

have had no comparable and concise gloss in translation covering all questions relating to death. The book gave full public attention to all stages of loss and the active roles for those involved to ensure the proper execution of matters like bedside confessions, rending mourners' garments, instructions for funeral and committal, and mourners' obligations and restrictions throughout the grieving period. The compendium also represented the first written manual in New York translating and detailing the hebra's most solemn work of washing the dead in preparation for burial. Those rituals would otherwise have to be learned and passed down by the very act of participation. The compendium divided all this information into two sections for easy reference and use. One part offered an overview of the laws of mourning. The other collected appropriate prayers and procedures in Hebrew with English translation for each step of the way. Commissioned by the Hebra Hased Va-Amet from printer Solomon Henry Jackson, who just a year earlier had translated and printed an English version of the daily prayer book, the compendium built on and contributed in its own right to a growing legacy of homegrown Jewish texts for use by New York and American Jews.[43]

The attention that the guidebook placed on mourners' obligations also underscored the crucial role of family involvement to carry out the proper mourning procedures in the wake of a loved one's death. This highlighted family members' active role in properly marking a loss for themselves and the larger community. Composers, for instance, detailed the laws of garment rending and mourners' restrictions, tying these rites specifically to those nuclear ties "on whose account we must mourn, viz. a father, mother, son, daughter, wife, brother, sister, whether by the father's side or by the mother's side."[44] Those allusions marked a shift from the synagogue's old tendency to elevate the communal whole over individual families. Focus on relatives' obligations also elevated kin and their active role in funeral rite. In that sense, at least symbolically, the compendium honored family members as participants rather than passive dependents leveraged in death to enforce communal norms and payments.

The book's nuanced treatment of two stages of bereavement highlighted those capacities: the regular mourning period following interment, "*Abeloth* [sic]," and a liminal stage beforehand, when mourners were designated "*Onan* [sic]." The latter period was initiated by death and active until the body's committal to the earth to signal the irregularity of an unburied corpse. Stressing a family's duty to lay a loved one to rest, the guidebook instructed that until that important task's completion, survivors were to forgo even quotidian religious practices like "the usual blessings . . . as also the observance of affirmative precepts."[45] Although they could not yet begin to mourn fully, bereaved family still had to mark this in-between stage in very deliberate ways. Ritual called on them to tear their clothing, to refrain from eating meat, to omit certain prayers, to avoid wine, and to obey a "strictly enjoined" mandate of "separation of man and wife . . . under all circumstances."[46] After interment, the week-long period of shiva began. Those family members whom tradition called on to mourn could not work, bathe, or again be physically intimate. Male mourners also could not shave for a month after the burial.[47] The compendium's composers aimed to educate the public about these rites and their many legal intricacies, but they also hoped to guide mourning families in all stages of observance. Even if the bereaved did not participate in the final ritual ceremonies over the dead, they would know their own personal obligations and engage in a larger performance to mark the loss of a local Jew for all onlooking contemporaries. Through the tattered clothes they donned, the foods they did not eat, the drinks they did not drink, the intimacies they did not enjoy, the labor they left undone, and the facial hair they did not remove, Jewish men and women performed their own shares of the funeral rites. In stressing those requirements that Jewish law posed for mourning family members, the hebra further increased participation and afforded the family new funerary recognition.

An impulse toward egalitarianism also shaped the group's interpretation of the purification ceremony by removing any hierarchy from the service and calling for the utmost dignity and deference to all departed Jews brought before it. The bulk of the manual's ritual section focused on washing the deceased and cast that rite as one of the most intimate dignities a hebra could provide. The compendium detailed a delicate process of moving with care from head to toe. It charged washers to ask mercy for the soul before them with lofty allusions to biblical prophets and kings. Accompanying prayers set the dead on par with those hallowed figures, and the body's actual treatment exuded reverence and respect. Attendants performed seven washings—cycling among water, soap, niter, and myrtle leaves—with careful attention to even fingertips and eyelids. The rite's conclusion called on hebra members to place the purified remains in the coffin and to invoke the traveling Ark of the Covenant as they carried the body on its final earthly passage to the grave.[48] That orchestration in early national New York stood in marked contrast to the one practiced among contemporaries in London. That city's hebra reserved "those additional solemnities" only for communal elites like respected rabbis, judges of religious courts, cantors, members of the *mahamad* (synagogue governing board), or other hebra brethren.[49] For all other departed Jews whom the English group attended, its manual prescribed a solemn yet far less deferential procedure devoid of those prayers and proud allusions and containing far fewer cycles.

That New York's hebra did not differentiate by social standing further indicated the permeation of early American values, particularly the Jeffersonian republicanism to which so many hebra leaders committed. As Joyce Appleby has argued, alongside political thought, Jefferson understood the need to deconstruct formalities in behavior and social interactions to promote political democracy, particularly in a society transitioning from colonial and monarchal rule. Realizing, at least among white men, that "the presumption of social superiority, conveyed in dress, carriage, voice, and gesture . . . served as a pervasive check to democratic action," Jefferson modeled new forms of White House etiquette and statecraft, symbolically elevating a sense of status among average white Americans.[50] Drawing on that impulse to counter rank or aristocracy, men like Seixas who guided the hebra in its holy work equally committed to promote egalitarianism and self-respect among members and those whom they attended. Mutual regard clearly underwrote the society's reason for being, but by universally offering the most regal purification to Jews of all walks, the group both departed from English Sephardic custom and forged a path for new American Jewish citizens, melding one of the loftiest promises of their people with that being set forth in their new home.

Those ideals made their way into subsequent Jewish burial societies, even if only indirectly by virtue of their organization in the model of the early hebra and their common use of its compendium. Whether later groups subscribed to Sephardic rites or not, they used the original handbook since no other English-language manual existed in New York.[51] Even if only unconsciously, a wide array of Jewish New Yorkers received firsthand exposure to broader republican values as they rose to a particular and intracommunal calling. As a result, the burial societies not only represented Jewish institutions as far more democratic in spirit and structure than any synagogue before them but enabled members to actively perform ideals of collective virtue on their contemporaries under the most intimate of circumstances.

The hebra also promoted mutualism through its efforts to expand participation among as many Jewish New Yorkers as possible, women and men alike. Just three years after printing the manual, the group sent out a call to formally organize a women's hebra. Since ritual law strictly segregated funeral rites by gender, the city's Jewish women had long performed the last duties even without a distinct society. They also oversaw the added task of sewing shrouds for all of New York's Jewish dead. Despite those responsibilities, women's funeral participation received little recognition. Reigning Sephardic custom limited the public space for women, as it prohibited them from marching in funeral processions or entering the graveyard at committals, even if they were immediate mourners.[52] A contemporary English Sephardic account even falsely claimed in 1870 that "the prohibition is universal—extending even to those countries where the most liberal ideas prevail," which its author justified in an ancient superstition that women's presence would entice the hovering angel of death: "He loves to dance among them with his sword drawn, the bare thought of the ruin which must follow from such an encounter caused the frightened sages at once to enact that . . . no woman should take part in any funeral ceremonial outside the house. If the Angel of Death were minded for a dance they at least would be careful not to provide him with partners."[53] Although Sephardic custom long defined New York Jewish practice, women and men both began to challenge that system in the 1840s through greater organization.

The absence of an official women's burial society in New York stood out, particularly in comparison to other locales like the German states or eastern European Jewish villages. In the former, women's publicly recognized involvement in burial dated to the early modern era. A women's burial society operated in Mainz, for instance, between 1650 and 1693, with a similar group founded in Berlin in 1745.[54] In locales farther east like Belarus, Jewish burial societies commonly cooperated with women to tend the dead or look after female patients.[55]

The emergence in New York of women's burial societies by the middle of the nineteenth century stemmed in part from those regions supplying larger shares of Jewish immigration, and from the spirit of collective responsibility and participation infusing the Hebra Hased Va-Amet on the eve of those new waves. When hebra leaders began to actively recruit women members in 1830, they issued a circular calling on "the ladies of the Jewish Persuasion" to form a women's hebra. They not only hoped that women would organize but put forth the idea that local women could assemble for themselves on their own terms, "bound by such regulations as they may deem proper to adopt at a convenient meeting."[56] Although bad weather initially prevented a sufficient first showing, the drive continued two months later with a new committee that divided the city into sections to "procure the names of such Ladies as are willing to become members."[57] That persistence contrasted the marginal funeral roles to which previous generations had limited Jewish women in New York. By 1841, Shearith Israel even incorporated a women's hebra that functioned independently for the next thirty years before the male and female burial societies merged in 1871.[58] With close ties to the Hebra Hased Va-Amet before then, the women's group continued sewing shrouds and attending the female deceased independently.

That movement spread beyond Shearith Israel as women of New York's second synagogue, B'nai Jeshurun, also formed their own burial society in 1841, the Hevrath Nashim Hased Vaamet (Ladies Benevolent Society). The group's first constitution reflected these women's sense of participatory agency from organizing themselves to take part in "time honoured institutions of the House of Israel" that "strictly enjoined upon all Hebrews, to attend the sick, soothe the dying, and bury the dead." The Hevrath Nashim underscored a conviction that a formally instituted women's burial society "is imperatively called for" and celebrated the fact that "a number of Ladies of the Congregation Bnai Jeshurun are animated by the holy desire of carrying those principles into action."[59] In a system that typically rendered women dependent on their husbands or fathers for the benefits of communal membership or relegated their funeral labor to unacknowledged private chambers, the group recognized its work's symbolic and social importance, and the infrastructure it established would promote it for years to come.

B'nai Jeshurun women also embraced larger currents of solidarity and self-reliance through the financial and medical securities they incorporated around the last rites. They affirmed a group "supported by and for the benefit of the female members" of the congregation and pledged to do so independently of male support.[60] If illness overcame a member, the group charged that "her friends shall apply to the first or second directress, who shall immediately wait on the sick person or appoint a visiting committee for that purpose." If that woman proved "in a dangerous or precarious situation," the society would enlist a nurse to intervene. And to ensure that limited resources would not preclude any woman from these benefits, the society pledged its own funds to cover costs "if the sick person or friends are unable to pay."[61] The group not only enjoined six women to sew shrouds and perform funeral labor for their peers but also specifically extended those services to affiliated women's daughters, notably making no mention of male children.[62] Like male counterparts, the group also adopted a system of fines to dissuade women from missing meetings or neglecting their obligations to the sick, the dying, and the dead.[63] Finally, even beyond the B'nai Jeshurun women's participation in mutualism, the ladies' society of New York's first non-Sephardic synagogue also directly reclaimed women's presence in funeral processions and at the graveside that reigning tradition had precluded until then.[64]

These moves in Shearith Israel and B'nai Jeshurun burial societies assisted fraternal and egalitarian trends to work their way into wider New York Jewish institutional structures. From the burial societies that Jewish women and men founded, joined, and participated in during the early nineteenth century, they received exposure to collectivism in death as much as in life. They also developed new mechanisms of social and material aid that complemented democratic systems of governance and organization. These structures had little precedent during Shearith Israel's tenure as the only official institution of Jewish social welfare in New York. As New York's Jewish population increased by midcentury, these trends replicated across growing congregations and affiliated burial societies. Fraternal and collective ideals reached more Jewish residents than ever before through their basic participation and attendance to contemporaries after death. That process not only cast funeral rites as a conduit for collectivism but laid the ground for some of the first Jewish fraternal orders in the city and the nation. These orders grew out of the many New York Jewish burial societies that detached from parent synagogues or simply developed autonomously in the 1840s.

"In the Case of the Occurrence of a Death in Our Congregation"

The rapid growth of New York's Jewish population by the 1850s further augmented those trends. From a few hundred residents in the 1820s, Jewish New Yorkers swelled their ranks to about forty thousand in just over two decades.[65] By 1859, in rapid succession, they had founded some twenty-five new congregations. The vast majority came into being after 1842, and most had at least one burial society founded under its auspices.[66] Although a dearth of Jews in previous eras had hindered an overly complex Jewish communal field, midcentury growth demanded that congregations quickly establish affiliated aid and burial societies. On the one hand, these institutions addressed increasing need among the city's immigrant Jewish population. On the other, the ability to offer funeral provisions and aid served as an important counterbalance to the intense competition among an ever-fragmenting field of Jewish congregations.

The establishment of new burial societies and independent graveyards went hand in hand among the city's new synagogues as two pillars of congregational autonomy. Given New York's still-limited Jewish burying spaces and the costs of land acquisition, most new congregations took pains to negotiate access to existing yards or to purchase land and set up societies of their own as quickly as possible. Affiliation determined congregants' eligibility for these services, and fledgling synagogues would not risk implosion for their inability to meet those basic needs. Still, some parent congregations were less amenable to cooperate with new offshoots. Shearith Israel set that tone early on when it rescinded the right of defecting members who founded B'nai Jeshurun to bury in its yards. The new synagogue understood that to maintain any autonomy it had gained, it could waste little time setting up a new graveyard. In 1826, just a year after the congregation's formation and even before establishing a place of worship, B'nai Jeshurun purchased burying land on East

Thirty-Second Street. That same year, it incorporated a burial society called the Hebra Gemilut Hesed, later to become the Hebrew Mutual Benefit Society.[67]

Similarly, when the city's third congregation, Anshe Chesed, split from B'nai Jeshurun in 1828, it also made burial a first priority. Founders attempted to delay buying grounds by requesting access to Shearith Israel's yards "in the case of the occurrence of a death in our Congregation, God keep us."[68] The new congregation met similar refusal. Not deviating from its long tendency to closely guard access to the graveyard, Shearith Israel replied that "like all other Corporate Bodies," it preserved its burying place as the exclusive property of its members and therefore could not "admit any interest or right of your Congregation or the members of it to the burying Grounds." The synagogue did grant Anshe Chesed temporary rights in case any member died before it could acquire its own land. Nevertheless, it made clear that that privilege could quickly lapse, "at least until we shall give you a reasonable Notice to the Contrary."[69] Uncertain autonomy thus led seceding congregations to acquire their own yards fairly quickly. When fifty members of B'nai Jeshurun broke away in May 1845 to form Shaaray Tefila, the city's eighth synagogue, they took special efforts to negotiate burial rights for the next fifty years in B'nai Jeshurun's yard despite their withdrawal. As if seeking added security, though, in under a year, Shaaray Tefila purchased its first burying place on 46th Street, between 9th and 10th Avenues, before settling on final grounds at 105th Street in 1847. Nevertheless, members did not relinquish their interment rights through the parent synagogue for another several years.[70]

The ability to offer the last offices remained just as crucial to new synagogues, so they established hevrot kadisha as quickly as they did new graveyards. When Anshe Chesed purchased land on Forty-Fifth Street, for example, it also established its Hebrah Ahavath Achim (Society for Brotherly Love) in 1832. When Shaare Zedek formed thereafter in 1840, it soon established a yard on Eighty-Sixth Street in the Yorkville neighborhood while creating its own Hebra Gemilut Hesed shel Emeth. Temple Emanu-El, New York's first Reform congregation, incorporated in 1845. Just months later, it purchased four lots for burial in the town of Williamsburg and soon founded a male Hebra Gomle Hesed in 1850 and a female Hebra Neshe Gomle Hesed in 1851. In rapid succession, New

York's first thirteen synagogues followed that trajectory, ensuring congregational viability and independence through access to funeral rites
and burial.[71] By midcentury, as Jewish graveyards speckled the physical
landscape, affiliated burial societies littered the city's Jewish institutional
field in kind.

As that pattern was replicated, these societies expanded, further incorporating new monetary relief alongside the last offices and burial.
They most closely followed the model of B'nai Jeshurun's burial society,
the Hebrew Mutual, which tended to burial and funeral arrangements
and also paid affiliates at times of sickness or mourning.[72] Over the coming years, as congregations proliferated, they incorporated payments
to help deceased members' widows and underage children or founded
additional societies specifically geared to that end. Anshe Chesed established four aid societies not long after its formation, including the
Society of Brotherly Love (1832), the New York Assistance Society for
Widows and Orphans, the Society Gates of Hope, and the Montefiore
Society (1841). The first dealt with widows and their children while the
rest focused on aid in sickness and burial.[73] These and similar developments filled a long-standing gap in the old synagogue aid system. They
offered greater social safety nets to secure member households before
poverty overtook them. In a significant departure, they paid all families
equally.

Splits in synagogue membership also laid the ground for fully autonomous burial and benevolent societies, especially in a system that tied
funeral entitlement to membership in parent congregations. The 1845
break between B'nai Jeshurun and Shaaray Tefila exemplified the issue
since B'nai Jeshurun's burial society, the Hebrew Mutual, did not follow
defecting members to the new congregation. Many seceding members
renounced society ties, but an equally significant number retained affiliation despite joining the new synagogue. The Hebrew Mutual responded
by extending its services and potential membership to all Jews in New
York, regardless of the synagogue they belonged to, as long as they affiliated to one in the city. The group required synagogue membership, since
congregations remained the only owners of consecrated Jewish burying
land, but the move still set an important precedent, further chipping at
the long monopoly over burial and funeral rites. In 1859, after burial
societies commonly purchased burying land for themselves, the Hebrew

Mutual took that precedent even further by opening its services to any New York Jews, whether they belonged to a synagogue or not.[74]

In addition to synagogues' semiautonomous burial societies, new Jewish immigrants from central Europe also formed totally independent groups to oversee funerary needs in this period. Their societies even began purchasing independent graveyards and, as a result, never had to associate with a parent institution. One of the first of its kind, the Mendelssohn Benevolent Society, formed in 1841. Among its first acts, it purchased a lot on Eighty-Seventh Street between Lexington and Third Avenue, impelled by "the proper burial of the dead," and soon pledged "mutual relief to the members . . . and their families, when in sickness, want and destitution or distress . . . and to defray the necessary funeral and incidental expenses, in case of sickness or death of any member, or of his family."[75] One institutional history later recalled that part of the impulse to organize independently stemmed from these Jewish newcomers' feeling of alienation from New York's established synagogues and aid associations. In that sense, they paralleled German immigrants, who were more comfortable affiliating with *Vereine* (voluntary associations) than churches. With common bonds of region, occupation, or political sensibilities, Vereine offered monetary as well as social benefits for new immigrants and their families.[76] A Jewish group like the Mendelssohn Society, or countless others it stood in for, had a rich set of models to choose from, drawing on American or other immigrant fraternal variations as well as the legacy of Jewish predecessors like the Hebra Gemilut Hasadim or Hased Va-Amet that had equally drawn on those forces.

Building on that array of fraternal examples, New York Jewish immigrants founded a staggering number of burial, benevolent, or widow and orphan societies by the middle of the nineteenth century. Nathan Kaganoff's careful study of city records between 1848 and 1860 suggests that they incorporated roughly ninety-three aid and burial groups in those years alone, a number that nearly equaled the ninety-six non-Jewish societies incorporated over the same period. That scope stands out in such a short time frame even more so given the fact that Jews constituted less than 5 percent of the city's total population.[77] Strong Jewish inclinations to avoid public charity may explain that overrepresentation, as does the drive for communal independence via self-sufficiency in matters of death. Continued competition and fragmentation among city synagogues may have only further driven that charge, particularly among those growing segments seeking secular Jewish communal options. Whether burial societies that detached from congregational auspices or wholly independent immigrant burial or benevolent societies, the field had greatly changed, providing Jewish families with options for financial or ritual security after death whether they affiliated with a synagogue or had no such desire.[78]

These trends also laid the ground for other independent Jewish burial societies to launch some of America's first national Jewish fraternal networks. Jewish residents of the city's German immigrant quarter, Kleindeutschland, famously founded B'nai B'rith in 1843 after the Freemasons refused their request to create a specifically Jewish lodge. From its inception, B'nai B'rith offered monetary entitlements alongside cultural and social outlets that swelled its membership. New payments to the members' widows and children, however, set a model for Jewish fraternities to follow. For dues paid in, members received sick pay for a set number of weeks, a lump sum of $30 to cover funeral costs, and sustained weekly pensions to widows for the rest of their lives, with smaller payments to children until they came of age.[79] B'nai B'rith expanded fairly quickly. In New York alone, Jews created nineteen lodges by 1854 and increased that number to twenty-nine in two years. Affiliated branches formed in Cincinnati, Baltimore, and Philadelphia in under a decade, with lodges in every state by 1861. The network formed a regional system with district grand lodges and a larger Constitutional Grand Lodge that recast the B'nai B'rith as America's first national Jewish fraternal order.[80]

The Independent Order Free Sons of Israel represented America's second national Jewish fraternity in 1849, but it also grew out of Jewish immigrants' local efforts to found a burial and aid group. Several Jews fleeing the German revolution of 1848 founded the Noah Benevolent Society when they arrived in New York. The group's initial aspirations closely mirrored the Mendelssohn Society and many others like it that were "built on the solid foundation of brotherly affection, and a broad idea of mutual assistance to each other, to the widow, the orphan and the needy." In their first moves, Noah founders purchased land for burial in the new Cypress Hills Cemetery outside of Manhattan and soon established funds to aid widows and their children. Within a year, two other lodges developed in New York, and Noah members recast their society as the first lodge of the Independent Order Free Sons of Israel.[81] Other similar societies and orders developed soon after, including local groups like the Lebanon Widow and Orphan Society (1851) and Zion's Widow and Orphan Society (1851) or larger networks like the Order Brith Abraham (1859) and the Kesher Shel Barzel (Band of Iron; 1860).[82] These groups represented not only America's first Jewish fraternities but also a new stage in Jewish end-of-life planning that forged deep connections among fraternal associations, funeral rites, and collective and preemptive security to affiliated member families. Although they drew on more immediate models like the Masons or the Odd Fellows, the synergy between wider fraternalism and that collective impulse that underwrote Jewish burial reflected a longer fusion sparked in the mold of New York's influential hebra created in the immediate aftermath of the Revolution.

Material benefits for members and their surviving loved ones drove the popularity of these groups as much as new access to Jewish burial, and detractors did not demur in showing disapproval. By the 1860s, New York's Jewish press regularly lamented waning synagogue affiliation, commonly connecting it to Jews' new ability to bury without recourse to any congregation. The *Jewish Messenger* printed a series of articles in the winter of 1861 titled "Burial of the Dead," in which it highlighted the role of lodges and burial societies in the decreased importance of congregations. It particularly noted the monetary benefits granted during sickness and the provision of funeral needs, since "those societies have burial grounds attached to their order." The piece marveled at "hundreds of Hebrews in our city unconnected with any synagogue, who never mingle their prayers with the faithful, who are scarcely known as Israelites, and who would never be known, were not their death to reveal the secret!" It also lambasted a supposed rampant belief among New York Jews that even after a lifetime of little other observance "being interred in a Hebrew's burial ground was a safe passport to Heaven."[83]

Whether or not members of Jewish lodges and smaller burial societies thought as much as their critics about posthumous spiritual security, they certainly valued the benefits that these groups afforded them in life, to say nothing of monetary protections and assured funeral dignities that they and their families received after death. Inasmuch as critics focused on a widespread recent shift away from congregations, the move could also trace its origins further back to those late eighteenth-century debates among Shearith Israel and the Jewish public at large. Whether those experimental alternative approaches to earthly well-being came in light of deficiencies of synagogue-centered relief or the gradual release of funerary control held by trustees, these initial developments set the tone for several decades. The beginnings of mass Jewish migration only encouraged that trend, particularly as Jewish population growth and increased incidents of death and death-related poverty strained an already buckling system. Incrementally, Jewish families organized to fill those gaps, valuing the self-determination and control over communal resources that popular initiatives around death and burial afforded them. From their beginnings within synagogue auspices, those ideals drove early Jewish aid and burial societies that helped pave the way for later Jewish New Yorkers to merge secular Jewish fellowship with the promises of an open American society, as Deborah Dash Moore has argued. As B'nai B'rith and other contemporary Jewish orders "affirmed" through fraternalism "that Judaism and Americanism were congruent,"[84] they built on the legacy of the city's first burial hebrot that devoted much of their mission to begin bringing those forces together.

After more than a century of New York synagogues closely controlling a handful of Jewish graveyards and most philanthropic matters, Jewish congregants ultimately organized and sidestepped their congregations. Burial remained a priority, one that Jews could not access beyond official Jewish circles. Even if they joined a broader trade society or fraternity, Jews seeking traditional funeral rites needed contemporaries at their side. The Jewish burial societies that took shape over the first half of the nineteenth century dovetailed with broader republicanism and fraternal values in the Revolution's wake. By way of Jewish obligations to the dead, these forces left their mark all the more on New York's Jewish social consciousness. Burial societies served as ideal institutions through which the city's Jewish women and men could drive those changes. They not only enabled households to address social and economic pressures around them, but they allowed them to do so without compromising on a priority to self-segregate in burial and to perform the intimate dignities in close-knit communal circles. Jewish burial societies not only soon surpassed the synagogues that had initially housed them but offered key transitioning bodies to bridge a gap between colonial congregations and nineteenth-century Jewish fraternal orders.

With those changes, new philanthropic models afforded Jewish families in New York several important instruments for communal autonomy. They also further legitimized family need and priorities after death alongside those of the community. The proliferation of Jewish burial societies and lodges in New York provided another important step cementing the alliance among family and material interests in Jewish end-of-life planning. At the same time, they marked a growing ability for Jews to organize at the grassroots. That foundation proved all the more important by the second half of the nineteenth century when old Jewish debates over family burial came to a head. When Jews, like most New Yorkers, embraced the Rural Cemetery Movement, the result set the stage for hundreds of new cemetery holdings just beyond the city, ripe for family lots. That development not only drove New York's emerging Jewish cemetery economy but further thrust commercial, family, and grassroots agency to the fore of Jewish burial in New York.

3

"Carry Me to the Burying Place of My Fathers"

Rural Cemeteries, Family Lots,
and a New Jewish Social Order, 1849–80

Boarding dedicated ferries from Manhattan to Williamsburg, eager New York Jews set off in 1851 to claim a piece of heaven on earth in the beautiful new Salem Fields Cemetery. The Reform Temple Emanu-El had just completed Salem Fields, and its leaders aimed to showcase America's first Jewish rural cemetery. Beautiful views, natural landscapes, and spatial innovations, they hoped, would inspire Jewish families to choose Emanu-El for eternal repose. More importantly, trustees gambled that "choice lots" for family burial would prove their crowning achievement. The congregation orchestrated a two-day auction event to promote those lots and advertised special rates every week in the Jewish press for more than a year.[1] Members responded so enthusiastically that most other synagogues quickly followed suit. When the congregation B'nai Jeshurun opened its own Beth Olom Cemetery in 1852, trustees not only laid out family lots but hailed the new cemetery as one in a long line of Jewish family resting places as far back as Abraham's purchase of a grave for Sarah.[2] In no time at all, Jews in New York City embraced family burial, and many even ignited heated controversies as they pushed the limits of Jewish law through requests to exhume loved ones' remains from old Manhattan yards in order to transfer their graves to recently purchased family lots. For all that fervor, one would hardly guess that synagogue trustees had forbidden burial among kin for more than a century, let alone that debates had still abounded just two decades earlier.

Despite that long taboo, unavoidable pressures led most Jewish congregations to embrace family burial fairly quickly. As rapid urban growth drove the city's northern expansion, most religious and benevolent groups sought new removed places to bury their dead. Otherwise, they struggled with city planners' aims to build parks and roadways through old communal graveyards. As a result, a wave of new "rural cemeteries" developed along the border of Kings and Queens Counties. As synagogue trustees imagined their own new rural grounds, pent up congregant demand led them to introduce family lots into these holdings. In light of members' petitions since the late eighteenth century to bury loved ones together and with synagogue competition increasing each year, boards of trustees saw new incentives to finally grant congregants the privilege to rest among kin. The significant revenues that family lots promised also drove even the most uneasy and traditional trustees to abandon old commitments to limit burial to sequential rows. For the first time since Jews laid one another to rest in New York City, synagogues considered the family of equal value to the community when organizing their burial places. That rapid midcentury turn not only spoke to growing market and family emphases in the city's Jewish funeral sphere but signaled new levels of influence that average member households were gaining over once-uncompromising trustees and religious officials.

But the Rural Cemetery Movement recast Jewish communal structures well beyond the synagogue. It also fueled the growth of new Jewish relief societies and fraternal lodges that, in just two decades, would outpace congregations as New York's primary institutions of Jewish social, philanthropic, and funeral provision. Although fledging Jewish burial societies had been developing earlier in the century, the ability to buy smaller cemetery parcels in commercial and nonsectarian grounds propelled their growth over the coming decades. That shift allowed Jewish women and men to sidestep heavy-handed synagogue governance steeped in burial monopolies. It also enabled them to better meet household needs. By pooling resources, members of these new groups not only bought cemetery land independently but also introduced widespread automatic pensions to surviving members' dependents, which protected families against death-related poverty. At the same time, they drove a growing alliance between family and material concerns in Jewish end-of-life planning.

The movement of Jewish burying places from old crowded yards in Manhattan to new sprawling cemeteries across the East River may not have seemed a likely cause for so much social change, but the project ushered in waves of modern conventions to Jewish cemetery spaces that quickly informed broader structures tied to the funeral realm. Whether advanced sale of cemetery land organized around the family, private ownership of family lots, or the ability of Jewish fraternities to incorporate independently around smaller tracts, each innovation elevated households with a new sense of entitlement as owners of cemetery real estate. The ever-present threat of urban incursion over loved ones' city graves also played an important part in the latter half of the nineteenth century. It validated family rights over matters of burial and counterbalanced traditional and communal dictates regarding death that previously outweighed most other concerns. Although America's nineteenth-century Rural Cemetery Movement aimed more broadly to preserve a sense of regional tradition and communal history against rapid industrial change overtaking city centers, for Jewish New Yorkers, it had precisely the opposite effect. Indeed, the establishment of Jewish rural cemeteries inadvertently set the stage to overturn old communal dynamics and the deference to tradition enshrined in city yards. In laying out the nation's first Jewish rural cemeteries, Jewish New Yorkers not only acted alongside other city residents to transform distant farmland into new cemetery real estate but laid the ground across lush new landscapes for an entirely new Jewish social order that carried well into the twentieth century.

An End to Urban Interment and the Rise of New York Rural Cemeteries

"When will our City Fathers put a stop to these burials in the City," the *New York Daily Tribune* criticized late in 1850. "London has abandoned the practice in full." Editors were responding to the recent evacuation of another city burial ground, this time on Twenty-Fifth Street. They described it as an effort "to make room for improvements for the living," but they also called it "another instance of the insecure resting place of the dead within the City limits."[3] New York's quick push north frustrated most city residents, particularly when old communal grounds fell in the path of that development. Pressures to empty the Twenty-Fifth Street yard echoed similar incidents leading churches, synagogues, and benevolent societies to vacate city yards. Members of the African Methodist Episcopal Zion Church, for instance, dealt with that challenge twice in just two decades when city officials claimed church burial land, first in 1827 to lay out Washington Square Park and then in 1851 as part of a larger project to build the city's Central Park uptown.[4] Scores of other churches and synagogues had similar experiences. At midcentury, as city planners raced to develop Manhattan for the living, those overseeing the city's dead faced unprecedented challenges to protect their eternal rest.

City officials, religious leaders, and enterprising land speculators all understood the need for new burying places beyond the city. Their efforts drove a parallel boom in New York's cemetery economy. In light of growing tensions over urban development, the Common Council passed an 1847 act to promote new burial far from the city. The act offered tax exemptions to religious groups and societies that established nonprofit cemeteries in Kings and Queens Counties. Churches and synagogues did so fairly quickly, but so did a wave of speculators who saw the gains in converting cheap farmland into resalable cemetery property. As larger congregations like St. Patrick's Cathedral, the Temple Emanu-El, or St. Paul's German Lutheran Church aimed to solve the challenges of urban interment by sculpting rural grounds like Calvary Cemetery (1846–48), Salem Fields (1851), and the Lutheran Cemetery (1852), respectively, private investors set up nonsectarian counterparts in their midst like Cypress Hills Cemetery (1848), the Cemetery of the Evergreens (1849), and Washington Cemetery (1850).[5] Commercial promoters targeted smaller societies that lacked the means to purchase or maintain large acreages independently. Through affordable rates on smaller tracts, for instance, Cypress Hills boosters promised any group "lots at a price that would exclude no one from participating in the advantages that have hitherto been enjoyed only by incurring large expenses."[6]

Beyond the increasingly popular new aesthetic, other immediate advantages of rural cemeteries included distance from urban development and a long-term solution to the new ban on city burial. Sooner rather than later, all parties realized, New Yorkers would have no place to bury other than in rural grounds. Most congregations and societies set about acquiring new rural land. In the process, many also transferred graves from their old Manhattan holdings. "Friends of the deceased are at work making removals daily to the various Cemeteries," the press noted in 1850. "No less than twenty-five bodies have been removed to one Cemetery within the last few days."[7] That rate only ballooned as the decade progressed, with congregations moving anywhere from hundreds to thousands of graves as city projects claimed portions or all of their graveyards. Some congregations, like Shearith Israel, waited for impending city construction before taking on the moral and practical burden of relocating affected graves from soon-to-be disrupted yards. Others, like the Methodist Episcopal Church, began preemptive projects in 1854 to remove entire yards over several years once the church had acquired tracts in rural holdings.[8]

Commercial cemetery boosters seized on these and similar episodes. Cypress Hills Cemetery touted its "[geographic] isolation from innovation or the inroads of improvements" and promised that the cemetery "is perpetually secluded and protected from all danger of invasion or desecration for all time."[9] By midcentury, religious and benevolent organizations engaged in mass disinterment across the East River. In Cypress Hills Cemetery alone, a handful of churches had moved thirty-five thousand graves by 1860.[10] Although New York City had maintained one hundred active burial grounds in 1820, only twenty-three remained in use by 1850.[11] Shearith Israel successfully resisted city incursions, but most other synagogues transferred their dead over the coming decades. Despite a growth of at least twenty-seven Jewish grounds in Manhattan between 1825 and the late 1840s, by the close of the century, only fragments of Shearith Israel's three yards remained in the city. Whether in response to urban development, bans on city burial, or simply seeking the status of ornate and modern burying places, all New Yorkers embraced rural cemeteries, enshrining them as part of the landscape by mid-1850s.

New York Jews Engage Rural Cemeteries

In style and structure, most New York Jews enthusiastically took part in the movement to sculpt new rural cemeteries alongside their ethnic and religious counterparts. Salem Fields rivaled the beauty of any neighboring cemetery and soon became a model to which most synagogues in

New York and the rest of the nation aspired. A proliferation of Jewish cemeteries—whether those of the larger congregations, the parcels they sold to budding synagogues and fraternal orders, or the tracts within nonsectarian grounds that smaller Jewish societies eagerly purchased—also all attested to growing Jewish demand for cemetery property.

Beauty and urban necessity explained only part of that drive. Equally important were the status and self-determination that rural cemetery ownership afforded Jews at all rungs of New York society. Elaborate and permanent memorials dotting these grounds offered symbols of Jewish economic success in America. And even as Jewish New Yorkers carefully separated their cemeteries from those of their Protestant neighbors, behind roadways, gates, and fences, the unprecedented proximity of these physical borders spoke to a new sense of Jewish inclusion in the American mainstream. So did the adoption of larger market trends in the city's developing Jewish cemeteries, from the family lots that synagogues introduced into their new modern burying places to the independence and viability that Jewish fraternal orders won through their ability to purchase tracts in larger Jewish or nonsectarian cemeteries. In style and real estate, each innovation further punctuated a long-fought challenge to synagogue authority in life and death. The Rural Cemetery Movement's commercialism and egalitarianism set the tone for much of its Jewish appeal, but the property rights and the decisions of communal affiliation it conferred to Jewish lot holders also made the movement's Jewish variant truly a grassroots phenomenon.

The ineffectiveness of New York's established synagogues during the early stages of the cemetery crisis set that trend in motion. Initially, the major congregations seemed stymied by competition or overwhelmed by the difficulties of building wholly new Jewish rural grounds. At the same time, some fledging Jewish burial societies took matters into their own hands, either lobbying against bans on city burial or simply purchasing tracts independent of the major synagogues in the emerging nonsectarian cemeteries.

Concerned Jewish onlookers noted both phenomena. Robert Lyon, editor of New York's first Jewish weekly, the *Asmonean*, used that platform to call on city synagogues for "prompt and efficient action, upon the very pressing and important question of a Cemetery for the Hebrews of New York."[12] Lyon did not shy away from highlighting what he saw as the failings in leadership and cooperation among established congregations. In particular, he targeted Shearith Israel for not addressing the cemetery question earlier or more effectively. He claimed that trustees had squandered the congregation's prestige as "the ancient—the first—and for a century and more, the ONLY" Jewish body in New York.[13] Lyon also criticized Temple Emanu-El. Despite trustees' initiative to purchase land for Salem Fields, they had refused easy access to the other synagogues, valuing instead the profits of independent action and ownership. When news soon broke that B'nai Jeshurun and Shearith Israel trustees had jointly purchased land for another Jewish burial ground alongside Cypress Hills Cemetery, the paper praised the agreement. On the one hand, it would prevent impending urban growth from menacing the city's Jewish dead by securing a place to bury that "may be perpetuated, without a probability of its privacy being invaded." On the other, he celebrated the congregations' cooperation as "the harbinger of a bright epoch for the Hebrews of New York . . . the first step to *union*."[14]

Unity was a regular theme in the *Asmonean*. In this instance, though, the cemetery crisis only amplified New York's ongoing communal fragmentation, particularly as new waves of Jewish immigrants established new synagogues and fraternal orders by custom, class, place of origin, and how recently they had arrived. "We are American by self-adoption," Lyon wrote in 1849, seeing Jews' common faith and minority status as cause enough to shed other differences. "We are Hebrews," he asserted, disturbed by growing communal fragmentation, "not English, or German, Portuguese or Polish, but Jews. . . . Heretofor [*sic*], there has been too much sectional feeling, dividing congregations and societies, impeding their healthy action."[15] Lyon's critique over the cemetery crisis reinforced these frustrations, especially as he bemoaned the communal initiative of other religious communities like "the Catholics, the Presbyterians, the Unitarians . . . surrounding us, witness their magnificent schools, colleges, cathedrals, hospitals, asylums, and then ask why Jews have done nothing, literally nothing . . . as a body."[16]

The cemetery crisis only amplified that point, especially as growing cohorts of central European Jewish immigrants founded independent relief societies that continued to chip away at the old cohesive Jewish social order. Burial and material aid proved central provisions, but so did a sense of alienation from New York's established Jewish circles. One origin story of the Mendelssohn Society (1844) recalled the "doubtful eye" that native Jewish New Yorkers cast on their "thriving and rising German brethren." Better-off native Jewish New Yorkers "with Spanish-Portuguese traditions" had "kept themselves socially aloof from the poor immigrants from Germany, who arrived here friendless and ignorant of the English language, and compelled [them] to band themselves more closely to obtain the social and religious advantages denied them by their flourishing co-religionists."[17] The Noah Benevolent Society (1849) also later recounted a similar drive among its early founders, "strangers in a strange country" who struggled to adapt and "sought each other's society for comfort and advice."[18]

United by collective funds to secure land for burial or guard against sickness and death, groups like these would not stand by and wait for the congregations to resolve the cemetery crisis. In fact, their sense of exclusion only quickened the pace for many of these emerging Jewish relief groups to purchase tracts of their own in the new nonsectarian cemeteries. The Noah Society represented one of the first to do so when it bought land in Cypress Hills Cemetery in 1849.[19] That move came the same year as the group's foundation and a full two years before any leading synagogue even broke ground on its own rural cemetery. Synagogue competition may have delayed trustees' actions, but fledgling Jewish fraternal orders acted collectively and for themselves. In fact, the Noah Society showed particular initiative. Even before it decided to purchase land in Cypress Hills Cemetery, it originally organized to challenge the city's ban on Manhattan burials. Founders' "primary object . . . for banding together," later members attested, "was for the purpose of bringing about the removal from the New York City Charter of the restrictions against the consecration of ground for burial purposes, so that they could have and own a Jewish cemetery."[20] Although early Noah leaders failed to change city policy, they did succeed in their mission to acquire independent grounds. Their actions foreshadowed a trend of grassroots organization around independently owned cemetery land that would upend Jewish communal dynamics for decades.

That phenomenon signaled an important change for New York's Jewish communal hierarchy that replicated in little time across other

American cities. Although smaller Jewish relief societies in New York developed only gradually in the late 1840s, greater access to commercial cemetery land fueled their growth within the following decades and rapidly fragmented New York's Jewish institutional landscape. Already by 1858, at least twelve other Jewish organizations had bought tracts in Cypress Hills Cemetery. These ranged from at least three subsequent lodges of the Independent Order Free Sons of Israel—the larger national fraternal network born of the Noah Society—to smaller Jewish burial and relief groups like the Magyne Reyim Ubicur Cholymm (Guardians of Friends and Visiting the Sick), the Beth Abram Society, or the Krakauer Society, to name only a few. Even some of the more recent Jewish congregations purchased tracts in Cypress Hills Cemetery, like Shaarai Rachmim (Gates of Compassion) or Ahawes Chesed (later, the Central Synagogue).[21] These varied initiatives proved how easily average Jewish individuals could organize on their own, even recent immigrants of limited means. Excess commercial cemetery land not only poised existing relief groups to marginalize congregations at midcentury but hastened their spread and allowed Jews at all levels to build and maintain independent societies with no recourse to older synagogues.

The inclusive ideology underwriting America's nonsectarian cemeteries encouraged that phenomenon. In fact, most rural cemetery advocates, especially in the North, genuinely committed to progressive ideals of social unity, religious liberalism, abolition, or democratic principles and committed to afford all groups cemetery access whether wealthy or poor, black or white, or Christian or other religious background.[22] The rural cemetery business model, in fact, hinged on the ability to develop cheap farmland into lush cemetery real estate and resell that property to as many groups as possible. Investors benefited from making cemetery tracts available to all groups that could afford them, regardless of creed or race. Well beyond early Jewish adopters, diverse denominations purchased tracts in Cypress Hills Cemetery, among them congregations like the St. Stephens Protestant Episcopal Church, the Duane Street Methodist Episcopal Church, the West Presbyterian Church of Manhattan, and the Madison Avenue Baptist Church. Several larger fraternities also purchased land there, from lodges of the Independent Order of Odd Fellows to the typically nativist Order of United American Mechanics.[23] Even several Tang (Chinese immigrant associations) established burial grounds there. Cypress Hills Cemetery also maintained tracts for African Americans that several black churches and associations established in the 1850s and 1860s.[24]

Investors valued that diversity and celebrated the cemetery's openness. They hailed Cypress Hills as "what has, it is believed, never before existed—a fraternal cluster of cemeteries, surrounded by one common enclosure, where every church and society may consecrate its own grounds according to its ideas of duty or feeling." The trustees' vision continued: "It is our ambition and our hope, to see all religious denominations, and orders of benevolence, and national and industrial societies, meet together on this common ground, and by proximity and good will, acknowledge that all men are brethren, having a common origin and a common destiny."[25] Commercial and ideological ends led a variety of New York's political, ethnic, racial, and religious groups to bury more closely than they ever had before. Significantly, and for the first time, they also afforded the city's smaller Jewish orders with ritually nonthreatening alternatives to synagogue-owned burial land.

If nonsectarian grounds served New York's smaller communal associations, larger churches and synagogues created their own self-contained cemeteries, particularly those with lower thresholds to mix the dead across communities. The Calvary Cemetery of St. Patrick's Cathedral, for instance, served only Catholic New Yorkers. Similarly, the city's three leading synagogues, Temple Emanu-El, B'nai Jeshurun, and Shearith Israel, created specifically Jewish rural cemeteries. Despite their preference to self-segregate, however, synagogue trustees laid out their new holdings directly alongside Cypress Hills Cemetery. In style and location, the Jewish cemeteries set a fine line between continuity and change. As the 1850s wore on, more Jewish congregations and societies invested in rural cemetery holdings. Many of these groups even bought smaller subdivisions on those first congregations' land. The trend forever altered New York Jewish burial.

"Because It Is a Comfort to a Man That He Should Rest with His Fathers!"

Although religious law and spatial taboos led Jewish New Yorkers to physically separate their holdings from those of their Christian counterparts, the nation's first Jewish rural cemeteries closely adhered to the movement's most popular elements like beautiful layouts, advanced sale of cemetery real estate, and much-anticipated family lots. The pressures of Manhattan's cemetery crisis enabled that reinvention. As city encroachment forced mass disinterment throughout the 1850s, the new realities of open farmland allowed innovation in New York Jewish burial spaces for the first time in more than a century. In Manhattan, Jews had isolated their grounds from city living areas and neighboring churchyards by buying land beyond city limits. Shearith Israel's long funeral monopoly also perpetuated Sephardic traditions of an earlier age that subsequent congregations internalized as reigning Jewish custom in New York. That situation prevented conventions like family vaults or elaborate ornamentation from entering Jewish practice. When the same underdeveloped areas that had incubated Jewish yards fell squarely in the path of city expansion, the uprooting of whole Jewish graveyards allowed a generation of Jews in New York to start anew. As trustees and laity both reimagined the contours of Jewish burial in New York City, they did so in the same spirit overtaking fellow enthusiasts of the nation's Rural Cemetery Movement.

Temple Emanu-El led the charge in its new cemetery layout and set an important precedent in Salem Fields, America and New York's first modern Jewish cemetery. Trustees purchased twenty-five acres in late March 1851 that they fashioned in the spirit of the broader Rural Cemetery Movement. They hoped it would rival the beauty of all other grounds around it. "As was never before the case with a Jewish cemetery," a congregational history still boasted decades later, "this was designed and laid out systematically with fine roads, well-ordered pathways, and beautiful alleys, and was stocked with plants and flowers; family vaults were built and neatly fenced in; and, in fact, all that was possible was done to make the place beautiful. To this day it presents the appearance of a lovely garden consecrated to the Lord, and the name, 'Salem Field Cemetery,' has become celebrated."[26] Emanu-El trustees continued preening Salem Fields for years to come. In 1877, just a decade after the architect, Henry Fernbach, had completed Emanu-El's famous Forty-Second Street synagogue in an exquisite new Moorish Revival style, trustees called on him again to design the cemetery's grand and imposing entrance.[27] At the project's dedication, Emanu-El's president, Louis May, lauded the congregation for what he called its "honor and credit of providing, with unstinted liberality, a Jewish cemetery second to none in the world. And if I am not mistaken Salem Fields is the first one ever laid out, adorned, and kept as such."[28] The cemetery remained a point of pride. When the congregation marked its fiftieth anniversary, a commemorative volume hailed Salem Fields as Emanu-El's "magnificent 'city of the dead'" and called it "one of the most beautiful cemeteries of the many fine ones maintained upon Long Island."[29] The book concluded with an entire chapter of twenty-eight full-page glossy photographs of the most ornate mausoleums. Emanu-El's embrace of that popular aesthetic set the stage for all Jewish rural cemeteries that followed. It also demonstrated how significantly these new Jewish grounds departed from traditional conventions, aiming to please the public through contemporary sensibilities.

Temple Emanu-El's other great innovation, the incorporation of family lots, not only spatially remade Jewish cemeteries but reshaped living communal dynamics through the consumer powers it conferred to congregants. Trustees divided Salem Fields into two sections from the start. In one, they arranged family lots that desirous members could purchase in advance. In another, they retained sequential graves that members in good standing received for free. The offer to bury among kin proved a highly welcome change, especially since reigning practice had long refused members that privilege. Trustees intended to capitalize on that demand and wasted little time promoting the option. As early as December 1851, they began advertising "choice lots" for family burial each week in the *Asmonean*. They even set special introductory rates at just $5 per lot.[30] The temple also orchestrated a two-day auction event to showcase the cemetery's striking design and layout. It arranged for interested parties to take the ferry from Manhattan to Williamsburg, where dedicated coaches carried them to Salem Fields. The trip culminated in heated bidding sessions over specific lots, further driving profits and the cemetery's allure.

Beautiful holdings became a status symbol, but members also invested them with the promise of future generations' security, given the cemeteries' removal across the East River. Early publicity commonly celebrated families' perpetual ownership of their lots, such as B'nai Jeshurun's cemetery regulations, which the press published in full with assurances to "[place] in the power of every member . . . to secure if he pleases . . . a burying-place possession, which he himself and his heirs, are to have and to hold for ever."[31] That promise was replicated in deeds across congregations with explicit emphasis on "perpetual Burying-place possessions" that members and their heirs could claim as long as they paid regular dues to the congregation.[32] To an extent, that strategy mirrored Emanu-El's pioneering approach in this period to the sale of synagogue seats. Rather than leasing them annually, it and wealthier congregations began to sell seats as permanent property. Members paid all at once for their initial claims and thereafter contributed smaller assessments each year to maintain their ownership.[33] Although seats and cemetery lots overlapped in promises of permanent ownership and a ready source of revenue, perpetuity—at least in the latter—struck an even deeper chord. On the one hand, families embraced the idea that the new lots they purchased would become multigenerational resting places, forever gathering loved ones to rest side by side after death. On the other, a Jewish head of household who bought a lot in Salem Fields or Beth Olom also bought into the hope that their geographic removal would protect an even greater investment, shielding the graves of him or his heir over subsequent years against the same kind of city incursions then disrupting thousands of New York City's dead on a regular basis.[34]

It is unsurprising that lot sales proved immensely popular and profitable, driving most other synagogues to follow Emanu-El's example. From $5 introductory rates in 1851, lot prices jumped to $25 in just one year. By 1860, they nearly doubled, rising to $40.[35] The press even speculated that revenue from family lot sales funded striking renovations of Emanu-El's synagogue. Soon, most other congregations viewed rural cemeteries as an asset too valuable not to pursue. As the city's growing Jewish population and their hunger for status demanded larger synagogue structures and ever-growing costs, cemetery innovations seemed an even more valued investment.[36] Amid the larger burial crisis and pressing competition among synagogues, even once-uncompromising trustees felt the need to attract and maintain affiliation, particularly given the broad appeal of family graves for most member households. Regardless of ideological leanings, synagogues running the gamut of New York's political and religious spectrum—such as Shearith Israel, B'nai Jeshurun, or Anshe Chesed—quickly embraced rural cemeteries and family burial within them.

Some boards proceeded more enthusiastically than others. At first, B'nai Jeshurun and Shearith Israel trustees did not imagine much difference between their old city graveyards and new rural holdings. They simply sought to solve the cemetery crisis and to keep pace with Temple Emanu-El. New York's first and second Jewish congregations refused to let this recent and nontraditional rival solve the cemetery question on its own. Accordingly, just weeks after Emanu-El's purchase of twenty-five acres for Salem Fields, B'nai Jeshurun and Shearith Israel joined forces to buy their own twelve acres alongside the temple's holdings. The older congregations, though, initially lacked their rival's vision for the revolutionary potential planted in their new cemetery. In early minutes, B'nai Jeshurun trustees commonly used traditional terms like "beth haim [house of life]" or "burial ground" to refer to their Long Island property. Only in late December 1852, a year after Emanu-El's Salem Fields met so much excitement and two months after B'nai Jeshurun began to lay out its own family lots, did leaders start to conceive of their new property specifically as a "cemetery." Now they typically reserved old language like "beth haim" for their city graveyard. On one early occasion, a recording secretary even crossed out the term *burial ground* when referring to the project on Long Island, replacing it instead with a more modern phrase: "the cemetery, Beth Olem [sic]." This was further refined a few days later to "Beth Olem Cemetery."[37] Although seemingly subtle, that shift marked a new understanding that the rural grounds developing under B'nai Jeshurun's auspices represented a revolution in New York's Jewish burial enterprise.

Along with that rhetorical shift, B'nai Jeshurun trustees embraced the exciting garden, market, and family principles defining the Rural Cemetery Movement. Two months after arranging Beth Olom into family lots, they composed a set of regulations that trumpeted family burial at every opportunity.[38] They defined Beth Olom Cemetery entirely through kin, labeling one of its sections "for the members of the Congregation who do not purchase family plots" and the other "appropriated for family, or personal burying-place possessions."[39] They even asked their newly hired rabbi, Morris Raphall, to pen a long preamble that celebrated the legacy of family burial in Jewish tradition. New York's Jewish press printed Raphall's treatise to advertise Beth Olom, but the piece also validated the departure from the old prohibition of family burial.

Since the Reform Temple Emanu-El had been the first to incorporate family lots, traditionalists had even more reason to look suspiciously at the practice. Raphall's endorsement, however, brought much-needed authority, for he was one of the first ordained rabbis to arrive to the United States and had become an emerging figurehead of traditional Judaism in America. Even four years later, as Jewish Cincinnatians began their own family burial debate, that city's premier Jewish paper, the *American Israelite*, reprinted Raphall's preamble, for "it shows plainly, how ridiculous the opposition is." More importantly, the paper sought to build common ground among emerging Jewish factions. As Raphall's support showed, "Laying out one portion of the cemetery in family plots . . . is subscribed not only by the reformers, but also by the principal leaders of the orthodox party."[40]

Raphall's preamble deeply drew on Jewish history and law to establish a legacy for family burial in Jewish tradition. Perhaps more pointedly, it framed those historic examples in terms that would clearly resonate with nineteenth-century Jewish families in America's growing urban centers. "It is a remarkable fact," Raphall opened the piece, that Abraham's purchase of a grave for Sarah represented the Bible's "first instance of sale and purchase of real estate." The patriarch also supposedly acted on his drive to secure for his wife "a burying-place possession, wherein the remains of the dead might repose undisturbed for ever." Raphall also empathized with Abraham's family instinct "that he in his turn might rest at her side; that his son and his son's son might come and mingle their dust with that of their progenitors; that his heirs should succeed to that possession, to have and to hold for ever."[41] That legacy continued down the biblical family line, as Raphall even embellished Jacob's final request. Along the shores of the Nile, Raphall painted the scene, the patriarch turned his dying glance to his forefathers' grave in Machpelah, entreating, "Act towards me with kindness and truth; Do not, I pray thee, bury me in Egypt, but carry me to the burying place of my fathers and there, bury me with them."[42] From prophets to judges to the books of Samuel, Kings, and Jeremiah, Raphall collected a litany of similar episodes enshrining family burial across Jewish tradition. Beth Olom regulations even drew on Joseph Caro's sixteenth-century legal manual, the *Code of Jewish Law*, and its emphasis to bury "'where the members of his family repose . . .' Because 'It is a comfort to a man that he should rest with his fathers!'"[43] Drawing far and wide, Raphall validated family graves while resurrecting a practice long banned by New York Jewish authorities.

B'nai Jeshurun trustees used all tools at their disposal to promote that exciting new endeavor. In addition to Raphall's well-publicized treatise, which doubled as an advertisement to encourage the sale of family lots, trustees also embraced other marketing techniques. Again, those proven effective by Emanu-El offered a ready model. When Beth Olom opened for sale in 1853, B'nai Jeshurun arranged its own day-long auction, at which "a large body" of members trekked out to Beth Olom and engaged in "a spirited [sale of lots] . . . highly satisfactory to the trustees."[44] If at first the congregation imagined little difference between its city grave-yard and its new rural cemetery, in no time at all, it came to see the modern trappings of family lots and advanced sale of graves as normal conventions that the synagogue enthusiastically promoted.

Those early years also marked a shift in popular will through the ac-quisition of cemetery real estate. The innovation to sell lots to members, after all, inherently conveyed a host of new entitlements to congregants as the owners of cemetery holdings. Realizing the potential to threaten old communal dynamics, particularly given the long-standing tie be-tween authority and burial, most trustees devised new fees and policies. These balanced members' claims of ownership by charging for the right to actually use family lots and make interments. At the same time, new fees, charges, and stipulations around cemetery access or appearance also preserved trustees' control, slowing burial's shift toward the realms of commerce and family.

Shearith Israel proceeded with greatest caution. One writer for the *Asmonean* remarked with surprise at "the tasteful manner in which sev-eral gentlemen connected with [Shearith Israel] . . . had fitted up and ar-ranged their family plots" during an early cemetery visit.[45] Nevertheless, resolutions in 1852 still stressed trustees' ultimate control, underscoring that "by the allowance of the privilege [to bury in those sections] Trust-ees do not relinquish the whole or any part of their control or authority over said plots." Rules for members who did not purchase private lots preserved something of the old status quo of sequential burial. Although trustees allowed spouses to reserve two graves side by side, they stipu-lated in all other cases, "nothing herein contained shall be construed to authorize interments in said Cemetery otherwise than in regular rows, as commenced and now practiced, without the consent of the Trustees."[46] They also emphasized that despite members' purchase of lots, trustees did not relinquish their right to charge members for breaking ground or, most pointedly, the right of "refusing permission of any interment."[47]

Even B'nai Jeshurun maintained what the press called "highly stringent" regulations governing transactions, despite eagerly promoting family lots. Trustees also instituted new fines, such as a $50 fee on families that violated stipulations.[48] Most congregations also instituted strings of extra charges for matters like digging or closing a grave or the right to bury nonnuclear relatives considered to fall outside of immediate relations.[49] The move regulated a family's use of its holdings and re-created the link between cemetery access and membership that private ownership of lots had initially severed. In all, as much as title deeds to lots and modern conventions of the Rural Cemetery Movement disrupted well-worn communal hierarchies, trustees tried to counter that revolution through financial and legal oversight.

Ultimately, though, those staid Jewish traditions could not counter American claims to the family, individual rights of property, and self-determination through grassroots purchase of cemetery land. Indeed, congregants pushed back on nearly all fronts. Some challenges played out in heated religious debates over families' desired use of lots and the transfer of loved ones' remains. Others involved members circumventing their congregations altogether by purchasing independent tracts in surrounding nonsectarian cemeteries. Either way, Jewish households sidestepped the synagogues' heavy-handed fees or regulations by asserting their rights as lot holders or simply taking their business elsewhere. Cemetery holdings and family lots thereby offered a platform for congregants to increasingly challenge the old communal order.

Gathering Bones of Beloved Fathers

The first tests came amid high-pitched disinterment controversies in the early years of Jewish lot sales. As purchase of family lots became more common, owners began unexpectedly seeking permission to exhume and transfer loved ones' remains from old Manhattan yards to new family holdings. Requests caught trustees off guard, since Jewish law strongly opposed disinterment. Tradition imagined the distress that exhumation likely caused the dead, stirring their souls from sacred rest or toying with their anticipation of resurrection at the final Day of Judgment. Beyond mystical concerns, intense fears of dishonoring the dead led most to simply prefer leaving graves intact and undisturbed as much as possible. As a result, Jewish law strictly prohibited the transfer of graves beyond a handful of scenarios. These included reburial in the land of Israel, relocation of a grave that had all along been designated as temporary, or transferring a grave because impending man-made or natural dangers threatened to disrupt it. Family burial also represented an instance in which Jewish law permitted disinterment, but most interpreted that allowance to apply only if a family grave had existed before a loved one's death. In mid-nineteenth-century New York City, of necessity, most Jews' family graves postdated earlier interments. That reality created the thorny issue of whether one could relocate a relative's earlier grave to a family lot proudly purchased only recently.

Despite those legal complexities, many Jewish lot holders pressed the issue, embracing American attitudes toward the family and the rights of private property owners. They cited, for instance, their desire to reunite loved ones and alluded to their sense of entitlement from purchasing their lots. The ever-present threat of city development only further seemed to justify those appeals. Nevertheless, each claim left trustees in a difficult position. While boards enthusiastically promoted the sale of family lots, they had never anticipated congregants would use them for anything other than *future* burials. Faced with challenges to Jewish law and communal power, synagogue leaders engaged in these debates with care in the early 1850s. They, and most onlookers, realized that the conflicts tested not only their own moral and communal authority but also the limits of increasing member influence amid new market and family concerns that were infusing the new Jewish cemetery economy.

The earliest debate came just months after Emanu-El sold its first family lots, in a case raised by Isaac Dittenhoeffer, a New York Jewish merchant gaining social and financial prominence. Sometime in October 1851, Dittenhoeffer suffered the loss of his mother, whom he buried in Salem Fields. The decision was not surprising. Among the founders of Temple Emanu-El and an eager promoter of its cemetery, Dittenhoeffer was one of the first to purchase a family lot. Controversy struck, however, when he informed trustees of his former congregation, Anshe Chesed, that he wished to remove his father and father-in-law's graves from that synagogue's Eighty-Ninth Street yard to the new family lot in Salem Fields. As debate flared in later weeks, Dittenhoeffer and his supporters—with little attention to his father-in-law—saw his parents' reunion in beautiful new family holdings as a sufficient basis for the claim. Those opposed cited the fact that Dittenhoeffer's father had died a full year before Salem Fields or the lot even existed. A strict interpretation of Jewish law, they maintained, would not permit the graves' transfer. On the advice of three separate religious authorities, trustees at Anshe Chesed ultimately refused the request. One included Dr. Max Lilienthal, another of New York's first ordained modern rabbis who would become a leading voice of Reform Judaism in America.[50] Soon after his arrival in the United States, Lilienthal served simultaneously as "chief rabbi" for Anshe Chesed and two other New York congregations. The issue could have ended with the board's ruling but for the many precedents at stake and Dittenhoeffer's own sense of justification. Broader debate raged in the coming weeks, and not coincidentally, Emanu-El representatives drove the discussion.

Dr. Leo Merzbacher, Emanu-El's rabbi and America's second one of European origin, offered the main dissenting voice. Whether he promoted the temple's interests as the city's primary Jewish seller of family lots or his own interpretation of Jewish law that often elevated popular sentiment, Merzbacher challenged the legality of Anshe Chesed's ruling. Importantly, he invoked family will at every opportunity. In a widely read editorial, Merzbacher cast Dittenhoeffer as an admirable son "gathering the bones of a beloved father, like a true Joseph, to that home destined to become a cave of Machpelah, a revered inheritance for his posterity." Why else, Merzbacher claimed, had Dittenhoeffer buried his mother there? And why else did he intend on "joining those 'who were lovely in and pleasant in their lives, and in their death not divided.'" Details of timing aside, if Jewish law allowed for disinterment in the name of family graves, why should Dittenhoeffer's request not come to fruition? Merzbacher also invoked another issue foremost in his New York readers' minds: anxiety over urban development threatening so many city graves. As waves of congregations were giving up their city yards, Merzbacher presciently predicted that "there will be by the general desertion of almost every burying place of every congregation in the limits of the City, a common interest felt in the settlement of this point of the law."[51] On the one hand, ruling against Dittenhoeffer may have set the stage for immense emotional anguish, precluding a families' ability to preemptively protect against urban growth. On the other hand, wary opponents feared that to rule in his favor might only embolden the notion that modern conditions in America justified other reevaluations of long-held Jewish law.

Rivals therefore countered with equal passion. Some paled at what they called an unjust "desecration," violating "an established rule, that the dust of the departed must not be disturbed."[52] Others decried what they considered Merzbacher's imprecise legal interpretation, especially regarding the family and its limited rights in such matters. Rivals pointed out that while tradition permitted disinterment to a family resting place, the grave must have existed before any such burial. Opponents clearly worried that growing enthusiasm for family lots might encourage local families to circumvent ritual taboos that had been put in place, they believed, to protect the dead and their eternal rest. If Dittenhoeffer could transfer his fathers' graves to a lot purchased well after their deaths for no other reason than sentimentality, the ruling might invite other families to do the same. As a result, Jewish New Yorkers might be enticed to use that precedent to realize their long-prohibited desire to bury their kin together. In the process, it would dramatically disrespect the dead as much as Jewish law in the wave of disinterments to follow. Dissenting voices, therefore, stressed the importance of timing in the purchase of a family grave. "It is plain that if a person has a private vault or family lot, it is lawful to remove the dead," one letter to the editor spelled out. "If, however, he purchased the lot afterwards, he certainly cannot be allowed to do it."[53] When Abraham Rice, America's first rabbi with European ordination, wrote from Baltimore, he further stressed that point: "It is only allowable when a family grave was long since in existence to bring a member of the family there, but not to disturb a father's grave to make a family grave. This last we call *arrogance* and *false pride*."[54]

Although in the end authorities did not allow Dittenhoeffer to move his fathers' remains, Merzbacher won the final word after a month's deliberation. He maintained that the case met all legal allowances for disinterment, and more importantly, he put his lot with the family, claiming that the bonds and wishes of kin outweighed those of communal authority. The urban expansion menacing city yards and the very security of loved ones' graves particularly emboldened him. Merzbacher reduced the authority of the trustees in question and any of their future counterparts to that of "an administrative body" guarding communal well-being. They could assess "what disadvantage might be sustained, if the requested permission is granted," but beyond these logistics, Merzbacher asserted, "far from it is the assumed authority of an ecclesiastical tribunal, to inquire into the merits of the case, and to expound the motives appertaining solely to the conscience and religious feelings of the claimant, who with a venerating heart approaches the grave, to gather the bones of his father." Although Jewish burial had long remained a public and communal issue, Merzbacher predicted the increasing sway of family will in the matter, especially as it aligned more closely with personal and commercial interests. The new ability to purchase graves seemed only to encourage an expectation of greater say over family repose.[55]

If nothing else, Merzbacher also predicted in a thunderous conclusion that urban growth would inevitably outweigh all other opposition. In moments of crisis, he warned, or even amid the disrepair facing so many old city yards, no congregation could deny a family's right to protect the graves of loved ones. Merzbacher personified that challenge as a Jewish son: he was fed up with congregations that managed city yards and lacked even "the smallest confidence in the protection [they] will be able to afford to the deserted buryal [sic] places and to prevent their desecration and destruction in a short space of time." Therefore, he asserted, "I will remove the sacred bones of my father to that place which will stand undisturbed for centuries, where my care can watch over the grave, where my love can adorn it, and where the endeared memory can be cultivated and brought down to posterity." Merzbacher never directly invoked Salem Fields or Emanu-El's responsiveness to family concerns, but each element saturated his affirmation. The argument anticipated New York Jews' shifting sensibilities and the understanding that most congregations, sooner rather than later, would have little other choice than to adapt to affiliated families' emerging consumer entitlements. "They might feel somewhat offended at such a bold utterance of distrust and fear," Merzbacher concluded, but inevitably trustees would "have to yield to the anxious and pious feeling of the son and dare not refuse his claim."[56]

As the 1850s wore on, the Dittenhoeffer affair predicted things to come, as the changing cityscape continued to reshape Jewish cemetery policies. The next notable controversy erupted within a year, this time in B'nai Jeshurun's Thirty-Second Street graveyard. Critics not only accused members of seeking to move their dead to family lots in Beth Olom Cemetery but also suspected trustees of conspiring to vacate all graves in order to sell that land for profit. Although synagogues had never pre-emptively abandoned their grounds when facing city development, the practice had become fairly common among other religious communities. Both the Allen Street Methodist Episcopal Church (1854) and the Brick Presbyterian Church (1856) transferred their entire churchyards all at once when bans on in-city burial led them to purchase new Long Island holdings. Other churches facing similar limits left Manhattan grounds intact for several years but ultimately transferred their dead to sell the old graveyards to the city for revenue.[57]

For synagogues, though, mass disinterment remained a clear taboo except in cases threatening an entire yard's security. Even then, New York Jewish authorities and rabbinic advisors overseas typically insisted on moving only the fewest possible graves. In 1855, for instance, when the New Bowery's extension forced Shearith Israel to transfer 256 graves from the old yard at Chatham Square to its Twenty-First Street and Long Island holdings, leaders only briefly considered abandoning the yard in full. Given the scale of the transfer and a sense that city development would only continue to crowd out Manhattan's dead, Shearith Israel questioned whether it should simply remove all remaining graves, but London rabbis forbade giving up the entire yard. They mandated instead that as "it is prohibited to disturb the repose of those who sleep in the dust . . . [it is] your sacred duty to surround with a wall that part of the [ground] which is not invaded by the public improvement and to adopt other necessary measures so that it may be effectually secured against desecration."[58] In 1856 and again in 1858, when Anshe Chesed's board discovered several graves exposed in its Forty-Fifth Street and Eighty-Ninth Street grounds, European advisors offered similar advice. They discouraged transfer of the dead to removed rural holdings, and despite the poor conditions of the city yards, they only condoned relocating the fewest graves possible. Even then, they advocated transfer only to another portion of the same burial ground followed by its enclosure with new protective walls.[59] In accord with the deep discomfort over disturbing or disrespecting the dead, New York trustees focused their resources for several decades on keeping old graveyards intact until there seemed no other viable alternative.

In this climate, outrage erupted in 1853 when the Jewish public learned that B'nai Jeshurun's board had requested city permission to rearrange some of its Thirty-Second Street graves and "to remove the remains of persons interred . . . in this city to their new grounds at Cypress Hills."[60] With the broader cemetery crisis on the rise and the Dittenhoeffer debate still fresh in public memory, even the mention of transferring graves set off deep anxieties. Editorials again rehearsed traditional arguments against disinterment, but this time the outrage focused on the trustees' alleged intention to empty the grounds in order to sell the land for profit. One writer charged, "Are the people blind or stupid, that they should fail to see that . . . the trustees sought more than our laws permit."[61] "I hope I do not err," another lambasted, "but it does occur to me that *money* alone stirs the parties . . . the trustees are shrewd businessmen—they know to a cent no doubt the value of lots running from 32nd to 33rd-st."[62] Although a few months earlier trustees had privately surveyed the yard "to obtain proper valuation," their public denial of the allegations never wavered.[63] Still, the broader trend among so many churches to vacate and sell their city grounds for municipal development only added cause for concern.

Many also believed that growing fervor over family lots drove the affair. As one editorial claimed, the trustees' actions were "founded on a desire expressed by some of the members to remove remains of a relative to the new cemetery. On this point turns the gist of the question."[64] On some level, that speculation may have been warranted. After all, preparations for lot sales consumed B'nai Jeshurun trustees just months before the public outcry. They had already put much energy into the composition and distribution of cemetery regulations and championed family lots whenever possible, even amid public uproar over the congregation's application for city permission to move some graves at the Thirty-Second Street yard. If synagogue officials did not directly encourage member families to transfer their dead from Manhattan, they clearly anticipated the possibility. When the board sought Raphall's advice on the legality of rearranging some Thirty-Second Street graves, it inevitably also asked, "Should any of the [lot] purchasers desire to remove the remains of deceased relatives . . . from their old ground into their new purchase are the Trustees according to Jewish law empowered to consent to such removals or not?"[65] After explaining exceptions to open or move a grave, Raphall again stressed the issue of timing: "It is, however, very doubtful whether . . . the Law can be construed to extend to the removal into a new ground, where as yet 'his kindred' do not 'repose.'" Far less assertively than before, though, he did remark, "Until this doubt be solved—and which I cannot take upon myself to do—the Trustees should not permit any such removal."[66] That emphasis on potential doubt—or, for that matter, its possible future refinement—signaled a clear awareness among trustees and religious leaders that the issue would not abate any time soon. Despite the scandal surrounding Dittenhoeffer's request just a year earlier, popular will through the purchase of family lots quickly shaped a new current in the court of Jewish public opinion.

Jews beyond New York City eagerly followed these debates, aware of the ritual and social precedents being forged in these new Jewish cemeteries. When Abraham Rice offered his opinion on the Dittenhoeffer case, he dismissed the affair for its clear challenge to Jewish law. He also fretted that Jews would be "so eager to imitate other confessions, without consideration of our holy religion."[67] In another letter to the *Asmonean*, a concerned Philadelphia reader explained that "this question has caused much trouble here for we fear the example set by New York may cause many imitators to break the sacredness of our humble [burying ground] and take the remains of their relatives to the more fashionable Laurel Hill."[68] Conversely, others admired New York's Jewish rural cemeteries and aspired to emulate their managing congregations. In 1856, as Cincinnati's two largest Jewish congregations discussed incorporating family lots into a shared ground, that city's Jewish press printed in full the constitution and regulations governing Shaaray Tefila's New York cemetery.[69] Two years later, an editorial praised Emanu-El and the cemetery policies it had adopted for nonmembers.[70] Whether expressing unease or enthusiasm over traditions in flux, Jews throughout the nation's burgeoning cities looked to New York as both a predictor and an exemplar for trends in American Jewish cemeteries.

Inasmuch as family lots and disinterment remained contentious issues, the mandate to protect the dead ultimately settled the matter, especially as large municipal projects at the doorstep of old Jewish yards made disinterment a pressing necessity rather than a theoretical issue for extended debate. In 1856, for instance, construction of the city's new Central Park forced Shaaray Tefila to abandon its 105th Street ground, shattering trustees' early hope that they had set the yard far enough beyond the city's reach.[71] Shearith Israel faced equally trying pressures just months earlier in 1855, when the city determined to extend the New Bowery through the old yard at Chatham Square. Although the congregation had prevented earlier plans to extend Henry Street there in 1831, this project proved far more formidable. Because of the yard's long legacy, members refused to fully abandon it. Instead, they set about the heavy task of disinterring only those graves directly threatened by the construction. They removed 256 in total, labor that none took lightly. Proceeding at a steady pace, they transferred at least 54 graves between the end of November and late December alone. Rates fluctuated, with the committee moving as few as one grave on some days and as many as six on others. Lists recording the process detailed biographical and family information for as many tombs as possible to identify.[72] Although exhuming the Jewish dead never lost its emotional and ritual complexity, it only became more common in the coming decades.

Even without looming parks or improvements, the ebb and flow of city life raised challenges for Jewish yards. Although most congregations had established burying places beyond city limits, New York's northern expansion quickly enveloped them over the nineteenth century. Mundane intrusions of chores, children, and the wear of time called into question those graveyards' respectability. In the spring of 1852, the city's general interest paper, *The Sun*, printed this stinging critique of how life in Lower Manhattan invaded the old Jews' yard:

> A house has been built over its entrance, its fences broken down, clothes are bleaching on the tombstones, kites are flown, and foot-ball and cricket played on this hallowed spot which is now the general juvenile military parade ground of the neighborhood. A small sum will fence the ground

and repair the fallen monuments. A few shrubs, flowers, and trees, would make the ground an ornament, instead of an eye-sore, as it is at present, to the respectable inhabitants of the house by which it is surrounded. We are sure the fair members of the synagogue will not allow the graves of their kindred to be any longer desecrated.[73]

Time only exacerbated that situation. In 1874, an editorial writer for the *Jewish Messenger* revisited the same graveyard. He highlighted the irony that although the New Bowery had not forced the transfer of his great-grandfather's grave decades earlier, an abutting tenement house brought daily steady disruptions through innumerable clotheslines of dirty wash hanging overhead or "slops and refuse of all kinds" thrown from neighboring windows, which "lay in heaps on the ground" throughout the hallowed grounds.[74]

Other yards scattered amid New York's manufacturing and residential bustle faced similar woes. The first installment of a *Messenger* series on Jewish cemeteries equally lamented B'nai Jeshurun's Thirty-Second Street burying place. Although trustees had made some clandestine removals at night during the 1853 scandal, much of the yard remained intact by 1875, albeit largely neglected and subject to incidental intrusions. "Bits of glass, old and broken bottles, shavings from the furniture factory, pieces of iron wire and hoops, sticks of wood, gravel stones covered with tar, and tarred roofing material, blown from the roofs of contiguous buildings . . . are strewed upon the earth in all directions," the piece lamented. Likewise, a band of local boys would scale the surrounding walls to play now that a neighboring workman no longer kenneled his dog there.[75] The prospect of vacating Jewish yards in the city remained controversial, but the threat of the teeming metropolis that was poised to swallow them up left congregants and religious officials ultimately more accepting of the need for large-scale disinterment.

In a fortuitous turn for those desiring to transfer relatives' graves from Manhattan to new family lots, the mandate of Jewish law to protect the dead from eminent domain or deteriorating grounds actually provided them cover to carry out those reburials. Most Jews accepted those transfers as long as city development or other physical dangers remained the primary reason. Accordingly, B'nai Jeshurun repeatedly invoked "security" to play down criticism in 1853. In 1856, Anshe Chesed also alluded to "the poor state of our burial places in [45th] and 89th Street" when it inquired abroad if "removing of the corpses from those places to our new cemetery would be a good deed as they would not be disturbed there."[76] Among the 1856 transfers from B'nai Israel's Ninety-Fifth Street ground to its holdings in Beth Olam Cemetery, at least two involved the transfer of graves to a plot just sold to H. B. Herz, with one belonging to an unspecified Mrs. Hertz, who may have been a wife or mother.[77] Even at Shearith Israel, so long the symbol of conservatism in burial matters, urban growth offered cover for members to move relatives' graves from communal grounds to new family holdings. When the New Bowery cut the Jews' yard at Chatham Square in half, Seixas Nathan had the grave of his grandmother, Grace Nathan, transferred to his family's private lot in Shearith Israel's new Long Island cemetery.[78] Although Grace Nathan's family had specifically paid the city's $250 fee in order to ensure her burial in the congregation's oldest burying place, her grave's transfer represented one of the first to vacate the old yard. The looming roadway provided her grandson the opportunity to move her grave to the physical and emotional security of a distant family lot. For many other families, these private holdings now offered the preferable and seemingly natural locus for the city's wandering Jewish dead. Echoing Merzbacher's earlier prediction, family values and individual lot holders' rights of private property rose to new prominence. The growth of rural cemeteries and an independent Jewish cemetery economy only further ensured that trajectory.

In coming decades, as need and the process became ever more routine, broad swaths of the Jewish public seemed only more sensitized to the issue. Importantly, they also accepted the notion of family responsibility for subsequent disinterment and reburial. By 1875, for instance, Beth El trustees, after an earlier merger with Anshe Chesed, finally decided to give up their graveyards on Forty-Fifth and Eighty-Ninth Streets. Trustees notified relatives "that the proper permit from the Health Department had been obtained, and that unless they removed their dead in due time, the Trustees would see to such removal."[79] The plan garnered some criticism but foreshadowed similar decisions by other congregations. Just eight months later, the press cast new ire on Rivington Street's Shaar Hashomayim for beginning to transfer graves from its Eighty-Ninth Street yard near Madison Avenue.[80] By 1879, news broke of excessive land assessments leading both the Clinton Street and the Henry Street Synagogues to vacate their shared yard at Eighty-Eighth Street near Madison.[81] Financial, physical, or family motives made that once highly controversial trend seem inevitable by the late nineteenth century. Indeed, even as the *Jewish Messenger* scolded congregations for giving up their burying grounds throughout the 1870s, its series on New York City's Jewish cemeteries ultimately claimed that although the historic legacy of Shearith Israel's oldest yard mandated preservation, "every other old graveyard in this city, should someday be torn up and dismantled, as is not at all unlikely."[82]

By 1883, the practice seemed so unavoidable that six rabbis of New York's Minister Association returned to the thorny issue that had plagued popular and rabbinic opinion at Dittenhoeffer's first request just thirty years before. Although this tribunal still encouraged Jewish New Yorkers to avoid disinterment whenever possible, they would be permitted to remove the dead to protect and respect them "as it not unseldom happens that by reason of the growth of cities, disused cemeteries become liable to encroachment and defilement." Even more importantly, and in light of that necessity, these rabbinic authorities set a new precedent by giving up the question of timing surrounding a family plot. "Under certain circumstances," they reasoned, "it is allowed to remove bodies from isolated graves or from the general row, to be re-interred in plots in which the mortal remains of family are resting. . . . So far from this being disrespectful to the dead, it is considered a mark of honorable consideration that our beloved ones who have gone the way of all the earth should repose side by side with those who were dearest to them."[83]

When Morris Raphall drew up an intricate guide to instruct a special committee of "shomrim [guardians]" in the delicate work of transferring selected graves from B'nai Jeshurun's Thirty-Second Street yard to the new Beth Olom Cemetery in 1853, neither he nor any representatives of other Jewish congregations likely imagined how regular those procedures would soon become.[84] Nevertheless, pragmatism and the realities of material and municipal pressures made that task ever more common in a shorter time than any would guess. Of so many Jewish burying places that had developed throughout New York City during the nineteenth century, soon only fragments of three belonging to Shearith Israel would remain. The anxiety over protecting the dead outweighed any doubts over the decency of disinterring individual graves or whole grounds. Jewish public opinion also became sensitized to removals as the need grew necessary and common. In the process, families' desire to relocate relatives' graves gained legitimacy, and the costs of inaction conferred new responsibility to do just that. By the century's end, the demands of modern America had left their imprint on both Jewish opinion and religious interpretation.

The Valley of Jehoshaphat and the Option of Being Independent

While crises menacing graveyards and tense deliberations over the permissibility of reburial received the most public attention, structural changes in the sale and management of Jewish cemetery land proved even more influential. Although synagogue trustees continued to refine their cemetery policies to appease current congregants and lot holders, they also curbed their influence. Members too capitalized on the broader cemetery economy to circumvent congregations altogether. They did so particularly as they came to understand how the system's imbalances worked against their interests, while larger market growth poised them to reshape it.

One representative case played out in 1856, when leaders of the congregation Shaaray Tefila gave up their city yard for new rural holdings. Trustees purchased a portion of B'nai Jeshurun's Beth Olom Cemetery and intended to adopt a standard policy governing family lots. A committee of displeased members spoke out vocally and early. "We are opposed to paying money for a *sham!*" they railed in the press, charging financial overreach and downright exploitation. Protestors reiterated, "The individual right to a cemetery or burial plot as offered under the [trustees'] regulations . . . is a sham, a delusion and a snare: a fiction of no value; a device to extract the means of paying for the ground, but conveying no privilege which the members do not already possess."[85] With a new sense of leverage, the committee threatened to break from the congregation and to purchase land on its own. Drawing on the example of so many fraternal lodges and burial societies around them, these dissenters declared, "[We] are in possession of the means to erect a cemetery affording every privilege, right, and immunity needed or desirable in a burial-ground." Like the founders of the Noah Society or other contemporary lodges, these Jewish congregants realized that if current policies displeased them, they could opt out by pooling money and buying land for themselves. They pledged that its use and control would be free of associational dictates or extraneous fees to bury non-immediate family members. The group even boasted that its holdings could furnish larger lots to individual families than those currently offered by trustees, all for a simple flat fee up front and with no additional charges. Foreshadowing a trend that only grew more common, the committee concluded with a warning to trustees and a reminder to contemporaries: "Uphold the laws you have adopted, but if they should be violently, illegally, or even under the color of the law, arrested in their efficiency, remember you have in this matter of burial plots, the option of being independent of the rules of the Trustees by the action of the undersigned."[86]

Fearing breakaway societies, synagogues continued to refine their policies. In this instance, they aimed to appease disgruntled lot holders and ease dissatisfied members. In others, they hoped less restrictive policies conforming to congregant demands might entice members away from their current affiliations. Following the 1856 protest, Shaaray Tefila gave in to congregants' complaints. Popular demand led Shaaray Tefila's trustees to emulate Emanu-El's policy, even rescinding requirements that lot holders' heirs retain affiliation or participate in the congregation in order to access family lots in the future. Despite trustee objections on that point, they saw little alternative than to meet members on their own terms. In that sense, Emanu-El's understanding that choice afforded congregants new leverage in communal dynamics again set a precedent for practice among competing congregations. Policies at Salem Fields remained the most lenient of the Jewish cemeteries, especially in terms of ritual stipulation. The few lot practices that Emanu-El did ban included refusal to bury non-Jewish individuals or spouses and a prohibition against setting up "improper" or potentially offensive monuments or inscriptions "contrary to this Jewish faith or creed."[87] Otherwise, trustees enforced few ritual dictates. They even abandoned old traditions that tied members' interment eligibility to religious observance. Despite the existence of so many long-entrenched communal and ritual traditions that had defined Jewish burying spaces in New York, congregations conceded to members' entitlement as property owners in several areas. They also affirmed the private rights of family, cultivating new standing and influence for Jewish congregants in cemetery and membership policies.

Beyond their congregations, Jewish households also enjoyed new social agency, as they continued to form collective burial and relief societies into the 1860s. Organizing around independent cemetery property, Jews in New York continued to claim greater self-determination in death. They refined their capacity to support affiliated families, steadily building up monetary aid like sick relief, funeral costs, and crude pensions to members' surviving widows and children. In this way, societies not only supplanted congregations as providers of funeral rites and burial but further decentered synagogues as key sources of philanthropy and Jewish end-of-life planning with their added benefits. Since early groups like the Mendelssohn and Noah Societies or the first B'nai B'rith lodges marked some of the first Jewish orders to combine these needs, similar groups followed and flourished in a matter of years. In New York alone, Jews created at least eleven B'nai B'rith lodges by 1859 as seven lodges of the Independent Order Free Sons of Israel had developed in the city alongside other fraternities like the Order Brith Abraham (1859) or its offshoot, the Kesher Shel Barzel (1860). The city also witnessed the formation of the first independent women's counterpart, the Unabhaengiger Orden Treurer Schwestern (Independent Order of True Sisters; 1846) that expanded to six northeastern lodges by 1851 and a small but notable national network of twenty-one lodges within decades. By the early part of the twentieth century, some sixteen national Jewish fraternities followed that pace, many with origins in New York and all boasting an abundance of loyal members across the country.[88]

These groups developed steadily beginning in the mid-1840s, but the ability to buy smaller and relatively inexpensive rural cemetery tracts propelled them in coming years. Lodges of the Free Sons of Israel, for instance, commonly purchased tracts in Cypress Hills. Other Jewish societies that may have remained uneasy about burying in close proximity to non-Jewish associations or nonsectarian land received encouragement from the city's flourishing Jewish cemetery economy. Early efforts among the leading congregations to sell sections of their new cemeteries offered an important alternative means to access Jewish cemetery land.

As in so many areas of the Jewish Rural Cemetery Movement, Temple Emanu-El played a significant role in laying that foundation by innovating the sale of portions of its twenty-five acres in Salem Fields to fledging Jewish burial and relief groups. The Mendelssohn Society was one of the earliest groups that bought land in Salem Fields after giving up its Eighty-Seventh Street yard in Manhattan in 1851. Other lodges followed suit, like the Brothers of Charity in 1854, Holche Zedek (Attendants of Justice) in 1856, Nesios Chaim ubikur Cholim (Journeys of Life and Visiting the Sick) in 1858, the Daniel Benevolent Society in 1859, and the Bruder Verein (Union of Brothers) in 1860, to name only a few.[89] In all, by 1877, within the first thirty years of Salem Fields' operation, at least twenty-three smaller Jewish societies had purchased tracts in Emanu-El's cemetery.[90]

Just as Emanu-El understood the value in selling lots to individual families, it was also forward thinking in applying market principles to sell portions of Salem Fields to smaller fraternal organizations. It was especially prescient since many of these groups did not have the means to set up rural cemetery land on their own. That innovation not only encouraged the formation of new Jewish relief orders that may have retained congregation ties in the absence of accessible Jewish cemetery land but also further infused corporatism into the city's Jewish cemetery economy. An early set of Salem Fields' statutes even built in incentives for smaller groups to purchase as many lots as they could. Although Emanu-El trustees had the final say in governing Salem Fields, they elected a five-member committee each year to direct cemetery policy. To any congregation or society that purchased seventy-five lots or more, Emanu-El promised the automatic addition of one institutional representative to that committee with "the privilege of attending the regular meetings, taking part in the proceedings . . . making motions [and voting] on such resolutions . . . as concern the general interest."[91] As policies like these further ingrained a precedent that Jewish communal standing would draw on broader purchasing power, holdings in both synagogue and nonsectarian rural cemeteries continued to fragment New York's Jewish institutional landscape. As an array of religious and fraternal organizations proliferated over the coming decades, their growth enabled and hastened New York Jews' transition away from synagogue-centered communal structures.

By the early 1870s, lodges and burial societies marked a new stage in Jewish funerary provisions and communal life. For the first time since

Jews settled in North America—and certainly in New York—only a minority now belonged to congregations, most favoring instead the plethora of local Jewish fraternities and benevolent societies as their primary communal, philanthropic, and funeral institutions. Just two decades after the congregations had first established rural cemeteries, the foundations they set paved the way for an abundance of Jewish cemeteries across the Cypress Hills area. One Jewish press correspondent marveled in the late 1860s when a funeral brought him for the first time beyond Salem Fields, Beth Olom, and the early cluster of Jewish cemeteries dating to the 1850s. Just over that horizon, he beheld "as far as the eye could see quite a number of acres set apart for different congregations and other societies." In disbelief, he imagined "an Israelite . . . visiting our city will be astonished at the number of Jewish burial grounds that will meet his view at or near Cypress Hills. . . . 'Is it possible,' will be his exclamation, 'that the Israelites of New York shall be so numerous as to require so many places for the repose of their dead?'"[92] He little could have realized that the sprawl would only continue to grow.

As Jewish cemeteries multiplied in coming years, similar accounts underscored that sentiment. "Every synagogue has its cemetery," an editorial complained in 1878, and "so has every benevolent organization. The sons of the covenant joined with a 'Band of Iron,' to the 'Free Sons of Israel,' 'Natives of Kalish,' 'Loving Montefiore,' the 'Women of Israel' . . . In fact, it would require more space than we can spare to furnish a complete catalogue of the number of separate and independent cemeteries." Jewish cemetery holdings stretched on so far that the editorial writer could not help but mock: "Talk of the extent of the valley of Jehoshaphat, and the number of bodies within the valley; in time, Cypress Hills and its environs will have a greater number."[93] By the late 1870s, New York's so-called Jewish cemetery question sounded far different than it had decades earlier. Where once the press decried the absence of a Jewish place to bury beyond Manhattan, now it lamented an excess in and around Cypress Hills.

That proliferation transformed the social structure of Jewish life in New York as much as the landscape of the Brooklyn-Queens border. As critics fretted over the shift away from congregations, they further warned that trading synagogues for the material benefits of lodges would come at the expense of New York Jews' moral and spiritual character.[94]

In short, the argument went, financial and family priorities in death not only undermined synagogue membership to the detriment of religious adherence but also fostered a misguided tendency among late-century Jews in New York to "centre all of their Judaism in six feet of sod."[95]

Despite these critiques, the advantages of planning for life's end through new Jewish fraternities far outweighed contemporary disapproval. At the same time, New York's Rural Cemetery Movement empowered Jewish families to set new terms for themselves, either pooling resources to purchase independent cemetery tracts or diverting funds that would have paid congregation dues in order to affiliate with one or several societies. Through grassroots orders that they formed and joined over the coming decades, average Jewish women and men took advantage of a ready supply of cemetery land to create new forms of self-reliance and to protect against death-related poverty. The movement also allowed those within the congregation system to reshape their rights of membership while validating the family and their desire to bury together as social principles of equal worth to community in matters of death. The Jewish turn at midcentury to rural cemeteries not only undermined long-standing congregational monopolies in New York's Jewish burial system but secured new options and priorities in Jewish end-of-life planning that previously had received far less attention.

That the family drove the bulk of these changes reflected its larger prominence in nineteenth-century American society. At the same time, it highlighted a great and unseen irony of New York Jews' adoption of the Rural Cemetery Movement. American city dwellers, after all, turned to rural cemeteries amid rapid industrial change in order to safeguard tradition and to create some sense of permanence around what they considered a rapidly fleeting past. To curb unease over urban growth and its disruptive modernizing forces, city planners cultivated lush cemeteries across America's new and rising cities between the 1830s and 1850s.[96] The tranquility and scenic flow of the rural aesthetic thus intended to counter the manufactured and artificial feel of burgeoning human-made cityscapes.

While these cemeteries aimed to preserve sites of nature against their nonnatural urban backdrop, the lots that associations, churches, townspeople, and families dedicated within their tracts added to that mission. Communal holdings enshrined local history and celebrated preindustrial life as much as they memorialized the dead. Family and the stability it provided amid so much physical and social change played a special role in that project. Cities not only displaced the countryside but reconfigured life, as new industrial networks and wage labor redefined households and individual roles within them. As a result, Americans found comfort in reconceiving the family as a more private and nuclear unit of conjugal ties. Charged with protecting emotional and economic well-being of immediate kin, the family also offered a constant and comforting anchor to balance the period's regional and social transformations.[97] Winding trails and pathways in new rural cemeteries not only celebrated the natural surroundings through which they led cemetery visitors but elevated the values and virtues of kin by inevitably bringing them to sentimentalized family graves. Industrial growth and the materialism of urban capitalism beyond cemetery borders may have stood as uneasy symbols of modernity and change, but sprawling cemeteries aspired directly to contrast that development. Romanticizing nature, family, and community in beautiful displays, rural cemeteries harkened back to several generations and a thoroughly idealized past.[98]

Despite the intention to safeguarded tradition and shield American urbanites from the city's modernizing forces, rural cemeteries did almost entirely the opposite for Jewish New Yorkers, as they drove social and ritual changes at almost every level. Far from creating stark spatial divisions to keep out the urban and material world, the shift to rural cemeteries flooded Jewish burying places with unprecedented commercial and modern innovations. While family graves preserved nostalgia for other American communities or served as monuments to local history, they wildly undercut long-standing Jewish conventions steeped in at least a century of New York Jewish tradition. They also displaced communal and egalitarian ideals that Jewish graveyards in Manhattan had arrested by their sequential rows and coded sections. The private ownership of family lots also introduced ornate decor and grave ornamentation along with market innovations like the advanced sale of cemetery real estate. Those changes repositioned Jewish individuals and benevolent societies with a host of consumer powers and entitlements that afforded them new ability to organize. They used that capacity to overturn premodern deference to tradition and communal introspection and to pursue broader interests of self-seeking individualism. If other Americans laid out rural cemeteries to carve their mark on the past, at least some of New York and America's Jewish variants also did so with an anticipatory eye to the future. Although burial in the city's Jewish graveyards had preserved medieval custom and top-down structures of social control for more than a century, adaptation to rural cemeteries brought with it new and fairly uncharted terrain, modern and unprecedented in its physical and symbolic structures.

Commercial innovations, family priorities, and grassroots independence proved some of the Rural Cemetery Movement's greatest legacies for New York Jewish participants at midcentury and well into coming decades. The Jewish relief societies and fraternal networks that proliferated around new commercial cemetery land in the 1860s recast old dynamics and also laid the ground for thousands of aid associations that would be founded by a coming wave of east European Jewish immigrants at the turn of the century. If the Jewish press stood in awe in the 1870s at sprawling cemeteries around Cypress Hills, it certainly could not have predicted the expansion just on the horizon. Later Jewish waves drew on the models that their native-born and immigrant forebears had set in the mid-nineteenth century. Their numbers, however, would drive New York's thriving Jewish cemetery economy even more than that initial sprawl. Their working-class profile in an industrializing society only further developed the monetary death benefits to families and surviving dependents that Jewish New Yorkers continued to tie to cemetery land and interment rights. The turn to rural cemeteries set a foundation for family and market forces to play a greater role in Jewish end-of-life planning, but the needs and innovations of more than a million counterparts soon to arrive only further entrenched those forces.

4

Wives and Workingmen

Protecting Widows and Orphans,
Affirming Husbands and Fathers, 1840–1940

"Buried cheaply!" rang the damning critique. By the 1870s, as Jewish lodge affiliation outpaced synagogue membership, uneasy onlookers belittled popular funeral benefits driving New York Jewish fraternalism. Defenders of the synagogue chastised Jewish fathers who saw no need to join congregations because societies would provide their funeral. Such men would save time, they thought, by avoiding congregation duties. More important, they would save money by avoiding congregation dues. While annually it might cost them $50 to belong to a synagogue, they could secure society membership for just a tenth of that expense. Nonetheless, critics warned that the long-term costs far outweighed short-term savings, especially if these family men considered the moral fate of their children. Without religious guidance, sons and daughters would "grow up to be as selfish, as narrow-minded and as small as their father." With no sense of decency instilled by their synagogue, these children seemed bound for incarceration. Then advocates claimed, "The father who wishes to be buried cheaply will take the money he saved by not being a member of a congregation, and spend it—and ten times more than it—in lawyers' fees, to keep his worthless sons and worthless daughters out of prison . . . all brought about through stubbornness and stinginess in not joining a congregation."[1]

Despite such arguments, New York Jews favored societies. In fact, most would have found it hard to believe that lodge membership could do otherwise than secure their family's well-being. They especially would have defended the monetary death benefits paid to their dependents. Like broader forms of fraternalism, New York Jewish variants aimed to support member households when they were otherwise at their most vulnerable. Jewish fraternities thrived by not only covering funeral costs but incorporating financial awards for a member's widow and children to guard against poverty in case of a man's death. Nearly all understood the dangers of America's new industrializing economy and the growing emphasis it placed on men as primary providers. Jewish lodges and benefit societies also knew that funeral costs alone could devastate a family's resources, to say nothing of a breadwinner's lost earnings. If synagogue proponents looked askance at Jewish fraternities, the wider public forming and joining these aid groups greatly valued benefits like new pensions to widows and, later, lump-sum death endowments to a wider array of beneficiaries. These entitlements not only preempted financial tragedy but fueled the next phase of the city's Jewish funeral economy and its ability to validate family need through material protections at death.

And yet far from the straightforward awards that widows' pensions represented at their introduction in the 1840s, the death endowments they evolved into over the next hundred years created complex new hierarchies between Jewish families and their burial societies. In the mid-nineteenth century, groups focused almost exclusively on nuclear married families with limited aid at death beyond pensions to widows and children. Conversely, by the time the Great Depression hit, they had actually spent several decades questioning obligations to affiliated widows. Although fraternal rhetoric still championed these women's support, the use and distribution of society money told a slightly different story. Indeed, groups still paid out death endowments to wives and beneficiaries upon a male member's death, but they ultimately retrieved that money over time through a host of new cemetery fees introduced against widows. These included charges like security deposits on headstones, costs to reserve graves in advance next to a spouse, new widows' dues to maintain previously covered interment rights for mothers and their children, and ongoing payments toward cemetery upkeep. Soon, groups even withheld portions of the death endowment directly, nominally applied toward many of these expenses.

Few Jewish widows may have realized it at the time, but the early decades of the twentieth century wholly recast them. From privileged recipients of aid, widows evolved into contributors in their own right. Over the course of their affiliation, they gradually returned the death benefits they had received from societies, and these payments also helped fund a host of growing expenses. Some groups funneled widows' payments into reserve funds for endowments or applied them to cemetery costs, thereby freeing up money for new entitlements to living male members and their families. These covered benefits like sick pay or emergency relief to compensate men for job-related injuries or unemployment. Other groups applied widows' dues directly toward those programs, despite policies excluding widow-headed households from receiving them in kind. Rather than an overt effort to exploit affiliated widows, those mechanisms simply reflected changing attitudes around relief. By the turn of the century, as the nation's industrial labor force massively expanded, Americans grounded their economic stability in men's providing capacity. As greater shares of New York Jews joined the working class, they also embraced that breadwinning ideal, and their burial societies and aid groups adjusted their priorities. As groups placed new focus on supplementing men's wages while living, new policies around cemeteries and death endowments made up some of the difference. Effectively, they retrieved and redistributed widows' aid in the long run. Although death benefits might help a family immediately after a father or husband's passing, the new system recast those payments as more of a short-term loan or reserve fund against which societies drew. For perhaps the first time as New York's Jewish social welfare system matured, groups moved away from hallowed emphases on widows' economic security to meet another pressing goal among their workingmen.

With family at the center of those changes, shifts in Jewish end-of-life planning also impacted domestic rhythms far beyond burial and death, marriage and remarriage in particular. The early emphasis on widows, for instance, when groups first incorporated and refined their pensions, privileged nuclear marital norms, and frequently limited other family models' ability to access aid. New policies by the turn of the century, however, conditioned surviving wives and children's funerary rights on maintaining widow-standing. After all, given advances in these groups' funeral insurance, remarriage not only would jeopardize the financial relationship to a first husband's society but could obligate a group to extend another set of burial and endowment benefits to more than one wife. To make matters worse, remarriage could lead a widow or widower to forgo double graves previously purchased with a first spouse. To avoid the difficult task of reselling stray single graves in a market driven by joint-spousal reservations as well as other obligations triggered by marriage and loss, groups introduced a bevy of charges and policies complicating a second wife's ability to easily gain coverage in a new husband's society. Whereas widows' pensions in the nineteenth century encouraged young and universal marriage among one generation of Jewish New Yorkers, one hundred years later, the convoluted financial ties among endowments, marriage, and cemetery real estate made the prospect of remarriage socially and economically costly. Perhaps even more ironically, with death benefits and cemetery transactions at the heart of their society status, widows bore the brunt of that evolving system over time despite the fact that they had been so central to its very creation.

Protecting Widows and Orphans

As Jewish cemeteries continued to flourish across Brooklyn and Queens throughout the nineteenth century, "widows and orphans" left their own ideological mark on the lodges, burial societies, and Jewish fraternal orders managing those grounds. After burial, guarding widows and their children became a centerpiece of nineteenth-century Jewish fraternalism. Most groups elevated families' financial protections to a task of equal importance with securing cemetery land. Just as central European Jewish immigrants did when they incorporated the Mendelssohn Benevolent Society in 1844, hundreds of counterparts would echo their two primary goals over the years. One included "mutual relief to the members . . . and their families, when in sickness, want and destitution or distress." The other was "appropriating money to purchase a suitable burial ground and to defray the necessary funeral and incidental expenses, in case of sickness or death of any member, or of his family."[2] While specific iterations varied—some giving only funeral aid, others medical relief or sick pay—a common pledge ensured assistance and protection to a departed member's wife and children.[3] Many Jewish groups of the period even highlighted that promise in the names they adopted: the Montefiore Widow and Orphan Benefit Society (1848), the Lebanon Widow and Orphan Society (1851), Zion's Widow and Orphan

Society (1851), or Washington Widow and Orphan Benevolent Society of New York (1858), to name only a few.[4]

The increasingly working-class profile of American and New York Jewish immigrants made financial death benefits and funeral provisions important reasons to affiliate with a lodge, especially as family economies increasingly relied on a husbands' earnings to anchor them. A proclivity among central European Jewish immigrant women to marry men far older than themselves increased this concern. As a result, widowhood and the prospect of need became increasingly likely for Jewish women over subsequent decades. In fact, widows made up a disproportionate number of needy American Jews, with Jewish children tending to enter orphanages at much higher rates after losing a father than a mother.[5] As grassroots burial societies and relief groups began erupting in the mid-nineteenth century due to more widely available cemetery land, the pensions that they devised for widows and their children complemented older funeral benefits, like the preparation of the dead and other ceremonial accoutrements. Although rituals still resonated among many of these groups, the need to provide financial aid to women and children cast new focus on surviving dependents and the earthly problems that death increasingly caused them.

In addition to poverty, Jewish aid groups focused on widows in an effort to spare them from broader public or private relief that seemed more harmful than helpful in assisting the needy. Although Americans began to pay greater heed in the nineteenth century to structural causes of poverty like insufficient wages or underemployment rather than divine will or individual failings, their efforts to help the poor struggled to balance good intentions with a tendency to moralize against idleness or vice. Mentalities that also questioned a mother's capacity to support and rear her children on her own posed another set of problems in a society that already privileged male earning.[6] Public aid institutions also tended to break up families. By insisting that recipients work, they forced mothers to give up their children and simply contribute toward institutional care. Overcrowding and poor conditions plagued those facilities. Limited funds among private charities also led to selective support, as groups tended to aid only those families deemed "deserving" of help. If private groups did accept women and their children, they closely monitored these households, imposing middle-class Protestant values as prerequisites for relief. In the absence of communal protections, nineteenth- and early twentieth-century widowed mothers in America faced difficult circumstances. As Ann Orloff aptly put it, "They were forced to depend upon the overseers of the poor for erratic, puny doles, lose their children to orphanages or foster care, or endure hardships in avoiding public charity."[7]

As midcentury Jewish fraternal groups placed increased attention to members' widows, they aimed to preempt their entrance into that system altogether. In offering monetary assistance to affiliated widows and their children, however, Jewish burial societies internalized broader notions that marriage and the family were the most effective institutions to guard against poverty, so early benefits replicated the state of marriage. Initially, Jewish fraternities devised extended pensions to widows and their children as male members stepped in collectively to compensate for the absence of deceased husbands and fathers. B'nai B'rith lodges, for example, paid a widow a lump sum of $30 to cover her husband's funeral expenses and then pensioned her $1 a week for the rest of her life if she never remarried. Lodges also promised smaller pensions to any children underage. Other contemporary groups adopted similar approaches. The Mendelssohn Society paid separate sums to a widow every three months for the rest of her life and to any children under thirteen.[8] For families facing the absence of husbands' wages, these new widow and orphan funds tried to make up some of the difference and offer these women a better chance at self-sufficiency without resorting to public aid.

Beyond financial support, Jewish orders also tried to compensate for the social deficiencies they imagined would affect fatherless families. B'nai B'rith policy pensioned a deceased brother's children, and if the oldest child was male, the lodges also saw to it that he learned a trade to promote self-reliance.[9] Groups also set up committees of brothers to look in on widows in order to monitor their health and social well-being. Early in its existence, the Mendelssohn Society instituted a standing committee that survived into later decades, consisting of its vice president and two other members who would stop in to "visit the widows . . . from time to time and to see that they and their children [were] comfortably situated."[10] By 1871, the Jonathan Lodge 14 of another order, the Kesher Shel Barzel (Band of Iron), also maintained "a committee on claims." It paid affiliated widows and their children but required that "one [member], at least, shall visit each month, and report to the Lodge . . . on the health of said widows and orphans."[11] Policies like these institutionalized another fraternal pledge to support brothers' wives and children after death socially as much as financially.

Nineteenth-century Jewish groups took those responsibilities seriously, especially those financial commitments. Often groups' earliest actions included setting up a widows' fund and the mechanisms to fill it into the future. In marked contrast to deviations by the twentieth century, most created budgetary barriers to make sure that money earmarked for widows was never siphoned off to other institutional expenses. When the Noah Benevolent Society set up a widow and orphan fund at its first meeting in 1849, for instance, it stipulated that a fourth of both initiation fees and annual dues would regularly go to the fund.[12] Other fraternities like the Order B'rith Abraham (1859) also established a "Widows' and Orphans' Fund" from the start and divided all income between that and a "regular Lodge Fund."[13] By the 1860s, when the group had grown into a national network, it even exempted individual lodges from paying any internal taxes on their respective widow and orphan funds despite demanding 6 percent of all other local revenue to pay regional grand lodge expenses.[14] Even smaller local groups like the Erster Ungarischer Kranken und Unterstützungs Verein (1865), later renamed the Mutual Benevolent Society, maintained clear financial divisions between a General Fund and its Widows' and Orphans' Fund until at least 1908.[15]

Had societies only served married members, that system may have gone unchallenged. As more single members joined, who were at least initially without wives and children to benefit from the funds they paid into, rumblings for a new system altered financial entitlements at death. They also shaped longer transactional perceptions that would overtake the death benefit and impact future widows' financial relationship to their societies. This change came through endowment awards, which allowed all members, whether married or not, to designate in advance someone to receive a death benefit in their name. Groups moved in that direction as they abandoned older head tax systems and began to establish reserve funds to underwrite the payments. Instead of ad hoc methods to collect money for surviving dependents, if and when a death occurred, reserve funds funneled portions of dues and other revenue into separate accounts on an ongoing basis. Under that model, members viewed monetary death benefits as a regular contributory effort in which everyone participated rather than a moral or fraternal obligation to safeguard a brother's wife in his stead. Members therefore felt entitled to the benefit regardless of their marital status. As groups transitioned to endowments by the late 1860s, they refined policies accordingly.

In a related turn, Jewish groups began to embrace a broader vision of the family by the late 1870s. These included multigenerational models in which single young men declared parents as beneficiaries or even siblings and their children. This shift linked to the move away from drawn-out pensions. Inadvertently, after all, death benefits designed solely for members' widows and children privileged nuclear families and elevated marriage. The latter became an institutional expectation and a promoted ideal as pensions rewarded members who married to the exclusion of those who did not. Along with these policies, the constitutions, financial mechanisms, statements of purpose, and groups' very titles put forth narrow domestic definitions that almost never strayed from wives and children when imagining beneficiaries.[16] Although marriage remained an assumed ultimate end for most members, the new system still challenged older definitions of family once limited to nuclear structures.

Alongside that broader view of the family, the departure from a pension system also set the stage for widows' transformation from a protected class to a reliable source of revenue in just a few decades. Perhaps ironically, however, most groups first turned to endowments in an effort to help these women by keeping entitlements solvent. Demographic shifts across societies by late 1860s already created a situation in which pensioned widows began to outnumber younger new dues-paying members. This was a by-product of spouses' earlier age differences, but it rendered widows' pensions too expensive to maintain beyond that cohort. These budgetary strains inflected attitudes toward widows. One Mendelssohn Society president even later assessed that "their number and with it the obligations of the Society increased from year to year, until the members felt the financial burden becoming too heavy for them." This and similar groups abandoned pensions "to adopt in its stead the so-called endowment plan . . . they consequently made a settlement with the widows then on the payroll . . . and started business again with a clean sheet."[17] In a similar arrangement in 1868, B'nai B'rith turned to endowments because members found the pension system "insufficient, unsatisfactory, and at the same time burdensome, aye, ruinous to our lodges."[18]

As lump-sum death endowments replaced open-ended pensions, societies began to pay larger awards to widows upon a husband's death. Between 1866 and 1871, for instance, the Independent Order Free Sons of Israel increased its benefit from $600 to $1,000.[19] That rapid increase even led the fraternity's founding branch, the Noah Society, to break from the national order. Nonetheless, it too established a fixed payment of $500 to go to its affiliated widows.[20] That range became standard across most groups. By 1869, varied national B'nai B'rith lodges even devised district-specific schemes to collect and reserve $1,000 endowments for their widows. Into the 1870s, despite several debates on the matter, districts eventually taxed their lodges at a member's death to raise that sum for a widow or legal heirs. They deposited any excess money in an endowment reserve fund that also underwrote future payments. At least while mortality rates remained low, plans like this safeguarded societies' ability to keep their growing financial promises to members and their beneficiaries.[21] Unlike their twentieth-century counterparts, they also taxed male members to fund endowment reserves rather than introducing fees on widows to refill those accounts for their sisters in the future.

As much as initial success bolstered societies, it also laid the ground for financial crises by the 1880s. Groups not yet versed in actuarial science did not account for fluctuations in their members' ages, affiliation rates or life expectancies, despite growing promises to pay ever-larger endowments. One B'nai B'rith historian reflected, "Some of the Districts had become exhilarated at the size of their growing reserve funds and were thinking of increasing the death benefit from $1,000 to $1,500, and even to $2,000."[22] Other groups similarly tied collective manhood to the largest sums they could possibly offer their widows. "This was toward the end of sixties," a historian of the Mendelssohn Society noted, "when the so-called insurance craze had seized all organizations and deluded their members to believe that with small assessments and still smaller annual dues, their lodge or society could afford to pay, at the time of their death, $1,000 to their widows."[23] It still took several years before fluctuating mortality rates jeopardized the system. As long as dying members did not outpace new candidates, the turn to endowments worked relatively well.

By the 1870s and 1880s, the new system enjoyed wide appeal. B'nai B'rith even boasted peaks in its membership outpacing other orders. Endowments fueled that climb. "The worker, the shopkeeper, the average professional man worried more than ever about what would happen to his family if he died," a historian explained. "Life insurance was costly, and society security non-existent. . . . A large number of men had joined B'nai B'rith, not for its 'higher objects' but for its material benefits . . . it made a big difference if a thousand dollars' worth of life insurance cost perhaps $28 a year (at a given age) in a commercial insurance company, or only $15 (regardless of age) in B'nai B'rith."[24] Many new orders sprang up trying to attract members with similar benefits for even lower dues. Membership in New York Jewish lodges not only peaked but led men to pursue multiple affiliations to several orders at once. In one group, the First Galician Sick and Support Society, thirty-one of at least fifty-two candidates who applied for membership between 1873 and 1879 belonged to at least one other society. Of those applicants already affiliated, ten belonged to at least two or three other groups. One candidate even affiliated to four other fraternities, and another claimed membership in as many as six![25] According to one B'nai B'rith endowment advocate, the death benefit alone drove Jewish fraternalism. "Demand for it was general and irresistible," he claimed. "Kindred Jewish organizations owe their rise to the demand for endowment."[26]

That appetite for large payments at death would reshape assumptions around family models and beneficiaries, particularly since unmarried men made up the majority of most new members. Remaining single for several years as they paid society dues, unmarried members felt no less entitled to awards for their next of kin in the case of death, whether or not they fit a long-standing married ideal. Between 1871 and 1885, for instance, only 69 of 342 young men enrolling in B'nai B'rith Manhattan Lodge 156 were already married upon initiation.[27] Even in member propositions for roughly the same period, the number of nonmarried applicants outnumbered married men.[28] While most married within five to ten years after joining, single men still provided large revenue streams. As such, they expected any listed heirs to receive $1,000 if they died prematurely. With wives and children no longer automatic recipients, the groups instituted new advanced declarations to identify legal heirs. In the process, unmarried members' declarations influenced policy more than any others. Married men, after all, rarely deviated from assigning wives as beneficiaries, as did all 69 married B'nai B'rith members entering Manhattan Lodge 156. Even among men who married later, no matter whom they declared in their original certificates, all issued updated declarations after marriage claiming wives as new primary heirs.[29] Among those 273 initially unmarried new members, though, original declarations had split among parents, siblings, and extended kin. The majority conceived of themselves as sons, but a smaller group listed sisters, brothers, combinations of siblings, and even cousins and nieces and nephews as their primary beneficiaries. Even if only temporary, those declarations reshaped the death endowment culture by highlighting other degrees of family responsibility. At the same time, they also forced policy makers to broaden conceptions of the family that societies aimed to serve.

Not surprisingly, fraternities and burial societies quickly refined endowment policies to reflect these trends. Although in 1878 the Independent Order Free Sons of Israel still called its endowment the "Widow and Orphan Fund," it had already expanded chains of entitlement beyond nuclear beneficiaries. Policy stipulated that after a member's death, the promised $1,000 extended "in the first instance, to his wife or children . . . or secondly if she is dead, to his children, or thirdly, if he leaves no children, to his father, or fourthly to his mother, and fifthly to his legal heirs." By 1888, the group removed any reference to widows or orphans altogether in a newly christened "Endowment Fund."[30] Similar changes played out across societies at the turn of the twentieth century, with many expanding entitlement to even include siblings.[31] By 1928, the Independent Order Brith Abraham (IOBA) maintained one of the most extensive models, covering, "Husband, wife, child or children (including legally adopted children), grandchild or grandchildren, parent or parents (including by legal adoption), brother or brothers, sister or sisters, nephew or nephews, niece or nieces, step-parent or step-parents, step-child or step-children, or a person dependent upon the member for support."[32] Although these hierarchies still elevated marriage, evolving endowment policies broadened official family conceptions well beyond a previous nuclear ideal.

Nevertheless, the transition from drawn-out widows' pensions and resulting entitlement hierarchies did have an important if unnoticed effect across societies. It unseated old assumptions underwriting widows' aid and allowed groups to question the very nature of the death benefit. With so many extended levels of kin now entitled to claim a death endowment, the benefit had moved a long way from its moral origins, steeped in collective gendered mandates to protect a fallen brother's wife. By the early decades of the twentieth century, mounting expenses, actuarial pressure, and demographic change among an ever-more working-class immigrant Jewish community built on these changes to challenge the very endowment system in unprecedented ways. For the first time, groups questioned whether costs of monetary awards at death merited the strain on their institutional budgets. They also reevaluated their priorities, measuring support for widows against new imperatives to provide greater aid to living men and their families to guard against poverty during that member's life. These shifts in entitlement spending and new attitudes toward widows laid important ideological ground for the introduction of new fees around cemetery rights that women had previously received automatically. By the 1920s and 1930s, new charges around death and burial not only targeted widows affiliated to groups but underwrote a complex system that drew back on these women's death benefits to help fund other expanding entitlements.

Affirming Husbands and Fathers

By the turn of the century, with endowments tied less to the image of despondent women and more to the complexities of legal heirs and budgets, Jewish benefit societies eased old convictions that once defined the death endowment. They also began to look more closely at the growing costs as they gained better understanding of actuarial risk. As a result, they became more cautious of members in poor health and their impact on long-term solvency. Realizing that ailments or early death would only tax the system, most groups adopted rigid medical exams to filter out risky candidates. Groups like the Noah Society already required an affiliated physician to review all potential members by 1889.[33] B'nai B'rith lodges began focusing more on health in applicant questionnaires in the same period. Mount Sinai Lodge 270 candidates gave basic background information, but they also responded to questions like "Are you now in good health, and do you generally enjoy good health?" and "Have you had any serious illness within the last year? If so, what?" Physician certificates also guaranteed that the group's doctor administered a private exam and whether he found the candidate physically worthy of membership.[34]

As medical exams became more common across societies, they also grew increasingly thorough. When the Kolomear Friends Association standardized its application in 1907, it constructed it around a detailed medical evaluation screening of twenty-four physical, respiratory, digestive, and neurological conditions. Physicians read candidates blood pressure, standing as well as sitting; measured heart rates and breathing; inquired about surgical history; and even tested the volume of their urine. Parts of the exam also anticipated long-term health risks or dangerous diseases such as "cancer or a tumor," "palpitation of the heart," and family history of consumption.[35] Just decades earlier, societies may have pitied contemporaries in poor health or the widows and orphans they would likely leave behind at an early age, but by the turn of the century, groups invested greater energy to weed out presumably risky candidates. Exams precluded these men and their families from even entering the system before they had a chance to burden group treasuries.

Medical concerns coincided with growing anxiety over death endowment costs by the turn of the century. Like broader insurance orders, Jewish groups faced increasing average death rates each year. With them, associated benefit costs only grew. As financial crises burdened younger members or led them to drop out, societies felt the pressure to refine their policies.[36] For many Jewish groups, this occurred around significant anniversaries or when they simply took stock of the many surrounding orders succumbing to financial ruin. The tenor of their debates showed far more pragmatism around endowments than in previous years. Preparing for a 1904 annual convention, the Independent Order Free Sons of Judah performed a massive audit after paying $123,870 in death awards in the 1902–3 fiscal year alone. As the group surveyed members who died in that period, it traced initiations back to 1891, assessing how many endowments it had distributed, the length of members' affiliation, and how much they paid in prior to death before finally measuring all those factors against causes of decease. Both the Grand Master and Grand Secretary spoke out against faulty medical exams that they believed could have prevented needless costs had they filtered out clearly risky candidates. "The cause and trouble lies in the loose and unworthy manner many physicians sign certificates for application for membership," the Grand Master criticized.[37] The Grand Secretary added that several death claims "occurred within a few months after the acceptance of the candidate." Pointing again to faulty exams, he chastised, "We are all liable to die any minute, but Heart failure, Nephritis and especially consumption could hardly develop so quick that the examining Physicians should not have detected them. With a little more care in the examination of candidates and especially their wives at least ten thousand dollars could have been saved for the members of the Order in the past two years."[38]

Other groups expressed similar concerns. While the Free Sons of Israel did not carry out as thorough a study as the Free Sons of Judah, a 1902 annual convention called for a "more perfect medical examination of candidates . . . which shall serve as . . . a protection to the Order." One finance committee member underscored the role of death benefits when he warned that including members "whose physical condition is not good, into participation in the endowment will nullify every safeguard, in the direction of contribution of dues, and accumulation of a reserve."[39] Findings of the IOBA proved even more pressing. In 1909, after commissioning its own audit, the group realized that although every member's family received $500 at his death, the average members were affiliated for just twenty years and paid in no more than $120. "In other words," it spelled out, "under the post-mortem system, a member gets more than $4 for each dollar that he pays in, which is not sound business."[40] Despite the actuarial gymnastics of the mid-nineteenth century in order to furnish the largest benefit possible to a member's surviving kin, pragmatism outweighed those ideals by the turn of the century.

Increased concern over medical and material risk not only shifted attitudes toward the death benefit but called into question previous convictions about the entitlement itself. Even widows came under escalating attack. B'nai B'rith debates peaked in the late nineteenth century, leading one member, Isidor Bush, to pen an eponymous tome of more than three hundred pages advocating for "our widows and orphans endowments." He chastised the opposition to costs as clouding members' sense of duty to affiliated widows and their children. Throwing aside material concern, he proclaimed, "There is a class of selfish men who say: 'Let the women and children earn their living as we did.' These are men with whom duty is nothing, greed everything; but such men, if such exist among Israelites, cannot be B'nai B'rith."[41]

As debates raged among contemporary orders, opinions wavered between need-based entitlements to wholly questioning the very principle of widows' aid. One 1916 deliberation in the Mendelssohn Society set "wan widows" against well-to-do ones: "The idea that the widow of the millionaire should receive the same financial assistance as the one whose husband died a poor peddler is absurd and in direct contrast with the principles and objects of our Society." The group even made light of the program itself when assessing rising costs. "Widows either were not a very much sought article in the matrimonial market," leaders explained, "or [they] preferred the Society's certain assistance to the problematic support of a second husband."[42] These sentiments signaled a weakening commitment to the once-serious task of protecting surviving wives as a matter of collective responsibility. Far from the celebrated examples of masculine noblesse that nineteenth-century Jewish burial societies had nurtured in widows' pensions, by the twentieth century, the death endowment seemed a burdensome obligation weighing on limited resources.

As much as internal financial constraints shaped those attitudes, so did larger debates framing early social welfare programs developing in America, particularly as they related to workingmen and widows. In the 1910s and 1920s, programs like workmen's compensation and mothers' aid represented the first steps toward government aid for the population at large. In a society highly suspicious of government assistance, gendered arguments around men's and women's labor and their contribution to the national good proved important to garnering support. Reformers placed new emphasis on the social and civic importance of male wage-earning, especially as they looked to the state to balance massive industrial change. In less than half a century, after all, the number of American factory workers had increased nearly fivefold from 1,300,000 in 1860 to a resounding 5,500,000 in mere decades.[43]

As American industrial capitalism vested financial well-being in men's limited wage-earning prospects, it also bolstered stigmas against women working outside of the home. In that context, the increased likelihood of men's workplace injury or death only predicted greater need for families at large. Still, a well-steeped culture of gendered individualism limited the extent of government safeguards for working families. As programs evolved, the state far more readily intervened for the needs of widowed mothers and their children than in previous periods. Nevertheless, public willingness and resources devoted to male heads of household remained far more uncertain.

As early policy architects created new programs to reach average men and women in need, they justified their campaigns through an earlier state program of limited pensions to Civil War veterans. The principle of "service to the nation" had justified that program, and here it became a useful concept as well. The terms of the twentieth-century debates around men's productive capacity, however, transcended military participation when discussing national "service" to encompass gendered day-to-day contributions to the nation's well-being. Proponents of workmen's compensation promoted it as a reward for men's labor and invoked state responsibility to ensure proper damages for the invaluable industrial workforce. Injury on the job, the argument went, or a worker's incapacitation would not only disrupt his wage-earning ability but also undermine his right as a citizen to support his family of private means. Mothers' aid advocates, in turn, pointed to women's own reproductive and domestic work. For bearing and nurturing future generations of Americans, mothers without men to provide for them also deserved state assistance if male absence would lead them to fall on hard times. By 1919, thirty-eight states had enacted workers' compensation laws, and thirty-nine had put into effect mothers' aid legislation.[44]

These broader developments became important reference points for changes in grassroots Jewish entitlement spending as did long-standing support for widows by Jewish philanthropies and charities.[45] With male provision also increasingly cast as a matter of civic and social importance, Jewish societies aimed all the more to underwrite the supporting capacity of affiliated men. As local and national programs created new sources of aid for impoverished widows, immigrant groups began to turn their focus from those left behind to the needs of so-called intact families.[46] The shape that workmen's compensation and mothers' aid programs took influenced that perception, as each commonly cast widowed mothers as primary beneficiaries. The fact too that mothers' aid programs did not tax recipients allowed them significant popular support. Workmen's compensation, on the other hand, seemed much less secure, since it depended on often insufficient payment schedules and the government did not finance those benefits but only ensured through the courts that eligible workers received damages for injury. In another important distinction, employers ultimately funded the program and also appointed the doctors to determine eligibility.[47] In short, the logic and limits of those broader programs raised the social stakes of living men's earning capacity, and widows and their dependents seemed to enjoy more far-reaching support and protections than ever before.

The changing profile of New York's Jewish immigrant community only amplified those concerns. Pipe makers, operators, tailors, and tinsmiths represented just some of the earliest applicants to the Kolomear Friends Association between 1907 and 1911. When Jewish newcomers from the city of Kolomea established the group in 1903, they did not center their founding principles on widows and orphans as they might have half a century earlier. Instead, they invoked male breadwinning as the group's driving concern. "Realizing the difficult task that workingmen as individuals have in coping with material and physical handicaps which arise in the affairs of men," their constitution's introduction proclaimed, "we a group of young men from the city of Kolomea, have organized this society for the purpose of mutual assistance in times of sickness and distress."[48] Ages and marital status also informed that focus, as predominantly young men, unmarried between the ages of nineteen and their midthirties, made up just over half of the group's applicants, with married men following close behind.[49] Waves of Jewish immigrants at the turn of the century shared a similar profile, vulnerable to the seasonal unemployment of the garment industry or the general insecurity of manual labor.[50] With higher rates of family migration, eastern European Jewish households also contained more elderly or young dependents so that, as one contemporary study noted, "even common situations—illness, unemployment, the presence of young children in the household, or old age—could easily overtax their meager means."[51] These pressures facing Jewish family economies only added to shifting priorities of aid groups that moved to supplement male members' earnings. Many groups would mirror Brownsville's Chevra Kol Yisroel, a synagogue and burial society that promised on its organization in 1912 to set up a dedicated fund "as soon as the treasury has at least $300" in order to fund wage compensation for men during illness or injury.[52] In contrast, the group did not establish a parallel program for widows' aid or an endowment fund to build up reserves. Instead, it adopted an outdated head tax to collect money ad hoc for surviving dependents whenever a member died.

Against that backdrop, New York Jewish aid groups readjusted their priorities. By the 1930s, most burial and benefit societies, like other ethnic aid groups, inflated aid and expanded entitlements for living male members and their families.[53] New and increased awards supplemented lost wages, provided emergency relief, and compensated for unemployment or injury on the job. In 1901, for instance, the IOBA completely retooled its relief fund. Over the next three decades, it paid out roughly $4,978,655 to men in distress. In 1913, the group also created an unprecedented disability fund "to provide for male members, who became incapacitated from their normal occupations through the loss of an eye, arm or leg." It would pay out $1,371,992 for such injuries in less than two decades.[54] Even early Jewish fraternities like the Noah Society, which had originated in the mid-nineteenth century to oversee burial and assist members' widows and children, incorporated relief for a member "incapacitated by sickness from attending his usual vocation." By 1906, it also provided new emergency funds to further stretch a member's wages.[55]

The challenges of industrial wage labor led dedicated burial societies to set new focus on their men's earning power, but those innovations also subtly marginalized aid and attention to affiliated widows. At the same time that the Noah Society expanded financial relief to living men and their families, it also began to alter accounting structures as old as the group itself that had ensured ready reserves for surviving wives. Despite the stark separation between the widow fund and the general fund in place since 1849, by the late nineteenth century, policy makers dismantled that division. In 1889, they consolidated the group's dedicated widow fund and general treasury into an unprecedented "Current fund" that combined all initiation fees, dues payments, miscellaneous receipts, and even charges toward the burial ground. Now all costs drew on that pool, including "sick benefits, burial expenses, presents, salaries, legal payments to Widows and Orphans, interest, [and] miscellaneous expenses." For the first time ever, the group no longer set aside or shielded widow reserves from day-to-day expenses.[56] By 1917, it even officially changed its name from the Noah Benevolent Widows' and Orphans' Association to simply "the Noah Benevolent Society."[57] Symbolic and financial displacements like these signaled shifting priorities in any number of extant Jewish burial societies. They also marked the next phase of widows' marginalization as groups recast these women and their death benefits.

Adjoining Graves for Spouses and the Redistribution of Widows' Aid

Like the great commercial innovation to sell family lots in the 1850s, the move to sell adjoining graves to married couples defined the city's Jewish cemetery economy in the first third of the twentieth century. It also paved the way for a new host of fees and charges against widows' funerary privileges that the groups had previously granted automatically. These included costs for cemetery upkeep and setting a headstone to more consequential matters like a widow or her underage children's very right to a grave on society grounds. Over time, groups introduced new widows' dues for interment rights while also withholding many of those charges directly from death endowments. This created a new system that, over time, retrieved most of the money paid to a widow when her husband died and funneled that sum back into a society's treasury during her remaining years of affiliation. By the time that system crystallized in the 1930s, the new aid flow not only helped pay for growing entitlements to living male members and their families but often funded benefits that these women and their children could not even access. In 1932, for instance, although the Loyal Benevolent Society split a widow's $4 dues between its "Burial Expense Fund" and "General Society Fund," it stipulated that "a female member is not entitled to any sick benefit."[58] Similarly, even though the Kolomear Friends required quarterly widows' dues by the late 1930s, it specified that after a husband's death, other than burial, "his wife is not entitled to any other benefits."[59] New family priorities and further commodification of Jewish cemetery spaces again drove those changes as they had for the last two hundred years. In this instance, however, they only hastened an ongoing realignment of priorities that set the needs of male-headed households over the one-time protected class of widows.

Although groups did not devise that redistributive system of aid all at once, the process began in the 1890s, when widows began reserving graves alongside their husbands in increasing numbers. They did so in the rows of single graves allotted to members who had not purchased family lots. Groups typically offered those holdings for free but filled them chronologically until the turn of the century. Then with widows leading the way, more and more couples began asking that proximate or adjoining graves be left open following a spouse's death. Soon after, a growing class of widowers followed that example. The practice not only became ubiquitous in most burial societies and synagogues but led to new fees around double graves and cemetery privileges, which had once been automatic rights of membership. Widows' overrepresentation in these early requests and the large sums their societies had just paid them likely only encouraged more and more charges around the cemetery by the twentieth century.

Trends in the Holy Society could stand in for any number of the New York Jewish burial groups. As early as the 1880s, for instance, widows there began reserving individual graves next to husbands who predeceased them or in corresponding adjacent rows. They also did so more frequently than their male counterparts. Among fourteen identifiable widows who lost their husbands between 1872 and 1922, only the earliest two in the 1870s did not reserve nearby graves. From 1883 on, all remaining widows reserved graves either next to their husbands or in corresponding adjacent rows. Conversely, identifiable widowers who outlived their wives over the same period only regularly reserved graves after 1910, reflecting the policy's standardization.[60] Reservations replicated in that manner across societies, with some of the earliest dating to women in the 1890s. Although Rebecca Marks of the Chevra Kadisha Beth Israel died in 1923, she made sure to secure her spot three decades earlier. When cemetery managers issued her burial permit, they noted, "Reservation on Bayside Cemetary [sic]—Grave Reserved 1893."[61] Similarly, minutes of Eldridge Street's Adath Jeshurun are replete throughout the late 1890s with either widows seeking to reserve graves next to their husbands or adult children making those requests on their behalf.[62]

The practice only grew by the early twentieth century, with wives, and soon husbands, showing more preference for graves directly alongside their spouses. To secure those holdings, they had to act quickly after a partner's death to ensure that those spaces remained available. Members of the Ceres Union, for instance, may have taken note when Henrietta Guggenheim arranged to be buried sometime after her husband Meyer's death in June 1898 in a grave in the next row that corresponded to his. Had she acted before July of that year, when the group buried its next member, she might have been able to reserve the grave alongside him. By 1899 and early 1900, respectively, the group's next two widows reserved graves alongside their husbands. All subsequent Ceres Union widows did the same, as did a widower, Nathan Green, who in 1903 reserved a grave next to his wife at some point between her death and that of another member who died the following week.[63] When Chevra Kadisha Beth Israel member Louis Schwabach died in 1916, record keepers immediately penciled his widow into the cemetery permit book just two receipts after his, noting "reservation of grave alongside of Husband."[64] At a regular 1919 meeting of the Henry Clay Lodge 15 of the IOBA, members immediately followed up a report of Brother Miller's recent death with a motion that "Sister Miller wishes to reserve a grave for herself, which was granted."[65]

Sentimentality likely led many of these widows to reserve graves at the turn of the century, but pragmatism also moved them. Society membership, after all, remained a male-centered institution, and most women's entitlements came through a father or husband's standing. Widows who reserved graves upon their husband's deaths sought to secure a place for themselves while their family's affiliation remained fresh in institutional memory. Otherwise, they might fall to the mercy of a son or son-in-law's society, to say nothing of the extra fees that groups charged to bury parents on society grounds. Congregations like Adath Jeshurun sold several graves to members' mothers or mothers-in-law in the early 1890s, but they also typically charged $25 for that privilege.[66] Even some decades later, groups like the Henry Clay Lodge still disputed the point. Only in 1918 did it decide "after very long debating that a member can buy a grave for his Mother or Father from the Lodge by paying $50.00."[67] Before groups began selling individual graves, some, like the Noah Society, only allowed members to bury parents in the cemetery if they owned a family lot. And even despite lot ownership, the group still charged $25 for that privilege in 1906 and doubled the fee by 1917.[68] Many early Jewish widows who reserved graves alongside their husbands may have hoped to reverse the old adage "Till death do us part," but an equal number also hoped to avoid extra charges or burdening their children by securing the entitlements for which they had already paid into the system.

As reservations occurred more frequently, though, societies began charging additional fees for the option. Cemetery managers could easily guarantee a widow the next sequentially open grave whenever her time should come, but allowing women to reserve specific spaces in advance seemed an entirely different matter. Officials not only justified charging for that privilege but imposed high fees for it too. There is little doubt that the large death endowments they had just paid to these women informed that logic. Whereas Adath Jeshurun regularly charged members $100 to purchase a grave throughout the 1890s, it more than doubled that fee for a widow, Dinah Rodin, who sought to reserve a grave next to her husband in 1897. It only agreed to leave a grave open for Rodin if she paid $250. It did so despite two earlier cases in which it only charged $100 each to adult children requesting the burial of their widowed mothers next to their fathers. Although the widow Rodin could not afford that sum in full, trustees offered a deal based on her death endowment. If Rodin agreed to "give back the $100 endowment that she officially received from the congregation" in order to pay the fee in part, they would allow another member to pay the remainder in four-quarter increments over the next year on her behalf. "When all [debts] would be paid," the congregation stipulated, "then Mrs. Rodin would have her right to the grave and from this right the two graves could be made."[69] Dealings with Dinah Rodin or her contemporaries demonstrated just how profitable those rows of single graves could be to societies and synagogues. Arrangements like these also laid important foundations for an evolving system that would draw back on endowments over time through newly established cemetery charges.

As women and men reserved graves more frequently into the twentieth century, groups standardized their policies in the hopes of making a profit. Although piecemeal arrangements may have sufficed in the practice's early days, its growing popularity recast Jewish cemetery real estate. Members, after all, witnessed reservation requests at regular meetings or saw graves for spouses left open at the funerals they attended. Although a 1906 constitution of the Noah Society had not discussed the matter at all, within a decade, a new version allowed members and their wives "the right to reserve the grave next to each other provided said deceased is buried in the single grave plots."[70] That "right," however, came with a charge of $50 and guaranteed that at least one spouse among the majority of married couples would pay for otherwise free burial privileges.[71] Little wonder the Mendelssohn Society celebrated in 1916 that "this valuable privilege" had been adopted after many years of "sporadic attempts to change the [cemetery] laws . . . so as to permit the reservation of a grave for a husband or wife."[72] Soon enough, reservations evolved into adjoining graves for spouses. Double graves could double revenue if couples paid for two plots all at once rather than only reserving one. By the late 1920s, some even reconceived of their single graves altogether, now referring to them as "the grounds laid out for double graves."[73] Across societies, these innovations garnered new profits from cemetery land. As spending and revenue challenges increased over the coming decades, that money buoyed group solvency.

At the same time that societies found new revenue in their cemeteries, they also experienced new budgetary obstacles from poor membership or competing commercial insurers. Although the highpoint of Jewish migration during the first decade of the twentieth century had reinvigorated New York Jewish aid associations, restrictive legislation of the 1920s greatly reduced potential membership pools.[74] Fewer younger candidates also endangered actuarial equilibrium. Groups continued to pay endowments and medical benefits to an aging roster, but they struggled to balance those expenses without simultaneously inducting healthy young dues-payers to make regular contributions while rarely taxing reserves.[75] Commercial insurers also enticed members away, as they targeted urban ethnic workers in particular by the 1920s.[76] Even some of the largest Jewish orders struggled with that trend. Despite the IOBA's popularity, one institutional history lamented, "Large numbers of [members] lost interest in the insurance inducements of fraternal orders. Instead, they acquired policies with regular insurance companies for sums greatly in excess of the $500 available in the fraternal orders."[77] Lacking new buy-in to balance these shifts, Jewish groups sought other means to counter the tide.

Adjusting cemetery fees and death benefits offered one avenue. So did new charges on widows that the groups introduced, since these women's financial relationship to societies tied so closely to the cemetery. After all, if groups faced difficulties finding new membership beyond their ranks, they could look to cohorts of widows within, who were already affiliated and flush with society money. Reining in spending, after all, was simply not an option. Relief expenditures overseas for war-torn hometowns only rose following World War I.[78] Thereafter, the Depression ravaged affiliated families as well as society budgets, with many groups reducing or unable to fulfill relief payments.[79] Overextended, many groups like the Moses Family Society consolidated their existing accounts in order to better "raise and distribute money to needy members, relatives and charities here and abroad." In 1924, it combined its previously separate "Loan & Relief Fund," "European Relief Fund," and "Widows Fund" into a new single entity called "The Finance Department of the Moses Family Relief Society."[80] As in previous eras, consolidation of widows' reserves in financial ledgers foreshadowed larger shifts in these women's institutional status. By the 1930s, building on innovative charges for grave reservations and double graves, many fraternities and landsmanshaftn applied the same logic to death endowments and burial itself among widows and beneficiaries. New fees for matters like setting a tombstone, cemetery upkeep, and even widow-headed families' interment rights retrieved money paid out upon a man's death, and the ability to increase those fees over time also offered new means to supplement expenses in the long run.

Security deposits on headstones first moved in that direction, as societies directly withheld portions of the death endowment to cover those payments. Cemeteries required markers on all graves, but because groups left stone purchases to individual families, they mandated that households pay a security up front. If a family lapsed in purchasing a monument, deposits ensured at least enough money for the group to set a stone without dipping into its treasury. Some groups, for instance, tiered costs for adult or child stones, while others favored lump sums.[81] Although the amounts and mechanisms varied, deposits only grew over time and were automatically pulled from endowments. Importantly, beneficiaries' awards did not typically scale with the increasing amounts that some groups required on stones. By 1936, for instance, although the Noah Society doubled the amount it withheld for stone deposits to $100, it still only paid surviving loved ones $500 as it had for several decades.[82] Similarly, the First Storoznetzer Bukowiner Sick and Benevolent Association not only withheld $75 for its headstone security from the total endowment it paid, but since the group collected those funds through a head tax at the time of a member's death, the money withheld effectively amounted to a new (if temporary) influx into its budget. Widowers, technically entitled to reduced endowments for their wives, did not even receive that money at all since the group withheld that entire amount for headstone security. The group thereby paid nothing out to these men—at least until a stone was set.[83]

While beneficiaries could reclaim security deposits after purchasing a stone, many opted simply to forfeit that sum. Some widows, however, could not afford them on their own. For those women, every endowment dollar mattered. The widow Y. Tow, for instance, of the IOBA Henry Clay Lodge 15, made sure to follow up three months after her husband's death, since the group had withheld $50 of her endowment. She reminded them of that deduction and pressed the matter of a stone. "You promised me that you would attend to such particulars," she wrote. "I cannot afford any more than the amount of money I left in your Lodge's care. I shall be very grateful to you if you would be kind enough to look after these particulars."[84] Other widows surrendered the deposit, hoping it would cover other long-term charges. In 1935, widow M. Folkman requested that the lodge use the $50 it had retained not only to erect a monument but also "to pay the yearly charge of four dollars . . . for the maintenance of the Cemetery as long as I live."[85] From an original obligation to widows in need, complexities overtaking endowments and cemetery real estate transformed the benefit into something far more transactional for all parties involved by the twentieth century.

Lodge accountants were not opposed to that inversion. In fact, as the Depression taxed individual and collective resources, groups drew against endowments for cemetery maintenance while also using the benefit to settle debt before paying beneficiaries. In 1931, as record keepers reviewed Henry Clay Lodge accounts, they scratched a note in the margins to "send agreements to all members who owe us money on cemetery that in case they die, they assign a part of the endowment for payment of bal[ance]."[86] In 1934, when the widow Folkman checked on her standing, she was informed of her frozen status because her husband had missed two dues payments before he died. "I deducted only one quarter from the endowment," the lodge secretary explained, "because I expected that you would personally pay the second quarter."[87] Interment rights and cemetery property defined the relationship between widows and societies, but they also discouraged households from falling behind in dues. The financial cushion of the death endowment proved all the more important as the Depression continued, since living members either fell into delinquency or had to leave society ranks altogether. Even those who maintained good standing taxed the limited funds through greater appeals for relief, which, amid mounting need and scarcity, could also go unmet.[88] Both cases only amplified already depleted resources. Whenever it could be utilized, the death endowment continued to evolve into a ready source of cash to draw upon for multiple ends. That shift, however, only encouraged an ongoing utilitarian approach to funeral and cemetery benefits as much as their recipients.

The institution of widows' dues marked a key step in that direction. On the one hand, they introduced charges against widows for funerary matters that had once been guaranteed as a function of their husband's membership and the dues paid throughout his life. On the other, they spoke to a process that had recast these women as financial proxies for their men after death in order to continue the regular contributions from their families to society coffers. A typical pledge by the Mutual Benevolent Society in 1908, for example, stated that it would provide burial "without charge therefor [sic], for the widow or a child not over 21 years old of a deceased member." However, this would ring far less true decades later without several added caveats.[89] By the 1930s, most groups introduced new fees for affiliated widows along with stipulations against remarriage in order to maintain affiliation. These often came only in exchange for funeral benefits for themselves and their children.

To be sure, some larger orders like the Workmen's Circle or IOBA had already created tiered classes of female membership that went beyond cemetery privileges. The Workmen's Circle early in the twentieth century offered women members lower sick pay for reduced dues and gradually introduced the option to apply for higher classes of membership.[90] Similarly, the IOBA maintained three classes of members (A, B, and C) and at least allowed women to apply for lower tiers. The differences in their benefits, however, mainly centered on higher or lower death endowments toward which they paid. Only men in Class A, however, could claim or receive additional awards for the loss of limbs or vision on the job.[91] Although smaller groups like the Plotzker Young Men's Independent Association may have paralleled those trends in 1929 by extending to widows the option of "social member" status, it did not expand their benefits. Instead, these women were "only entitled to burial ground, funeral expenses and a committee to follow her hearse." Despite the much reduced $1.50 quarterly dues, the new status still maintained revenue from those households. This came in addition to a one-time $5 initiation fee in order to officially recognize a widow's membership.[92]

Although rates and clear divisions between general funds and cemetery funds varied across groups, most ensured that even after a husband's death, his household would not dry up as a source of much-needed income.[93] Some groups folded widows' dues into general treasuries, while others at least limited their contributions to reserve accounts for cemeteries and endowments. Above all, whether groups limited widows' rights to interment or even extended to them reduced regular benefits, these women's financial transformation created a new class of members who paid in with far less risk of draining funds retooled toward living men and their earning capacity. Smaller groups, especially, like the Loyal Society, collected dues from their widows while simultaneously stipulating "a female member is not entitled to any sick benefit." Nonetheless, it divided her dues between its "General Society Fund" and "Burial Expense Fund." That general treasury also worked "to aid members of the society who are in distress."[94] Directly and incrementally, that new system and the web of fees leveled against affiliated widows gradually cut into their death endowments and redistributed them over time.

Mounting cemetery charges and widows' dues clearly worked together. They returned much or most of the endowment over the course of a widow's lifetime, but by largely limiting these women to cemetery privileges, groups also gained a class of contributors who could not claim unexpected or episodic costly awards. The system established by the Kolomear Friends offers one of the most direct examples. By 1937, the group stipulated that after a member's death "his wife is not entitled to any other benefits," but "she may, if remaining unmarried, be entitled to a cemetery plot for herself and her children." For those entitlements, she was required to pay $1 every quarter for the rest of her life. It also deducted another $50 "from the death benefit she received for her husband's death as security for a tombstone for herself or for her children." That $50 came in addition to another $100 already withheld for a tombstone on her husband's grave.[95] Between security deposits and quarterly dues, by the end of a widow's life, maintaining affiliation to the Kolomear Friends would have effectively returned more than half, if not the bulk, of the $300 endowment that she had received when her husband died. In this way, along with up-front charges for reservations and stones, new dues for burial rights funneled back endowments while swapping departed husbands for their widows to maintain contributory ties between a group and a household. Although a man's death in previous generations would have severed those financial links, in this instance, a widow not only bridged the disruption of his dues but served as a highly efficient member who would claim far less than the amount she repaid.

Given that financial role, groups pursued incentives to ensure that widows continued their affiliation. Cemetery privileges remained important points of leverage. Groups tied widows' financial obligation to their interment rights as well as those of their underage children to justify new widows' dues. In 1936, the Kolbuszower Society extended grave rights, funeral costs, and a hearse for a widow or her child's funeral, provided she began to pay $6 annually as soon as her husband died.[96] Even when a group like the Noah Society nominally did not charge a widow for her own interment, in 1936, it still instituted and justified widows' dues through her children. Perhaps balancing the hefty $5 fee, the group offered fairly expansive protections to underage children as well as adult daughters if they never married. It also pledged coverage to sons who reached adulthood but would be ineligible for coverage on their own for physical or cognitive disabilities. If widows bristled at the new dues, the protections extended to their children after death may have made the policies easier to accept.[97]

Along with children's interment rights, stipulations against widows' remarriage or policies that made the prospect costly further discouraged these women from cutting ties to a first husband's society. Parallel fees that were required of male members who married again and wanted groups to recognize their second wives also alleviated societies from duplicating obligations. Most policies flatly denied paying a second endowment, but they also created profits since groups typically charged an entirely new fee just to bury a subsequent wife. The complicated state of cemetery real estate also had a hand in these stipulations. Given preferences for prepurchased double graves by the early twentieth century, groups especially worried about unused plots that spouses had reserved and the difficulty of reselling them should remarried widows or widowers opt to spend the afterlife next to subsequent spouses instead. Although men and women each bore the brunt of these anxieties, widows faced greater limitations since their financial and social status was so closely defined by funeral policies.

Debates and innovations soon abounded to manage and discourage remarriage among widows and even male members. In 1926, for example, Bizoner Chebra members debated a case "at length" in which a brother who had reserved a grave next to his first wife tried to apply that original claim to another grave in the cemetery after he remarried. He sought a new grave next to one purchased for his second wife, but he hoped to sidestep additional series of fees for the new grave by invoking his original entitlements to burial on society grounds. Striking down the claim, the group ruled in pained specificity: "Any brother who has a grave reserved next to his first wife must be buried in the reserved grave next to this first wife and under no circumstances shall a grave be given him in any other part of the cemetery." It also took the opportunity to establish a $100 charge to extend interment rights to second or subsequent wives in society holdings.[98] The problem of members remarrying and trying to alter previous interment arrangements extended across groups by the 1930s. Although the Holy Society had only included one reference to widows in the lean four-clause benefits section of its 1907 constitution—offering a grave "if desired" and as long as they did not remarry—revisions in 1930 included five new detailed clauses. Each filled a hefty paragraph anticipating not only several scenarios of widow or widower reservations but also all the ways in which one spouse predeceasing another or remarrying would complicate rights to a plot.[99]

Although these intricacies raised as much alarm over affiliated men's remarriage as affiliated widows, policies disenfranchised wives even more because their remarriage not only jeopardized interment plans but also interfered with the mechanisms to retrieve endowments paid out at their original husband's passing. If men remarried, after all, groups in fact gained some extra revenue through additional charges to bury new wives. If widows remarried, in contrast, they would not only take the remainder of their endowments with them but also leave empty graves that would weigh on group treasuries. Open single graves on their own may not have posed significant challenges, but if widows had invested in double stones over the joint plot, those monuments would only interfere with the resale value of single graves. The prospect of removing such double stones came at society expense, and the outrage it would invite from surviving family members seemed wholly unpalatable. As a result, some groups like the Bizoner Chebra spent several meetings in 1932 debating the institution of an additional fee to widows who erected double headstones on reserved graves in case these women "failed to keep" membership in the society.[100]

In this vein, groups devised penalties and new fees and even rescinded interment rights to anticipate the complications of remarriage. While societies may not have consciously sought to make remarrying costly, they aimed if nothing else to preempt imagined losses that subsequent unions might cause institutional finances. Widows again, for their evolving status, faced ever more challenges than their male peers. Orler Society policy in 1937 spoke for many other groups when it directly stipulated that "when the widow of a deceased member remarries, she becomes automatically suspended and shall be stricken from the membership list."[101] Only in the 1950s did this and similar groups finally allow widows to keep their rights to burial and graves even if they married again. Until then, however, most societies nullified remarried widows' burial rights or even forced them to forfeit reserved graves despite the fees they had already paid on them in advance. Even as early as 1917, when the Noah Society first instituted the right to reserve graves, it stipulated that "in case of re-marriage, the said reserved grave is to revert back to the Society."[102] Later groups maintained similar policies, many even stipulating that they would not refund reservation fees.

Of equal or more importance to widowed mothers, policies on remarriage also threatened their children's interment rights. As regulations evolved over the first part of the twentieth century, nearly all original groups rescinded underage children's rights to graves if a widowed mother remarried. Most did so regardless of the dues that these women had already contributed. Perhaps more significantly, although some groups previously conditioned children's interment on their father's membership during his lifetime, the institution of widows' dues came to nullify that obligation over time.[103]

Had receiving societies accepted a second wife's children without their own set of stipulations and charges, that shift may have been more benign. At least until the late 1940s, however, many groups also explicitly refused interment rights to a new wife's children or charged significant sums for the service. The Chevra Kol Yisroel stipulated as early as 1912 that "if a member marries a woman with children from her previous marriage, those children have no right to any benefits in the chevra."[104] By 1937 and even as late as 1957, the Orler Society still refused a second wife's "children by a previous marriage, and should any of said children die, the society shall not furnish a free burial plot nor any funeral expenses."[105] Others showed a bit more flexibility, recognizing some obligation to subsequent wives and the children they hoped to bring under new society coverage, but their benefits were allowed only after payment of additional fees that could range from $25 to $100 by the 1930s.[106] Even with these charges, many groups added other obstacles like requisite medical exams for new wives or refusing any above the age of forty before they would even consider extending funerary coverage to these women or their children.[107] In short, more often than not, a widow's remarriage not only meant new costs for her own interment in a new husband's society but risked the easy or already guaranteed burial of her underage children, coupled with additional charges to gain a new society's coverage. And even if she and a new husband paid additional fees for the new family's burial privileges, she would have to resign herself to forfeiting all the payments she had made to an original society before remarrying.

If these and other complications did not discourage at least some widows and widowers from remarriage, the prohibitive social and financial costs may have given others initial pause. One whimsical anecdote pictured a woman on her deathbed, pleading with her husband to marry the widow of another member: "She is a good woman, she made a good home for Morris and she'll make a good home for you. . . . Think of the children and don't feel guilty when I'm gone. You can even give her all my clothes to wear." The punchline lands with this woman taking her last breath after her husband's dismayed demand: "How can I marry Sadie? She takes a size six and you wear a size ten!"[108] Humor aside, a kernel of truth stands out. Consideration of remarriage here, as in many societies' policies, centered on the well-being of men rather than the implications for the widows involved. The same could be said for this widow's interment rights or the fees she might face in abandoning a grave alongside her first husband, Morris—all matters obviously ignored in this joke. The constitutional weeds overwhelming society cemeteries and marital policies may not have always been at the center of these calculations, but they mattered. If nothing else, they spoke to drastic changes that had overtaken Jewish end-of-life planning in just a century. The impact that these shifting ideals had on widows and their families stood out in particular. That nexus not only influenced the funeral realm by the mid-twentieth century, but it worked its way back so that policies surrounding interment rights and financial awards at death framed the options and obstacles of family life well beyond the graveyard.

Widows, of course, acted within a host of considerations and ultimately made decisions at their own discretion. Some, like M. Folkman, left their societies altogether. Folkman severed ties to the Henry Clay Lodge in 1934, shortly after her husband's death. So many charges, add-on fees, and unexpected dues soured her to the group.[109] Other women, like Eva Hammer of the Weinreb Benevolent Society, lost their husbands at later periods after the system better accommodated widows. Although Hammer's husband died in 1973 and she remarried in 1975, Hammer continued paying society dues. Only in 1992 did she resign from the group because she "made plans to be buried in Florida, since most of my family has retired here."[110] Despite the money paid in for two decades, Hammer felt little sentimental need to make use of the grave she had reserved.

Other widows, however, took equally different courses. Although Bertha Schiffman maintained affiliation to the Bolshowcer Sick and Benevolent Society for decades after burying her husband in 1938, she only learned that a grave did not await her in the late 1980s. The group was facing insolvency, and despite nearly five decades paying toward a plot she had reserved, the society had run out of graves and could not furnish one next to her husband. Founders had long since passed on, and one volunteer remained to settle society business before the group liquidated.

Although he promised that the society could provide a grave on a wholly different ground, Bertha and her family refused outright. "Being there are NO MORE graves available in the Mount Hebron Cemetery where my father is buried," Schiffman's daughter wrote on her behalf, "NO WAY are we interested in a plot at the Beth David. Therefore, we have to seek a grave on our own . . . for my mother, when her time comes." In addition to requesting the return of Schiffman's $50 security, the family also sought "a refund that is due her for all the years she had the confidence in paying her dues to the [society] to hold in reserve a plot for her where her husband was buried."[111]

Although Bertha Schiffman found that promise ultimately unmet, her experience and those of so many others highlighted the central role that dealings among Jewish benefit societies and widows played in driving much of New York Jewish fraternalism and the cemetery economy between the nineteenth and twentieth centuries. While B'nai B'rith widows received $1 a week throughout the 1840s for the rest of their lives, just a century later, widows like Bertha Schiffman returned anywhere from one to eight times that amount every quarter until they died. Despite a basic consistent pledge to protect, provide for, and assist members' widows over that period, a larger and less-visible system also developed. It recast widows from privileged aid recipients to long-term contributors in their own right. Their payments helped fund a larger system of relief that they and their families could often not even access. The roles that Jewish widows played over that long century of aid not only highlight the malleability of gendered ideals of dependence but underscore an added field in which family and material priorities reshaped Jewish efforts to plan for life's end. In response to evolving industrial concerns and despite convictions around the needs of widows and orphans, developing priorities for living men and their dependents ultimately eclipsed those of widow-headed families. While these women and their dependents benefited from short-term funds, changing priorities surrounding men's earning capacity retooled death benefits as much as the very conceptions of entitlement.

Rhetoric of "protecting widows and orphans" remained consistent into the twentieth century, as did the importance of monetary benefits at death. Both persisted, enshrined in society policies as monuments to an old fraternal mission to bolster women and children after a male head of household's death. At the same time, Jewish benefit societies also devised an invisible system of new fees primarily targeting widows to draw back on those rewards. By the early twentieth century, groups not only questioned old obligations amid industrial insecurity but created an unprecedented hierarchy between widows and workingmen while a challenging new economy threatened the very ideal of male breadwinning. Jewish aid groups and burial societies did not give up support to widows or their children, but they constructed a complex system so that endowments became, in effect, something more of a short-term loan. These payments helped widows and their dependents avoid sudden falls into poverty, but by way of new cemetery fees, annual dues, and unprecedented charges around women and children's interment rights, groups incrementally retrieved and redistributed that money. They supplemented living members' wages and inaugurated a new system of relief. That structure entitled families leading up to loss and just after it but recast families of departed members as soon as they became recipients of funerary aid. Through widows in particular, groups underwrote new family ideals, privileging households before death rather than after a loss. By the twentieth century, commitments to widows remained ideologically important, but groups recast those women in order to reaffirm their men and the needs of their dependents in life.

At the turn of the twentieth century, while massive industrial change underwrote the introduction and evolution of monetary benefits at death, the rise of private Jewish undertakers only complemented the material priorities that underwrote them. Professional parlors would play their own role in commoditizing Jewish funeral rite, and their spread elevated the family even more in Jewish New Yorkers' strategies to plan for death and burial. As benefit societies and synagogues devised new programs to maintain relevance in an increasingly crowded funeral market, consumer entitlements targeted individual families from all sides. These shifts ensured that New York's Jewish funeral industry would crystallize around the family and its commercial needs. That seemingly inevitable outcome also sparked a renewed drive among synagogues at midcentury to reform the industry entirely and, in the process, return supposedly wayward religious ideals and practices to Jewish death and dying.

5

"Fine Funeral Service at Moderate Costs"

New York's Jewish Funeral Industry, 1890–1965

"Is that an undertaker shop," several onlookers puzzled, "and do the people down here use unpainted pine coffins for their dead?" On Hester Street in 1895, visitors to Lower Manhattan struggled to make sense of a carpenter's shop that also sold Jewish funeral wares. The coffins "had no lining," they recoiled, and "there were pine shavings in the bottom of some and they had not even been planed or smoothed with any care." Pity overcame one visitor: "How pathetic for these exiled Jews to be so poor that they must bury their dead in this fashion!" "Not so; not so!" the carpenter corrected, explaining the widespread practice among many Jews to prefer unassuming accoutrements: "They might buy better, but they believe that it is right to have the coffin plain and to have a poor funeral. One man I know is rich, but when his wife was dead he got her a plain coffin like that in the corner." A girl among them still wondered, "Then they do not have fine funerals in this quarter as they do in many sections even among the very poor?" "No," the carpenter answered. "They don't make anything of funerals down here."[1]

If immigrant Jews at the turn of the century could not afford or had little taste for extravagancies in death, it certainly did not mean a lack of professionals to assist them. Just blocks from this Hester Street carpenter, enterprising men like Abraham Gutterman or Louis Meyers established modest livery stables on Orchard Street and East Broadway in 1892 and 1897, respectively. Although they founded these businesses to deal mostly in transportation, they quickly laid the ground for some of New York and the nation's best regarded and oldest Jewish funeral parlors. Steadily adding to their responsibilities, liverymen like them soon graduated to licensed undertakers or better-regarded funeral directors. From minimal service in the nineteenth century, they offered all-inclusive packages by the 1920s. Now in addition to supplying hearses, shrouds, and coffins, Jewish undertakers also performed key tasks like ritual washing and planning and hosting funerals in elegant new Jewish chapels. Although Jews in New York had performed most funeral rites among family and friends for more than two hundred years, turn-of-the-century standards led many to call for new professional oversight. Style, modernity, professionalism, and material care were well within reach. By 1942, Riverside Memorial Chapel, heir to Meyers' stable and one of America's largest Jewish funeral chains, coined a winning formula: "Fine funerals at moderate costs."[2]

The rise of private Jewish chapels in New York drove new materialism in death, but it also wholly recast long-standing communal structures. As Jews ceded funeral oversight to third-party professionals, they also repositioned the aid groups and synagogues that had until then handled those matters almost exclusively. As early as the 1910s, some Jewish undertakers even began selling cemetery plots in addition to other provisions. For the first time in nearly three centuries, Jewish New Yorkers could secure funeral needs without drawn-out affiliation or a lifetime of dues payments. In an effort to maintain funeral relevance, burial societies, synagogues, and landsmanshaftn all assumed new intermediary roles. They championed themselves as brokers between members and chapels and pledged to hold undertakers accountable for dissatisfactory service. They also adjusted monetary benefits that had long covered funeral costs and bereavement rituals to now apply to services beyond parlor purview. Facing competition from the city's expanding Jewish funeral industry, those traditional Jewish funerary providers stressed the importance of membership for privileges that individuals would sacrifice if they hired undertakers on their own.

Although most Jewish institutions realized by the 1950s that cooperation with private parlors offered the most effective strategy to navigate a changing industry, synagogues weathered the shifts most successfully by the postwar era. With the conclusion of mass migration decades earlier and immigrants enjoying economic mobility, subsequent American-born Jews found far less relevance in their family's landsmanshaft leaving groups struggling to stay financially or socially afloat. Conversely, synagogues not only enjoyed a renaissance as Jews flocked to the suburbs but naturally asserted themselves as overseers of life-cycle ceremonies. Access to cemetery land ranked high among funerary provisions,

but nearly all synagogue and rabbinical associations also won new credibility as they seized on mounting criticism facing the funeral industry
at large.

As the nation reckoned with excessive funeral costs and supposed
consumer exploitation into the 1960s, synagogues stood especially
poised to proclaim themselves obvious custodians of Jewish death in
America. Of course, funeral homes still provided most services, but congregations touted their ability to protect members from ritual laxity or
industry upselling. They accused parlors of ignorance of Jewish law
or simply cutting corners to increase profits. They also claimed they
were the only responsible intermediaries who could protect distraught
families from expensive displays and coffins. In striking uniformity,
whether they were a part of Orthodox, Conservative, Reform, or Jewish
Renewal movements a decade later, all proponents agreed that pressured
purchases not only failed to comfort a loss but countered the dignity and
simplicity prescribed by Jewish tradition. Without religious guidance,
the argument went, Jewish families could not reasonably navigate the
funeral industry on their own. These twentieth-century shifts punctuated the deeply entrenched ties between the family and the market that
had defined centuries of Jewish end-of-life planning in New York, and
in their continued jockeying for household loyalties, the synagogues, aid
associations, burial societies, and professional undertakers thoroughly
enshrined the family at the center of Jewish death and dying.

The Rise of Jewish Undertakers

New York's private Jewish funeral industry grew out of many the same
forces driving the nation's broader funeral economy. In New York
especially, urban and medical developments complicated average city
dwellers' ability to deal with death without professional assistance. Rural
cemeteries, far from residential neighborhoods, created new distance
between sites of dying and burial. Increasing instances of hospital death
also complicated arrangements to transport the dead. Carriagemen and
owners of livery stables took advantage of those difficulties and created
thriving businesses, conveying the dead and the bereaved to funeral
proceedings. Early Jewish undertakers enjoyed even more of a niche
market, as most of their customers, whether observant or not, could

simply not concede to Christians handling their dead. Issues of comfort and consumerism also drove professional undertaking. Like that Hester Street carpenter who sold caskets and shrouds to local Jews, woodworkers had been building coffins for Americans since the middle of the nineteenth century. With the exception of those selling to traditional Jewish consumers, these carpenters soon offered more ornate caskets, providing silk or fabric linings for extra charges. While they invoked the comfort of the dead, the comfort of those left behind drove the enterprise. Finally, after the Civil War, many early undertakers also began to specialize in embalming, a technique that had proven its usefulness when transporting fallen soldiers during wartime. For many commercial undertakers, embalming also offered them a means to elevate their standing as skilled medical practitioners. For loved ones seeking their services, though, they emphasized the procedure's sanitary benefits and the comfort it could offer to the departed one last time. As professionals refined the process, Americans also came to appreciate the natural appearance it afforded the dead. Due to its novelty and sentimentality, embalming slowly gained popularity in the decades after the war. By the 1880s, most Americans, especially city dwellers, hired private undertakers to handle a range of services like preparation and placement in the coffin, embalming, transport, and even funeral planning. Given so many new considerations, many came to believe that nonprofessionals simply lacked the skills to tend the dead on their own.[3]

Although New York's Jewish funeral industry paralleled national developments, Jews tempered that transition far more slowly by ceding only the most incidental or pragmatic matters to early Jewish undertakers. While Jewish New Yorkers began hiring professionals as early as 1849, these contracts only covered transportation needs or supplying funeral accessories like shrouds or coffins, which most groups had previously produced independently.[4] Beyond those incidentals, Jews still maintained close-knit hevrot kadisha within their lodges and synagogues that continued to sit with the sick, watch over the dying, lay the dead to rest, and pray among the mourning. Although less common by the late nineteenth century, some women's burial societies still produced ritual shrouds in specialized sewing circles for themselves and affiliated male institutions in addition to other funeral services.[5] Accordingly, when one of New York's first Jewish undertakers advertised in 1855, he promoted shrouds and coffins "prepared by members of the Jewish faith" and promised even his vehicles would be "driven by a Jew," but notably he made no mention of purification or other ritual labor.[6]

That division of duties between the Jewish public and early funeral professionals continued for several decades. Most societies and congregations preserved their internal hevrot to oversee the last dignities, even as they regularly contracted professionals for other tasks. In the 1870s, one Jewish immigrant group, the Samaritan Society, still maintained a set of "funeral utensils" for its committee although it already purchased shrouds, coffins, and hearses.[7] Throughout the 1880s, congregations like the Kahal Adath Jeshurun of Eldridge Street regularly divided funeral expenses between its internal burial committees and external carriagemen and gravediggers.[8] Although America's broader funeral industry offered new room for Christian undertakers to assume more intimate responsibilities, Jewish ideas of communal obligation kept funeral ceremonies among family and friends for an extended period of time.

That cooperation continued into the twentieth century, even among some of the city's older Jewish immigrant communities. In 1906, one of New York and America's oldest Jewish fraternal orders, the Noah Benevolent Society (1849) still maintained a "Burial or Thara [sic] [Purification] Committee." Its revised constitution that year still charged six volunteers, on the death of a member or his family, "to repair to the house of mourning at an appointed time in order to attend to all the ceremonial Jewish rites." Further indicating its commitment to oversee the last offices, the group fined a volunteer if he "neglects his duty . . . in default of a legal excuse." Even the Noah Society's president, on word of a member's death, faced the charge to "see to it that the proper directions according to the Jewish rites are given, or direct them himself."[9] More recent immigrants also kept that work within their circles. When Adath Jeshurun composed a new constitution in 1913, for instance, it too still detailed the structure and organization of its male and female *messaskim*, a committee of attendants who performed the last rites on fellow congregants.[10] A congregation in Brownsville, Brooklyn, Chevra Kol Yisroel made similar guarantees in 1909, and even into the 1930s, it still paid its own internal hevra kadisha for that work while regularly listing other undertaker fees as a part of its funeral expenses.[11] Similarly, the Bronx-based Tiferes Beth Jacob established a hevra kadisha in 1923, barely a decade after most founders' arrival, and sustained that body well into the 1950s.

That internal Jewish oversight stood out, particularly as undertakers beyond Jewish circles had already assumed most funeral work by the mid-nineteenth century. Across American cities, undertakers consolidated tasks that had once fallen to friends, family, and other community members like liverymen, sextons, and carpenters. These ranged from "providing 'services' at the home, notifying family and guests about the death and funeral, tolling the bell, supplying the pall, placing the corpse in the coffin, carrying the coffin to the hearse and from the hearse to the vault or grave . . . and digging the grave or opening and closing the tomb."[12] Most Jewish New Yorkers, however, resisted that trend. Although the nation's broader funeral industry created new space for Americans to accept professional intervention, Jewish funeral professionals would not gain the same oversight for several decades.

Nevertheless, Jewish undertakers did find a niche to expand their operations at the turn of the century. Particularly in New York, amid growing medical and logistical concerns, the complexities of moving the dead among homes, hospitals, chapels, and cemeteries called for new levels of professional assistance. For one thing, increased regulation over the dead required new credentials to navigate city bureaucracy, secure transit permits, and organize processions. For another, as cramped city apartments lacked sufficient space to host funeral proceedings, most New Yorkers turned instead to private parlors. Hygienic concerns also mattered. As early as the 1870s, some Jewish groups even began relaxing practices like sitting overnight with peers ailing of contagious diseases. In those cases, they allowed members to "hire strangers" to do that work instead.[13] Jewish professionals seized on those practical concerns, touting their expertise and well-equipped facilities. In time, they would encourage burial societies and congregations to turn over most funeral responsibilities, even the most personal ceremonies like the ritual washing of the dead.

Groups with longer ties to New York began that transition as early as the 1920s. The Noah Society, for instance, despite its previous commitment to have members perform all funeral rituals on one another, did trim old provisions. When the group reissued a constitution in 1917, it wholly dissolved its burial and purification committees. It also did away with the position of "messenger," once charged to "provide everything necessary for the burial," and even removed the president's earlier obligation to make sure the deceased members received the traditional rites.[14] The Holy Society, another group that central European Jewish immigrants had founded in 1849 explicitly for burial and ritual needs, took a similar trajectory. In 1907, its constitution still promised that upon a member's death "the Society shall, at its own expense, provide 'watch' until the time of interment; [and] also provide for the tahara [purification] of the deceased" along with a coffin, hearse, carriage, and accompaniment to the grave.[15] By 1927, however, revised policies removed all references to traditional funeral rites and only guaranteed a grave in the society cemetery.[16]

More traditional Jews did not entirely outsource oversight to parlors, but they did begin allowing professionals greater involvement at this time as well, particularly when members lacked resources or personnel to handle death on their own. Early in the twentieth century, one traditional burial society arranged with undertakers on the Lower East Side and outer boroughs to furnish rooms on chapel premises where its members could perform the purification.[17] Jews of a Polish town, Biezun, who had formed the Bizoner Chebra B'nai Shaul, a New York congregation and burial society in 1872, even contracted with Meyers & Company in 1920 to hire one of its undertakers to replace the sexton that the group lost that year. The choice played out organically since Meyers' undertakers had already handled the society's last funeral.[18] That gradual cooperation was common as Charles Rosenthal, who would develop Meyers into Riverside Memorial Chapel, had already been acting as a sexton for the West End Synagogue (Shaaray Tefila) for at least a decade.[19]

Cooperation like this only encouraged expanded professional oversight over the coming decades. Since most societies and synagogues already hired funeral directors for so many other services, undertakers gradually incorporated purification rites as well. Many Jewish parlors, like the Guzeit and Smith Funeral Chapel, even developed all-inclusive packages. For set prices, varying only by the age of the deceased, clients received "hearse auto, Coffin, Tachrichim [shrouds], Tahara, and Sexton." For additional fees, Guzeit and Smith also provided "removing and Icing" of the body as well as "zinc lined coffins."[20] In the same way that earlier nineteenth-century undertakers had won over most Americans by stressing skills and medical prowess, later Jewish counterparts made similar inroads with gestures of expertise and technological innovation. E. Bernheim and Sons, for instance, hyped "an up-to-date funeral parlor" as Sigmund Schwartz promoted his "first class" establishment, equipped with separate purification facilities and "beautiful private quarters" that surpassed the old livery stables.[21] When Meyers & Company expanded its smaller funeral operation into a four-story structure on Manhattan's Upper West Side in 1926, its imposing French Neo-Renaissance architecture testified to the style and efficiency of the Jewish funeral services carried out within. The building included a large chapel that rose two levels as well as pews and vaulted ceilings. As funeral goers there bid farewell to their loved ones, other parts of the building contained arrangement rooms and a showroom for caskets. The chapel also greeted visitors with an inviting and spacious lobby. Its three elevators further highlighted the state-of-the-art operation.[22]

Even smaller and traditional Jewish undertakers stressed a commitment to modern and conscientious care. "Day and night, telephone Orchard 4857," an ad for Perlshteyn's Undertaking Establishment instructed readers of the Yiddish press in 1929. "Funerals personally attended to the best satisfaction." Another professional, Louis Diamond, implored New York's bereaved observant Jews to contact "the well-known Orthodox undertaker, Reb Haim Leb Diamond . . . who has overseen the finest funerals among the most prominent departed for the last 15 years. All will be fine, Jewish, and promptly attended."[23] By the 1920s, most ads for Jewish parlors reflected the appeal of modern equipment and facilities, touting credentials as "licensed undertakers" or "funeral directors." Some even added embalming services to their offerings, like Joseph Garlick, Abraham Gutterman, and even Louis Diamond, the earlier self-proclaimed "Orthodox" undertaker.[24] Another ad celebrated Diamond's small facility on Broome Street as home to "a modern chapel with all comfort and conveniences for the living." One of Brooklyn's oldest Jewish funeral directors, I. J. Morris, also stressed a "modern chapel on premises."[25] Despite centuries of close-knit and closed-off Jewish burial societies preserving most oversight around Jewish dying in New York, modernization in the early twentieth century pushed Jewish undertakers along with their clients to take a new approach. As Jews in New York internalized broader American funeral values and the currency of professionalism, they endorsed the idea of undertaking as a skilled and necessary profession. Managing Jewish death in the twentieth century, they came to believe, could only benefit from expert and external assistance.

"I Make Contracts with Societies for the Cheapest Prices"

That expanding role of private Jewish undertakers significantly reshaped Jewish communal structures, particularly internal dynamics within societies and congregations. Greater professional funerary oversight not only threatened to displace old traditional institutions but forced Jewish groups to retool their death benefits to remain relevant to their members. Although Jewish institutions had long hired professionals to furnish funeral accessories or manage transit, retention of the last offices and provision of society cemeteries continued to incentivize Jews to affiliate. As commercial groups branched into cemetery provision and more Jewish undertakers took up the purification rites, new market access to those provisions decreased the consequences for households if they opted out of society membership. To compensate, Jewish groups created new subsidies and entitlements and incorporated new end-of-life services to make affiliation more appealing. They also assumed a new brokering role, touting themselves as representatives between members and contracted professionals. Their charge was protecting affiliated families from an exploitative and profiteering funeral industry. As congregations and societies attempted to navigate the advent of professional funeral chapels, they further elevated family well-being in New York's Jewish funeral industry. Consequently, their packages combined with those offered by commercial providers to nurture a growing sense of consumer entitlement in death among the Jewish public at large.

Continued growth of New York's Jewish funeral and cemetery economies set the stage for communal restructuring. As early as 1913, groups like the Independent Burial Association specialized in an array of services sold "for Jewish burials exclusively." For just a flat fee of $35, the association provided an "entire funeral complete, including the grave, coffin, Shrouds, Hearse, etc., also a carriage for the family." The Burial Association also furnished cemetery land—with "small family lots of two graves" included in that $35 fee and larger plots priced proportionately—boasting desirable funerary real estate in Mount Judah Cemetery near private well-to-do plots of neighboring Union Field Cemetery. In one of the period's most significant turns, the association offered these packages not just to societies but also to individuals. No matter "private families, societies" or "individual members of organizations," it pledged, all "are equally accorded the same liberal and careful attention."[26] Cemeteries, like the recently founded Riverside Cemetery also specifically marketed to "private families" as well as societies and congregations.[27] Appealing to members directly, these and similar groups sought to carve out a new market beyond traditional Jewish funeral providers. At the same time, those commercial advances created a means for individuals or whole households to sidestep once-dominant Jewish communal institutions.

Smaller and larger Jewish funeral parlors adopted similar business models. Advertisements for Louis Diamond's chapel noted in the 1920s that, in addition to trappings and parlor services, he also offered "single graves for sale in all Jewish cemeteries." Mount Judah, Mount Carmel, and Washington Cemeteries made up just some locations where Diamond maintained plots.[28] Another undertaker, A. Bretschneider, also advertised "single and family graves in all cemeteries at cheap prices" alongside other services. Even individuals with no apparent credentials in the city's funeral industry tried a hand at profiting from cemetery real estate. One broker who identified himself only with a traditional aggrandized title "the Rav, Rabbi Doldzinas" appealed to "all lodge committees, synagogues, societies, *khevras*, and private individuals looking to buy CEMETERY lots and private plots, come see me before you go elsewhere."[29] In this expanding field, as Arthur Goren argued, "By 1910 if not earlier, it was possible to bypass synagogue, hevra kadisha, and lodge and go directly to a funeral director who would provide all necessary services, arrange for the purchase of a burial plot, and secure the ministrations of a rabbi and cantor for the funeral."[30] Traditional Jewish institutions had to reassess their functions or face a difficult reality in which members simply no longer needed them to plan for the end of their lives.

As enterprising undertakers consolidated old funeral provisions, synagogues and societies evolved alongside them. Although groups had long paid for outsourced funeral expenses like carriage rentals and gravediggers, the early twentieth century stood out since families could now act in their own right, purchasing all-inclusive packages. Some groups attempted to find a middle ground. In one transitional effort in 1906, a Noah Society policy offered flat, scaled reimbursement rates for different family members' funerals. It stipulated, though, that if members desired the society to "supervise and conduct" the funeral itself, it would deduct incidental costs, shrouds, and payments to two watchers to fulfill the traditional mandate of *shomer* (a dedicated guardian who would never leave a body unattended until its burial). Families would then receive whatever difference remained. Perhaps it is unsurprising that by the 1930s, the society's ritual committee had disbanded, and the group simply promised a flat sum toward all funeral costs.[31]

Other groups contracted with undertakers early on but still showed a willingness to reimburse members who acted on their own. They offered reimbursement in addition to all existing funeral benefits, as groups realized the need to cooperate with private chapels. In June 1921, for instance, the Bizoner Chebra paid a $48 head tax to the widow of Brother Pologe as well as an extra $50 funeral expense "owing the fact he was buried by a strange undertaker."[32] In 1923, when another member lost his wife, he successfully turned in his bill for society coverage although he had dealt with Meyers & Company on his own.[33] The group was also quite expansive regarding the charges it reimbursed. In 1925, even after paying $58 for a member's funeral, the Bizoner Chebra also paid his wife back for several larger elements, "as the widow . . . paid for the coffin, shroud and Icing."[34] The group even covered spontaneous religious costs. When Daniel Goldstein's wife passed away in 1910, the Bizoner Chebra paid several days' worth of watcher's fees, since Mrs. Goldstein had died on a holiday, delaying interment and requiring a longer shomer period.[35] As groups tried to cooperate rather than compete with the private funeral industry, they attempted to make it clear that forfeiting affiliation would also sacrifice unexpected forms of coverage.

In that spirit, they also innovated benefits that not only expanded the protections they offered but appealed in new ways to families' economic interests. To continue with the example of the Bizoner Chebra, for instance, the group built on expected funeral insurance to spouses and their children by also offering more flexibility to cover adult children as well. Across groups, a father's membership typically only extended to sons until their coming of age at eighteen or twenty and to daughters until they married and accessed coverage through a husband's society. When Brother Louie Silber's son died at the age of twenty in March 1910, the group decided after some debate to pay his funeral costs and appointed a committee the following June to officially raise the age for adult children's funeral entitlements.[36] In a buyer's market, the group understood the long-term gains of maintaining families in its ranks by relaxing rigid structures to appeal to individual families. And even if members could hire undertakers on their own, professional charges also varied by age—some graded individuals above twenty-one years old as adults, while others set twelve years as a sufficient age to trigger adult rates.[37] Unaffiliated households would have to pay those costs on every loss, but by extending age brackets for internal benefits, groups like the Bizoner Chebra afforded members and their dependents longer coverage for everyone in the family at just the cost of a father's dues.

Similar logic may have informed another group, the Ceres Union, to craft a new policy for the family's well-being at times of loss, even if domestic obligation seemed at odds with tradition. The group still provided free graves in the society cemetery to members and dependents in 1921 as long as "the deceased was an Israelite." Despite the society's unwillingness to bury members of mixed or uncertain religious background, it committed nonetheless that "should the child of a member be of a different creed and not entitled to a place of burial by another organization," the Ceres Union would at least fulfill its financial obligations. It pledged to contribute anywhere from $10 to $30 toward burial costs despite its inability to provide for interment directly.[38] As private Jewish undertakers hoped to entice away business by marketing to families at large, traditional Jewish funerary providers appealed to them in kind, expanding the most valuable commodities still in their arsenal: funeral coverage and individual family interests.

Many spiritual concerns to which synagogues and religiously oriented landsmanshaftn focused financial resources had similar aims. Despite the allure of all-inclusive packages from commercial parlors, there were still important kinds of religious concerns that families would have to forfeit if they discontinued their affiliation, and synagogues and other groups used those to their advantage. Traditional Jews in mourning, for instance, would refrain from work for seven days after losing immediate relatives like a spouse, child, sibling, or parent. Unable to leave their homes, they opened them up instead so that neighbors and friends could visit, pray, and offer condolences. Adult Jewish men would also have to recite the kaddish mourning prayer every day during morning and evening services to memorialize the dead in the presence of at least nine other adult Jewish men. The need to take time off of work to fulfill these traditions meant a significant loss of wages for those in mourning and their peers. To enable families to observe these customs, turn-of-the-century synagogues and aid groups—as so many before them—offered small subsidies. Account records of Adath Jeshurun in the early twentieth century were filled with payments of *shiva gelt* (funds to subsidize the week of mourning) or small awards classified as *minyan* (prayer quorum), earmarked for recently bereaved member families.[39] The latter may have compensated peers who took at least some time away from work to fill prayer services in order for males to recite the required kaddish prayer. By 1913, the congregation enshrined these benefits in its constitution. It promised $5 shiva benefits and, perhaps to avoid the need to pay for a quorum, it guaranteed to arrange and send a "minjon" to bereaved members in good standing after a funeral and to any members seeing out the week of grieving.[40] In addition, if a deceased member did not leave an immediate male heir to recite the kaddish on his behalf, the congregation also promised to arrange its recital during the shiva week and on all anniversaries marking the death as well as other holidays when the prayer had to be said.[41]

Beyond congregations, even landsmanshaftn without religious leanings paid bereaved families the shiva benefit. Some societies created shiva committees that visited affiliated households in mourning and offered condolences while also verifying that members actually refrained from work and had real claim to the small wage compensation.[42] In some groups, the expanded payments to underwrite mourning rituals became exceedingly costly. The Bizoner Chebra once reimbursed up to $35 to one deceased brother's family for "minon" expenses in 1920. It continually debated doing away with the payment and, by 1928, finally abolished the award.[43] Regardless of their duration or sustainability, those religious monetary benefits aimed to ease a family's mourning experience and to guard economic as much as spiritual well-being. They also represented a form of ritual coverage that members could not get elsewhere, even if Jewish funeral chapels offered otherwise quite inclusive packages.

Realizing the benefits of their respective specializations, synagogues, aid groups, and funeral parlors coalesced into new partnerships. In a model that paralleled health care provision among Jews and other ethnic communities, Jewish groups contracted undertakers as they did local physicians who, for annual fees, provided medical care to member families.[44] Although the physicians in these arrangements ultimately did not benefit and cut ties, the model offered a useful framework for funeral benefits. If nothing else, it tempered the appeal for households to make funeral arrangements on their own. It also enabled societies and congregations to recast themselves as brokers, protecting members in times of loss and from pressures of an industry ripe for exploitation. As New York's general and Jewish funeral industries underwent robust growth and internal competition into the 1930s, that reputation would especially trouble them.

Although most Jewish funeral professionals were still coming into their own by the 1920s, it did not take much time for the public to suspect them of profiteering. In part, early Jewish funeral directors' efforts to divvy the market likely played into that reputation. Although the Jewish Undertakers' Association of Greater New York by then included most regional members of that profession, the group disbanded in 1929 amid charges of intimidation and violation of antitrust law. The office of attorney general Hamilton Ward already had the group under investigation for setting territory, clientele, and funeral costs among members. To add insult to injury, though, it also charged that the association did so through "the use of strong-armed men and through an alliance with a Labor Union of Hearse and Cab Drivers."[45] Independent undertakers and former members also accused the association of prohibiting patron societies from changing undertakers without its permission. Finally, they claimed that the professional order punished uncompliant members with increasing fines. Louis Kasten, a Lower Manhattan undertaker, testified to such fines on at least two separate occasions, which he claimed were retribution for performing society funerals below the association's set prices. He also alleged that for refusing to pay those fines, the Jewish Undertakers' Association had vandalized his parlor's plate-glass window, hired men to attack him during a funeral to prevent him from directing it, and disrupted another ceremony by dismissing union drivers so that no one remained to drive the hearse but him.[46] Within a month of Kasten's testimony, although the association refused to admit any wrongdoing, it disbanded amid claims that "in view of the criticisms publicly advanced, it was felt that this was the best move to satisfy every one."[47] Although certainly not the last time that charges of unscrupulous behavior would dog Jewish professionals, the scandal went a long way to realign the industry and all its players.

Into the 1930s, societies and parlors actively courted each other. Common refrains like "I make contracts with societies for the cheapest prices" or "Contracts for societies in all cemeteries, with moderate prices and courteous dealings" echoed in ads throughout the Yiddish press. Jewish undertakers also took out smaller or larger advertisements in synagogue and landsmanshaft anniversary journals. Joseph Garlick pitched his services in highly visible full-page ads, typically at the back, of various anniversary souvenir books of the Plotzker Young Men's Independent Association, claiming "contracts with societies a specialty."[48] Louis Diamond ran an ad for his services in an induction program celebrating new members to the Velier Progressive Benevolent Association.[49] At the same time, aid groups and congregations also pursued local undertakers. Diamond regularly received invitations like one in 1934 from the Dockshitzer Benevolent Society requesting his presence at a special upcoming meeting, as members "wish[ed] to hear estimate prices for conducting funerals for our society."[50] Working together, new and older Jewish funerary providers carved out roles in the city's changing funeral industry. They also laid the foundation for growing tensions by midcentury.

"For Your Own Peace of Mind . . . in Kindliness to Your Loved Ones"

As regular contracts staved off the uncertainty of the role of Jewish aid groups going forward, they also effectively divided responsibilities. Communal institutions increasingly focused on coverage, while Jewish funeral homes specialized in service. As a result, into the 1930s, aid groups and synagogues presented themselves more fervently as protective intermediaries. They stressed the importance of dealing with contracted undertakers to save families money in the long run. They also stood ready and able to hold those professionals accountable for any and all dissatisfactory service. As a major selling point, benevolent societies, landsmanshaftn, and even synagogues touted members' interests as their primary concern. In what would become a familiar charge for the remainder of the twentieth century, Jewish groups—emboldened by their new brokering role—continually began to question the scruples of a widening field of funeral professionals. Whether commercial undertakers or monument makers, the received wisdom seemed to be that family exploitation served as their bottom line. Trusted communal groups, in contrast, would remain fiercely dedicated to the emotional and financial well-being of affiliated households in death.

Those claims continued with relative ease in the middle of the twentieth century, and private Jewish funeral directors, like most of their peers, would only continue to fight them into the 1960s. Among all parties, however, family anxiety and obligation became new central themes. Although most synagogues and societies disparaged the funeral industry for supposedly preying on emotional fragility, those same traditional Jewish providers invoked their own brand of funeral angst to entice advanced cemetery purchases or warn against falling behind in dues. Similarly, even as private undertakers tried to soften their image, they did so through appeals to the family, marketing the care and compassion that their operations offered. As all parties jockeyed for household loyalties and business, Jewish families would ultimately gain ever more centrality in the city's emerging Jewish funeral market.

The protective stature that Jewish groups settled into laid the ground for much of that family-centered dynamic. In addition to early insurance benefits that groups introduced to balance their partnerships with private Jewish chapels, societies' growing broker role led members to turn to them early on to hold undertakers accountable when they were displeased or dissatisfied with service. In the initial years of their contract with Meyers & Company, for instance, the Bizoner Chebra heard mounting grievances from several members. In 1924, Brother A. Simon "lodged a complaint against Meyers & Co. as to there [sic] attitude and treatment at the funeral of Sister Ruth Simon." Other members in attendance corroborated the charge, also citing dissatisfactory service at the funeral just before it. In response, the group charged several leading members to form a committee to "call on Mr. Meyers—as to his actions" and then to report back.[51] Another complaint the following year about overcharging a member's bill led the Bizoner Chebra to order its secretary "to see Mr. Meyers and have him adjust same."[52]

Synagogues took on much the same function. In 1926, a financial discrepancy between the Congregation Beth Israel of Brooklyn and its undertaker, Louis Diamond, moved the synagogue board to write Diamond directly of their intent at an upcoming meeting to raise "the matter of your returning of the money due the Congregation for the burial of a Mr. Neumann." In less subtle language, leaders spelled out their real aim: "[We] give you an opportunity to adjust the matter before we take any drastic action in reference there to. Kindly give this your immediate attention to avoid thereby considerable expense and trouble."[53] When members turned to Jewish communal groups to settle such disputes, representatives did not shy away from flexing their collective purchasing power. Likewise, they did not demur from reminding their members of those protections at every opportunity.

Growing inquiry into an increasingly crowded field of New York undertakers soon amplified those claims. In 1934, mounting concerns over excessive funeral costs led the City Affairs Committee to investigate New York's entire funeral industry. Its report found that single funerals alone yielded hefty profits, a direct result of an excess of practicing undertakers. Whereas two thousand professionals operated in the city, just one hundred could handle the same number of deaths with no negative impact on service. Findings also made clear that average consumers bore the brunt of that intense competition. In just reducing the number of undertakers, the report suggested, New Yorkers could cut costs and overhead by $10 million each year. As one solution, the committee proposed consolidating resources and creating a Municipal Funeral Home to centralize service and rein in a runaway market.[54] Although far from its intention, the report and its findings offered Jewish institutions a powerful alternative against which to measure their accomplishments and the benefits they extended to their members.

The Workmen's Circle's Cemetery Department, for instance, excerpted whole sections of that city investigation in its annual report. It regularly used that organ to demonstrate member benefits, but that year it flaunted its credibility by reminding readers of their good fortune to affiliate to a national network. By "arranging over 500 funerals a year through one undertaker," the report stressed, the fraternal order not only stood out as a pioneer of centralized funeral provisions, but it was also poised "to abolish undue profiteering and exploiting of our members in times of death."[55] An earlier issue in 1930 made a similar point when it announced a decision to contract headstones directly from monument engravers rather than leave that business up to families. A national network could not only purchase stones at cheaper rates "than a private-individual," but the department underscored its ability to combat the industry's urge "to encourage a customer to purchase the largest and most expensive stone."[56] By centralizing a network of contracted providers, the Cemetery Department often repeated, it successfully ensured lower rates than outside providers.

The Workmen's Circle frequently pointed out its experience of years dealing with commercial providers and the savings it afforded its members. Far beyond branch treasuries, however, that money mattered most for individuals, especially "the widows and orphans" whose death benefits paid out by branches would otherwise be negatively impacted by higher funeral expenses. Appeals therefore doubled down on family protections. Although individuals may have managed funeral matters a handful of times, they could never compare with the Cemetery Department's daily negotiations with professionals. Its agents' savvy not only assured they would never fall victim to predatory prices but also drew on the order's national leverage, purchasing funeral goods and services wholesale. On the one hand, that ability translated into savings for families as long as they did not attempt to navigate the funeral market on their own. On the other, it contributed in the abstract toward greater financial security for those most vulnerable: wives and children surviving departed members.[57]

Ironically, although any number of Jewish fraternities and synagogues chastised professionals for emotional profiteering, these groups appealed just as opportunistically to family insecurity in death. They did so not only when boasting society protections but also when encouraging dues payment or boosting their cemetery holdings. Many a souvenir journal, for instance, echoed one celebrating the Independent Order Brith Abraham's fiftieth anniversary in 1937. It rehearsed the emotional and financial anguish facing unaffiliated families "when losing the bread-winner" and the godsend of a society membership that laid him to rest and "covers the expenses thereof."[58] Synagogues sounded similar notes. "DO YOU HAVE PROVISION FOR CEMETERY PLOTTAGE?" the Society for the Advancement of Judaism asked its bulletin readers every week throughout the 1940s. Highlighting beautiful holdings in Mount Hebron Cemetery, ads endorsed plot acquisition as "one form of protection your loved ones should have. Why not arrange for it now?"[59] Like their counterparts on Manhattan's Upper West Side, members of the Brooklyn Jewish Center received similar sage advice in the form of cemetery marketing: "Obtain peace of mind by knowing that you have spared your dear ones the tragic confusion that arises in a bereaved home when a cemetery plot has not been provided. The Brooklyn Jewish Center has reasonably priced plots in the beautiful Old Montefiore Cemetery at Springfield, Long Island, which may be bought on convenient terms."[60] Although benefit societies and congregations proudly claimed the mantle of brokers, protecting member families from the exploitative arm of the funeral industry, they also traded in family well-being and funerary unease as powerful tools to promote membership decisions.

Although the growing role of private undertakers in the first part of the twentieth century altered synagogue and society roles as they related to funerary provisions, the ways in which those groups responded to an emerging industry laid important foundations for decades to come. Their arrangements with Jewish funeral parlors and the protective stance they embraced ensured that most Jewish families would not stray too far from their synagogues or fraternities when navigating the Jewish funeral market. When Jewish mobility and demographic change after World War II led to a decline in immigrant aid groups, prewar foundations in New York's Jewish funeral industry well-positioned private parlors and synagogues to fill that void. Although Jewish chapels, congregations, and aid associations differed in the ends they pursued, their decades-long common targeting of households in marketing appeals, membership campaigns, and benefits packages still went a long way in that centuries-old alliance between family and market concerns in New York Jewish funerary affairs. As Americans turned against the funeral industry by the 1960s, and as family dignity in death became a commodity all its own, synagogues especially rode those tides to reclaim greater responsibility over funerary matters and to promote their relevance in a communal landscape once more in flux.

Fraternal Decline, Synagogues, and "the American Way of Death"

The decline of Jewish aid groups began subtly in the 1930s, and most of these societies ultimately became insolvent within three or four decades. In the war's immediate aftermath, Jewish immigrant societies enjoyed a new sense of purpose through relief efforts for old hometowns, refugee resettlement, and commemorative projects abroad and at home. Despite those activities, Jewish movement into the middle class undermined any real future for the groups.[61] Members who moved out of state or city often cut ties to their landsmanshaftn or made new burial arrangements in the suburban or Sunbelt towns to which they retired. Others aged and ailed in New York, taxing society treasuries with medical and funeral costs that exceeded decreasing revenue among remaining members' contributions. Immigration restriction decades before had prevented a younger cohort from replenishing society rosters, leaving American-born children the most likely crop of members to steward these groups into the next phase of their existence. With only tenuous sentimental links to immigrant parents' places of origin, though, adult children felt little emotional incentive to invest in the immigrant orders. Their own mobility or access to commercial and workplace insurance likewise left them few incentives to join.[62] Although robust at the turn of the century, landsmanshaftn and Jewish fraternities proved to be largely a one-generation phenomenon.

Synagogues, conversely, enjoyed new primacy, especially as young Jewish families came of age and sought out new forms of community beyond the neighborhoods of their youth. Whether they associated those streets or institutions with their parents' old-world mentality or simply embraced the promises of suburbia, as postwar Jewish families moved on from older urban enclaves, they built and affiliated to congregations in unprecedented numbers. The life-cycle provisions and other social needs that synagogues offered drove that renaissance, especially amid lacking Jewish infrastructure in new areas of settlement. Burial and funeral oversight composed an important part of those offerings, particularly given the continuous legacy of congregations owning and managing cemetery land and the relationships they had nurtured with private undertakers over the first half of the twentieth century. Likewise, from Catholicism to Unitarianism, postwar American denominations increasingly challenged the consumerism they felt was stripping death of its spirituality in America. By throwing down that gauntlet, churches and synagogues alike staked a claim to reassert their oversight of death and dying in America. Even if families could do business with funeral homes independently, most of those businesses still held the profiteering image of the funeral director that popular culture and commercial practice had fostered for several decades. As a result, Jewish families came to expect the protections and entitlements that their synagogues and societies had fostered since the early twentieth century, and postwar congregations happily continued to stress those benefits while sounding the alarm about their commercial counterparts.

Jewish residential shifts offered one important boon to synagogue affiliation in the postwar years as American Jews became suburbanized at significant rates. One national estimate between 1945 and 1965 claimed that roughly a third left the cities for surrounding suburbs. In the 1950s alone, another survey calculated that Jewish suburbanites more than doubled as Jews relocated at a rate roughly four times that of other white city dwellers.[63] In and around New York, the city's postwar apartment shortage or aspirations to homeownership led young Jewish families to either leave traditional Jewish enclaves for new Bronx and Brooklyn neighborhoods or settle new communities altogether in Queens, Nassau, Suffolk, and Westchester counties. These areas saw a significant Jewish population increase between 1957 and 1970 as the city experienced some of its starkest Jewish decline. New Jersey suburbs and emerging Sunbelt cities like Miami also enticed them. By 1959, New York Jewish transplants made up 43 percent of Miami's Jewish population.[64]

Accompanying those moves, more American Jews joined and built congregations than at any other time in their history. Expenditures for congregation construction soared from $500 million to $600 million between 1945 and 1950, and by the end of the 1950s, synagogue affiliation among American Jews had peaked to roughly 60 percent, far outpacing any other period.[65] Most historians agree that lacking communal infrastructure in new areas of Jewish settlement played an important part in that growth, particularly as internal Jewish migrants sought out social or communal services through their synagogues in the absence of older social networks or family members who did not make the move from urban ethnic neighborhoods.[66] Generation clearly mattered in laying out postwar Jewish landscapes, whether city or suburb, as well as the institutional models that one generation of Jews continued in the city and a new style that another created in its outer reaches. Those factors would prove important in shaping postwar Jewish funeral provisions in New York and surrounding Jewish communities, as they tended to narrow among congregations and private funeral parlors.

In that sense, new Jewish residential patterns in and around New York City combined with the waning relevance of fraternalism to lead this generation, like counterparts elsewhere, to fill deficiencies in certain social provisions by turning to congregations or an emerging field of postwar Jewish centers. In the Bronx, Queens, Nassau, and Westchester counties and nearby New Jersey suburbs, congregations grew as more Jews came to live there. Nearly fifty Conservative congregations sprung up in Queens and Nassau counties in just a decade after the Second World War.[67] Many adopted a "synagogue center" model, like the Rego Park Jewish Center, the Forest Hills Jewish Center, or what some historians consider the "quintessential" postwar Jewish congregation in suburbia, the Israel Community Center of Levittown.[68] Although analysts at that time and since have devoted most of their attention to the youth of postwar Jewish families and their "child-centered" needs that fueled internal migration and affiliation, funerals and cemetery provisions still ranked as an important concern that motivated synagogue membership even if it stood among others more immediately relevant. Congregations and their national institutions understood that reality as well, and they made sure to consider the issue in their membership drives and financial planning.[69]

Throughout the 1950s, the Conservative movement's United Synagogue of America put out guides to assist affiliated congregations in growing their ranks. These guidebooks often alluded to the best uses of cemeteries for institutional advancement. One 1956 manual, *So You Want New Members*, recognized funeral needs as one of several offerings to entice paid affiliation. "The (One Dues Payment) Package Plan, which includes High Holy Day seats, Bar Mitzvah and wedding arrangements, cemetery privileges, CAN work," it advised. It stressed that requiring membership for the most valued services could best transform "synagogue 'customers' into synagogue members."[70] Another series, called the *Congregational Handbook*, affirmed that logic with an entire section dedicated to "Cemeteries." Investing in cemetery land, it reminded, could meet congregants' spiritual and emotional needs "that all will be taken care of properly after they are gone." Members' peace of mind aside, though, cemetery sales would also serve congregations' long-term fiscal health. They not only provided a "cushion" to draw from in hard times but could help *maintain* members in the long run. By charging new members extra fees for graves and burial rights and then refunding that surplus after several years of membership, synagogues could "discourage people from joining congregations just for cemetery privileges only to drop out the following year."[71]

Of course, postwar congregations also faced new competition in an ever-crowded market. Members' cemetery satisfaction therefore factored into synagogue calculations in new and meaningful ways. Despite its legacy as one of New York's oldest congregations, even B'nai Jeshurun found itself focusing on that bottom line in the early 1950s. It repeatedly scolded its cemetery keeper for poor maintenance of family graves, reminding him that "cobwebs in the mausoleums which are under annual and perpetual care . . . is a serious situation for a Temple which has its own cemetery." The warning continued, "Our Congregation cannot affort [sic] to receive any such complaints because of the fact that not only are these people interested in the cemetery, but as Temple contributors it reacts seriously on our finances."[72] A follow-up stressed the point more clearly: "We must satisfy the vault owners, many of whom are members of our Temple. We are in a different position from other Temples who have transient owners. Our people are contributors and if we do not give them the very best of services, it will react on us unsatisfactorily."[73] At a time when most Jews in New York and the suburbs naturally gravitated to their synagogues for cemetery and funeral needs, congregations once more bandied a crucial factor in affiliation. After years of targeted ad campaigns and family-centered benefit packages from synagogues, fraternities, and funeral homes alike, congregants complicated the old formula by way of the market and consumer entitlements vested in their funeral and cemetery purchases.

Following Jewish families as they moved from older neighborhoods, New York Jewish funeral homes reinforced that standing. They expanded their businesses into chains across the outer boroughs, Nassau and New Jersey suburbs, and some even extended as far south as new

Jewish centers in Florida. Many transplants or later retirees, for instance, may have remembered Garlick Funeral Home, once boasting a mighty Workmen's Circle contract, or its Grand Street origins in 1916. Attuned to residential shifts, Garlick partnered with Larry Goldstein in 1950 to grow the business "to better serve Jewish families" in their new frontiers. In little time at all, they had built two new modern locations on Jerome Avenue in the Bronx (1952) and Coney Island Avenue in Brooklyn (1954). By 1961, they had built a funeral home in Forest Hills, Queens, later landmarked for its architectural allusion to the Sinai Desert. Within a decade, another branch graced Flatbush Avenue to serve Jews residing in Canarsie, Mill Basin, and Marine Park, Brooklyn.[74] More-established counterparts spread even farther. By 1963, for instance, in addition to its famous branch on the Upper West Side of Manhattan, Riverside had established locations on Ocean Parkway in Prospect Park, Brooklyn; Central Avenue in Far Rockaway, Queens; Mount Vernon in Westchester County; and two separate branches in Miami and Miami Beach, Florida. Gutterman's Funeral Directors, New York's other onetime modest nineteenth-century livery, similarly expanded offices across Manhattan, Brooklyn, Miami, Rockville Centre, and Jersey City.[75]

That growth propelled the Jewish funeral industry as much as it commodified the funeral homes themselves, bringing within reach some of the oldest and most trusted names in New York Jewish undertaking. As new congregations and funeral chains followed Jewish settlement across greater New York and even down the East Coast, they naturally built on partnerships in the making since the 1920s. That cooperation reinforced synagogues as key providers of cemetery land and brokers between families and the funeral market. It also filled an important void, as aid groups and landsmanshaftn did not make that move themselves. Importantly, however, synagogues and commercial chapels did not settle into that transition without tension. In fact, the confrontation about to overtake American funeral directors offered all movements within American Judaism and their local and national networks of synagogues and rabbis a prime point of entry to reassert their religious bodies as legitimate custodians of Jewish death and dying in America.

The American (Jewish) Way of Death

The early 1960s marked a moment of reflection on the nation's excessive funeral industry. Whether *Time, Coronet*, the *Saturday Evening Post, Collier's*, or even special-interest magazines like the *Progressive*, popular media outlets one after another opined the high cost of dying in America. They set their attention on elaborate displays and leveled familiar accusations of funeral directors' "high-pressure salesmanship" preying on surviving relatives.[76] Even denominational magazines like the Roman Catholic *Jubilee* criticized the outsized role of undertakers, supposedly edging out the clergy and diminishing death's finality through the artifice of embalming. Then, in 1963, Jessica Mitford's scathing critique, *The American Way of Death*, took the nation by storm. With just the right combination of wit and investigative journalism, it reinforced long-standing caricatures of American undertakers while affirming the heinous suspicions of industry profiteering.[77] Although Mitford's exposé was not the first work of its kind, it further sensationalized a reevaluation of death that had been ongoing in the United States for several years. As funeral directors and the public responded to the onslaught, the questions and conclusions they raised reverberated for decades.

Drawing on that sentiment, Jews of all stripes began their own reappraisal of America's Jewish funeral industry. In striking uniformity, a chorus of Conservative, Orthodox, and Reform voices derided the costliness of Jewish funerals and the ill-effects of consumerism. By the decade's end, most echoed the United Synagogue's early critique that "the hallowed *mitzvah* of the burial of the dead is fast becoming the exclusive domain of commercial entrepreneurs, bringing with it many abuses and the loss of time-honored Jewish values."[78] These typically focused on industry norms ubiquitous in Jewish parlors like viewings, embalming, and ornate caskets and flowers. All appeared to undermine Jewish law and inspired calls for simplicity. One after another, each denomination issued condemnations and funeral standards to guide rabbis and synagogues in dealing with Jewish funeral homes. Conservative and Orthodox groups in particular also engaged in citywide and national projects to reform the funeral industry. These included chapel surveys, information campaigns to educate congregations and sisterhoods on funeral law, a trial program to launch a citywide and national hevra kadisha to circumvent the industry, and by 1963, a historic agreement with the Jewish Funeral Directors of America (JFDA) that allowed, among other things, Orthodox supervision of affiliated parlors. Although specific strategies varied, nearly all Jewish onlookers saw a return to simplicity and tradition as the best solution to industry maladies. To do so required greatly diminishing the role of Jewish funeral chapels. As a means to that end, nearly all Jewish movements reaffirmed the synagogue as a central (if not the only) communal body equipped to oversee members' funeral arrangements.

To an extent, there was some truth to the claim that commercialism had marginalized or inadvertently undercut ritual practice. Some causes were as simple as payment structures or additional fees that Jewish parlors charged for religious services. A 1961 survey of New York's Jewish funeral homes performed by the Union of Orthodox Jewish Congregations (OU) and its Rabbinical Council of America (RCA) found that while many chapels standardized services like embalming as part of all-inclusive packages, they charged extra for unique Jewish rituals. *Shomrim* (watchers to sit with the dead before funerals), washing and purification, and ritual shrouds all inflated a family's bill. While some undertakers did not profit from watching or washing, they did benefit from upsold religious accoutrements. For instance, the report cited $20 for cotton *tachrichim* (shrouds), $35 for linen, and $75 for hand-sewn Irish linen—the last of which cost only $22 to produce. The state of facilities could also discourage families from purchasing ritual services. Whereas most Jewish funeral homes invested in state-of-the-art equipment for general industry practices, those related to Jewish rites were either highly out of date or simply off-putting to average customers. "The Taharah room is to be found in the basement next to the boiler room," the OU report complained. "Refrigeration is still the kind that was used generations ago and there are no facilities or at best poor facilities for a Shomer to sit with the body under these conditions." Families seeking "kosher" funerals would find that situation "of such poor quality and unesthetic [sic] that they usually change their mind and accept the newfangled approach outlined to them by the funeral director."[79]

Then, of course, critics focused on consumerism. They chided pressure on families to purchase lavish displays, and they lamented its affront to rituals that were intended to promote dignity and solemnity.

"The simple funeral for which Jews were known and which our Christian neighbors thought sensible . . . has developed into an undertaker's delight," Rabbi Aaron Blumenthal, the recent president of the Conservative Rabbinical Assembly, editorialized to his congregation in Mount Vernon, New York. "Gone is the plain pine box; the shrouds; the Psalms; the immediate burial; the simple ceremony . . . the cost of coffins has climbed to three and four figures, in violation of Rabbinical injunction."[80] "The artistry of cosmetic morticians is not for us," Henry Rapaport asserted at the United Synagogue's 1963 convention. His recent survey of Jewish parlors as chair of the Committee on Congregational Standards left him particularly perturbed by the false comfort of costly funerals, eclipsing old practices like shiva, the week-long mourning after loss: "[Grief therapy] is not to be found in excessive expenditures for copper-lined caskets, public and ostentatious exhibition of slicked-up corpses, lying in state, soft music, flower-scented funeral chapels or drawing rooms and all the other newly created practices which have given rise to commercial exploitations of funerals. Flowers are not the equivalent of instant Shivah."[81] That year, the United Synagogue codified a set of funeral standards to counter most of those industry practices. These guidelines also influenced those soon adopted by groups like the Orthodox Union, Union of American Hebrew Congregations, Central Conference of American Rabbis, and the Synagogue Council of America, all of which formally issued funeral standards by 1965.[82]

Perhaps none did more than Samuel Dresner to inaugurate and promote that campaign by widely publicizing his community's example in Springfield, Massachusetts. While briefly serving there in the early 1960s after a time studying in New York with Abraham Joshua Heschel, Dresner lamented an increase in wakes, embalming, and other ornate offerings in Jewish parlors. He galvanized the cemetery committees of Orthodox, Reform, and Conservative synagogues to set new funeral regulations to counter that drift. Rules banned flowers, called for simple wooden coffins draped in black, and rejected viewings and embalming. Others called for renewing neglected rituals like shomer or reviving hevrot kadisha. Dresner frequently publicized the Springfield initiative, writing on it in denominational organs, speaking at conventions, and in Mitfordian style, dedicating an entire scathing chapter to "The Scandal of the Jewish Funeral" in his own widely read 1963 book, *The Jew in*

American Life. He also used his editorship of the Rabbinical Assembly's journal, *Conservative Judaism,* to model a congregation's capacity to re-orient the industry.[83]

Similar messages echoed throughout the 1960s at annual conventions of the United Synagogue, Rabbinical Assembly, and the National Women's League (the association of Conservative sisterhoods), permeating pulpits, institutional organs, and meetings of local congregations and sisterhoods and spurring change from below.[84] With increasing attention to commercialization of the life cycle, for instance, the National Women's League president, Mrs. H. Herbert Rossman of East Midwood, Brooklyn, addressed the United Synagogue's 1961 biennial on women's ability to "bring back a spiritual touch" to religious occasions from birth to death that were so often filled with "ostentation and often boisterous celebrations not befitting the religious motivation of the event." As one example, she charged women to prepare food for neighbors to "quickly eliminate those posters in catering establishments that blatantly adver-tise *Catering for Funerals.*"[85] A rousing address and debate at the United Synagogue's 1963 convention inspired a year-long survey of affiliated congregations and their dealings with Jewish chapels.[86] At the National Women's League's own 1964 biennial, a session devoted to "Jewish Family Living" inspired women present to discuss new strategies to take to their sisterhoods to best promote "proper conduct" in and "thorough understanding" of services like bar and bat mitzvahs, circumcision, naming ceremonies for baby girls, and, of course, funeral practices. The last topic in particular "aroused spirited discussion" with a focus on shiva and decorum in houses of mourning to understand tradition and impact change at the communal level.[87]

Like their Conservative counterparts, the OU and RCA undertook their own projects to reform the funeral industry. These included an ex-tensive survey of New York's Jewish funeral homes in 1961, and on find-ing "intolerable violations of Jewish tradition" in almost all of them, a project was formed to launch a national hevra kadisha, based initially in New York. Realizing the impossibility of circumventing the entire indus-try, the Orthodox groups moved toward cooperation, negotiating first with the Metropolitan Association of Jewish Funeral Directors and then signing an accord with the JFDA that allowed Orthodox rabbinic super-vision and certification of affiliated parlors.[88] Although these strategies differed or stressed finer points of Jewish law, Orthodox critiques similarly found in industry commercialization a laxity of tradition and pressure for Jewish families to use expensive services. Although standard across most American funeral homes, those elements challenged Jewish law and the simplicity of tradition.

Establishing a national hevra kadisha seemed at first the best way to solve those issues. Ironically, at least in terms of how to institute such an organization, the OU looked to the model of the secular Workmen's Circle and its Cemetery Department. Endowed with a robust insurance program, the Cemetery Department enjoyed not only popular influence among its members but the broad purchasing power that gave it significant leverage across the industry. By subsidizing members' funerals, the OU imagined, it too could make all decisions and thereby emphasize religious services and priorities. It would also remove the allure of expensive procedures and trappings contrary to Jewish law from unwitting family members. Finally, with the potential for massive buy-in among Jews seeking "kosher" funerals, the OU believed it could create a large member base with sufficient consumer clout to force Jewish chapels to prioritize tradition.

A trial hevra in New York not only revealed the scheme's limitations but also led the OU and RCA to realize that cooperation with existing parlors would better serve their ends. For one thing, poor actuarial odds stymied the effort as the OU tried, ex nihilo, to transform itself into a benevolent association. The likelihood that elderly members would compromise the majority of interested constituents did not help insurance rates. The campaign also created undo competition with existing burial societies. Perhaps most importantly, the OU also quickly realized that most congregations or burial societies would not so easily sever commercial and communal links with their funeral parlors. The bulk of synagogues, after all, had developed ties to Jewish chapels "from which they receive generous contributions and advertisements in their bulletins, and are reluctant to give up this association."[89] For better or worse, any hope of righting the industry would require the OU to work with parlors rather than supplant them.

In that spirit, the OU and RCA embarked late in 1961 on their next plan to contract standardized funerals among amenable chapels in return for certification as Orthodox-approved businesses. Fairly rigid standards would have enabled immense influence over endorsed ceremonies. One early contract stipulated no less than twelve rules for a "kosher" funeral. These included familiar prohibitions on flowers, music, embalming, and viewings, as well as rules regarding matters like Sabbath violation, requirements that only Jewish employees prepare a body, approval of shrouds and hevrot kadisha, the presence of a *mashgiach* (ritual observer) to supervise procedures, a shomer to sit with the dead until a funeral, and stipulations over the processes of burial and the rending of mourners' garments.[90] The trial run centered again in New York with Garlick's four branches in Brooklyn, Manhattan, Queens, and the Bronx serving as test parlors. Conflicts over funeral prices and Garlick's desire for exclusive endorsement rights derailed the contract.

Despite another failure, the setback ultimately fueled the OU's decision to give up on individual parlors and to work instead through the broader industry. Within a year, the OU and RCA began talks with the Metropolitan Association of Jewish Funeral Directors. The negotiations foreshadowed many of the basic compromises in the 1963 national accord signed among the OU, RCA, and the JFDA. According to that agreement, Orthodox representatives would oversee performance in participating funeral homes and offer their own personnel for purification and other rituals. Parlors with all-inclusive packages also agreed to fold in the costs of ritual shrouds. Finally, funeral directors would disseminate an OU and RCA guide detailing Jewish funeral law, which was intended to educate the public on Jewish standards and sensibilities in death. Echoing long-standing critiques against many pillars of the industry, the guide discouraged, among other things, ostentatious funerals and detailed why embalming transgressed Jewish law.[91]

Even if the accord marked a new moment of cooperation, it by no means signaled unquestioning trust. In fact, in their calls for industry reform, nearly all denominations aimed to monitor Jewish funeral homes and to create a wall between Jewish families and funeral directors. They did so in internal deliberations and overtly in the funeral guidelines they issued and renewal movements for hevrot kadisha in local congregations. They also aimed to ensure that synagogue committees, rabbis, and trusted representatives would always be on hand to prevent Jewish funeral directors from upselling families offensive accoutrements like metal or fancy wooden caskets and services like embalming. The OU, for instance, continually discussed creating a funeral hotline that families could call as soon as a death occurred so that representatives could handle arrangements in their place or at least be present with the bereaved at parlors when finalizing funeral plans. The RCA similarly encouraged affiliated rabbis to drill the message into their congregations that the first call after a death should be to the rabbi. Likewise, even after signing the accord, internal memos of the OU and RCA reasoned that in addition to *mashgichim* (ritual overseers) monitoring chapel practices, these observers could also make sure that funeral directors handed out the OU guide to patrons before discussing funeral arrangements and intercede if customers opted for unacceptable packages or services.[92]

The guidelines adopted and stressed by the Conservative movement had a similar aim. Most not only intended to curtail offensive funeral practices but saw local communities and their synagogues as the only reliable institutions to curb the influence of funeral directors and reshape industry practice. Many agreed with Rabbi Moshe Goldblum of Middletown, New York, who boldly claimed in 1961 that "there is only one organization in American Jewish life which is sufficiently strong enough to demand the loyalty and respect from the individual Jew. To re-introduce Jewish tradition in American Jewish burial practice will demand the guiding yet demanding hand of the synagogue."[93] He especially celebrated his own congregation's innovations, which refused families any input over the funeral save the ceremony's time. Otherwise, the Middletown Hebrew Association strictly imposed uniform simple services for all, regardless of wealth or standing. It also left all preparations to the synagogue's funeral committee so that "relatives are not permitted to make any arrangements on their own . . . none of the families ever meet the funeral director, for all negotiations are carried out through the committee."[94] Even calls for a renewal movement of local hevrot kadisha had a similar aim. In fact, curtailing industry excess stood at the heart of Dresner's original efforts to encourage the institution's revival. Versed in custom, hevra members could ensure proper ceremonies and reject elements offensive to Jewish law. As an added benefit, their collective input would spare surviving family from the daunting task of facing funeral directors alone and possibly succumbing to emotionally charged decisions over funeral services. "It is Jewish tradition," Dresner asserted, "that protects the rights of the mourner against those who would manipulate grief to their own advantage."[95]

In that sense, although few if any Jewish proponents ever directly invoked a parallel movement in America, these midcentury hevrot kadisha and synagogue funeral committees closely aligned with a larger crusade of so-called funeral societies and memorial societies. Buoyed by the sensation of Mitford's book and her and her husband's own support of these groups, nonprofit funeral societies had a simple aim. For small fees in advance, members or families joined a funeral society and left detailed instructions in the group's care for the services they desired. Memorial societies sought to do away with wakes and funerals altogether, favoring quick burials among the closest friends and family. They only held memorial ceremonies after initial grief had subsided. Prearrangements in this manner allowed for decisions in a "rational rather than emotion charged atmosphere." When the time came, societies drew on their collective leverage to see that the funeral home held to those simple arrangements.[96] Although groups would honor a member's wishes, they advocated modest ceremonies with *closed*, inexpensive caskets to cut down on embalming, one of the greatest funeral expenses. Churches overwhelmingly endorsed this approach, with Unitarians particularly well-represented. Although Jews did not explicitly cast their hevrot kadisha or even synagogues as funeral society variants, those groups arguably filled and aspired to many the same functions. Anchored by collective support and the sobering weight of Jewish tradition, synagogues and traditional burial societies not only drew on centuries of Jewish practice to assert their oversight of death and dying in America, but they stood poised in the early 1960s to tip the scale in the favor of simplicity and solemnity. As an added bonus, they were sure to emphasize, they protected affiliated families' financial, emotional, and spiritual well-being.

Marketing Funeral Rites, Commoditizing Family Dignity

Jewish funeral directors and their peers in the nation's larger industry squarely rejected detractors' claims and attempted to diffuse them by invoking a family's right as a consumer to send off loved ones in whatever style it wished. The funeral service industry's trade journal, *Casket and Sunnyside*, frequently attacked American clergy on that point. One 1962 issue even ran two editorials pledging solidarity with the JFDA and attacking the United Synagogue of America for challenging industry practice among the wider Jewish public.[97] No matter the denomination, it saw the decline of Protestant, Catholic, or Jewish subsets of the industry as a potential tidal wave that could implode funeral homes across the United States. Echoing some of its red-baiting leveled against Jessica Mitford, the wider industry brought in family will to counter both churches and synagogues. Far beyond a religious intrusion into the nation's funeral economy, opponents claimed, "It is a direct attempt of the . . . church to encroach on human freedom. Contrary to the ways of the American democracy, in which people can decide how they will bury their dead as well as other aspects of the their personal life . . . [this is] stripping away from bereaved families the right of any free choice."[98] Although Jewish funeral directors agreed, they stressed family decency over democracy in ads to consumers like one Riverside appeal to the diverse forms of comfort sought at that universal time of loss: "That is why we, at Riverside, have learned to help families on an individual basis, performing those services, which the family wants and needs, to the extent that the individual family desires . . . always quietly and unobtrusively . . . always respecting the family's dignity."[99]

By the 1960s, most Jewish New Yorkers not only embraced "fine funerals" but turned to a coalition of synagogues and funeral parlors to see that ideal fully met. Few would have predicted that shift after several hundred years of strong communal commitment to familiar hands tending the dead. Nevertheless, the permeation of professionalism and market concerns early in the twentieth century passed on most oversight to private parlors. The importance of family security and consumerism, however, tempered that transition. It also set much of the tone, as postwar synagogues and Jewish funeral homes stressed their commitments to family dignity and care. Those emphases drew on longer legacies, particularly the targeted campaigns of congregations, aid groups, and undertakers that consistently appealed to family interests as they competed for Jewish business and loyalties. Commercial growth worked to vilify the industry, based on popular perception and the profit-seeking in practice. By invoking protections over family budgets as much as souls, synagogues found several inroads to reassert themselves as the primary institution to which most Jews naturally turned when planning for life's end.

Although congregations benefited in those postwar years from the decline of Jewish fraternalism or new Jewish residential patterns around the city and the nation, their own drawn-out adaptation to a maturing Jewish funeral industry enabled them to weather these changes. Midcentury synagogues and their rabbis found powerful foils in Jewish funeral homes and their directors whether dealing with the cemeteries they owned, the contracts they had long ago brokered with undertakers, the void they filled amid Jewish fraternities' slow decline, or the expertise they claimed over Jewish law in an industry riddled with laxity and affronts to tradition. They used both to great effect to motivate and sustain Jewish membership. Still, after decades of ad campaigns, consumer packages, and society benefits appealing above all to family interests, congregants and their households emerged as an equally important party in New York's funeral economy, to say nothing of its larger Jewish communal landscape that was tied so closely to that industry.

Those developments recast old communal structures and norms as much as the traditional institutions that had long overseen the last acts of loving-kindness that Jews performed for one another and the land in which they laid their dead to rest. In their efforts to maintain relevance amid all these changes, policy makers of synagogues and benefit societies not only retooled their models but played an equal part alongside private professionals in setting their members' needs above most concerns. In the decades that followed, nearly all actors in New York's Jewish funeral industry asserted the family's centrality and affirmed their consumer entitlement. If an alliance among the family and the market had developed gradually since the late eighteenth century, the competition and cooperation to secure Jewish funeral business and communal loyalties among the masses firmly set that bond by the decades after World War II. Well beyond old monopolies that Jewish cemeteries or end-of-life provisions had represented three hundred years before, members' purchasing power and their very claim to private holdings afforded families influence as consumers and congregants that few could have imagined when early New York synagogues overwhelmed most funeral matters. Nonetheless, that shift left an important imprint on New York's Jewish communal structures as much as the city's Jewish cemeteries and its primary funeral providers.

Conclusion

To Be Buried among Kin, To Be Buried among Jews

When the dust settled after three centuries of Jewish interment on and around Manhattan Island, New York's Jewish burial enterprise looked very different in the 1960s than it had on first breaking ground in 1656. Dutch officials and the Jewish settlers to whom they sold a small hook of land for their dead would have looked on in disbelief at the thousands of Jewish cemetery holdings threading New York's cemetery belt as far as the eye could see. Early nineteenth-century families that had pled for the right "of being near to those in death, we loved most to be near in life" might have been pleased with the family lots and spouses' graves brimming within those grounds.[1] Widows like Hanah Louzada, whom synagogue elders had suggested "be dispatched to Lancaster" while her son remained in New York to alleviate her poverty, might marvel at the widows' death endowments driving thousands of Jewish fraternities in just over a century.[2] And early congregants like David Franks, Judith Pettigrew, Samson Myers, or Henry Phillips, who faced stigmas in death for marital choices or congregational debt in life, may have looked on in awe at the vigorous Jewish funeral industry, developing and thriving around the will and satisfaction of individual households. Despite these pivotal changes, one stark continuity would have remained as recognizable in the twentieth century as in any other period over the previous three hundred years: the continued Jewish commitment to be separate in death.

The central role that death and burial maintained in New York and American Jewish communal systems stemmed from that duality. It was both the dynamism to innovate and the gravity afforded to safeguard tradition. On the one hand, Jewish cemeteries and the evolving institutions around them proved integral for city Jews to navigate urban, industrial, and communal life in New York. On the other, that persistent dedication to maintain a separate funeral realm allowed Jews, at different times and in different forms, to limit integration and to negotiate larger social freedoms. Evolving Jewish strategies to plan for death proved unexpectedly malleable, even as the weight of eternity rendered many rituals and traditions strikingly persistent. Innovations offered Jews material protections against new social and economic dangers threatening their families' livelihoods, especially in an urban industrialized setting. At the same time, although Jewish New Yorkers eagerly embraced social opportunity and economic mobility over time, they did not take either lightly. In fact, they worried about inherent challenges to continuity so that the boundaries they maintained in death proved an important strategy to balance integration. Jewish burying places, therefore, along with associated funeral provisions, simultaneously embodied profound sites of change and deep bastions of tradition. They helped modern American values like self-individuation, democratic governance, elevation of the family's material and emotional security, and collective agency through consumption to permeate Jewish communal structures. At the same time, and despite those innovations, the funeral realm also offered stability and comfort in hallowed tradition by maintaining some social divisions among the living as much as the dead.

The capacity of New York's Jewish funeral realm to drive internal change and grassroots empowerment stemmed from the growing priorities around the family between the seventeenth century and the twentieth. At nearly all stages of that long evolution, the family's emotional and economic security—to say nothing of growing consumer powers—ran like a central thread through changing Jewish strategies to plan for death. In the process, a consistent alliance among family and market forces enabled average Jews to place individual concerns on par with those of the collective. Whether broader attention to family economies in the light of rapid industrial change or growing entitlement in a society centered on family and free market ideals, those priorities offered Jewish women and men new agency to act through the cemetery holdings they purchased or the funeral benefits they came to expect. They challenged the system when they found it did not meet their needs, and they did so precisely through newfound purchasing power in the city's thriving Jewish cemetery and funeral economies that targeted their households at nearly every turn. As a result, all those elements remained closely connected to Jewish communal dynamics for more than three hundred years.

Debates around New York's earliest Jewish graveyards highlight the beginnings of that trend. For early republican Jews, the family embodied a cause for protest and change as much as it offered their leaders a source of communal leverage. Family took center stage in debates around the graveyard, whether they were regarding marriage in or out of the community, children's religious upbringing, receipt of life-cycle rites, or even threats to deny dependents interment due to debt to the congregation. The far-reaching influence that synagogue elders wielded through their graveyard monopolies drew on the ability not only to grant or rescind a right to burial but to penalize spouses and children as much as individuals who had not met expectations. As we have seen, if members accepted that system for most of the eighteenth century, they challenged it in greater numbers by the turn of the next. They did so especially through sentimentality and by pushing back against the old ban prohibiting family interment. Eagerness to overturn the sequential "Row" stirred popular dissent, especially among those who simply wished to rest in proximity to their loved ones. Through appeals to family values, the power of the market, and inventive uses of official city burial fees, early New York Jewish families legitimated bonds of kin in death as much as those already well established around the community. They also set the framework for a new alliance to consumerism that would help them sidestep the status quo and to realize individual desires.

The nineteenth-century shift to Jewish burial societies represented another key innovation toward grassroots family protections. The proliferation of early Jewish burial societies and the fraternities they launched went a long way in reshaping the centrality of New York synagogues as the primary sources of Jewish social welfare. They also drastically undercut the reliance of the many on the personal wealth of the few. A vestige for over a century of Jews' corporate status in Europe, the centralization in one congregation could not withstand turn-of-the-century republicanism and popular will that elevated individual households over collective ideals. New Jewish burial societies placed as much value on egalitarianism as they did on family units. The fraternalism and mutuality that these burial societies promoted among their members influenced reforms of older top-down synagogue hierarchies. The competition that they posed to congregation monopolies also forced trustees to adopt family lots and the option to bury among kin that synagogues had long delayed until the 1850s. Finally, Jewish burial societies' incorporation of regular pensions and aid to surviving dependents, long in use among other ethnic and religious benefit societies, set an important precedent that elevated families' immediate needs as a key priority in Jewish approaches to death for decades to come. By the late nineteenth century, as New York Jewry swelled with working-class immigrants in industrial occupations, the real threat of death- or work-related poverty made the legacy of those earlier groups all the more important.

By the twentieth century, family and market emphases only continued to saturate New York's Jewish funeral industry. Like family lots decades earlier, the new option of adjoining double graves geared to spouses became a defining element of Jewish cemetery real estate. New fees to purchase or reserve those graves worked alongside charges for cemetery maintenance and interment rights that recast marriage and beneficiaries through new financial mechanisms related to death. At the same time, the advent of Jewish funeral chapels that pitched emotional care and dignity in their all-inclusive packages promoted a brand of family consumerism all their own. Competition with these new professionals led synagogues and societies to find new value in catering to constituents. New benefits like families' funeral reimbursements, extending parents' funeral coverage to unmarried adult children, and the pledge to protect against supposed industry profiteering at the expense of survivors' emotional fragility all aimed to preserve household loyalties through family-centered support. By the postwar period, even as synagogues cooperated more closely with funeral providers, each party still understood the importance of projecting itself as the champion of everyday Jewish households at times of loss. That general thrust over three centuries of evolving Jewish strategies to plan for life's end empowered New York Jews to act through the funeral realm itself and to drive social and institutional change through the legitimacy of their family concerns.

And yet, even as Jewish New Yorkers innovated all these funeral provisions, their cemeteries, their burial societies, and their subset of the city's funeral industry also all preserved centuries-old traditions and Jewish particularity. The maintenance of those customs proved no less important than evolving entitlements for affiliated Jews to navigate modernizing American forces like urban or industrial change. In fact, in light of broad civic and social opportunity that rendered most divisions among Jews and Christians seemingly far less relevant over their formative centuries in the United States, the widespread proclivity of Jews to value self-segregation in death acted as one important counterweight to their integration in American society.

Time and again, Jewish burial in New York City anchored traditions and tempered Jewish mobility. Those earliest few Jewish graveyards, for instance, set the backdrop for larger debates over social fluidity, religious conformity, interfaith exchanges, and the challenges facing a small and underdeveloped community to maintain authority or adjust tradition to a new setting. New York's first Jewish graveyards addressed elders' anxiety over continuity while charting a path to navigate new access to mainstream life.

The same applied in the 1850s as congregants and trustees together reinvented old Jewish graveyards into new rural cemeteries. Although those holdings enabled Jews to embrace the Rural Cemetery Movement's broader universalism, cemetery regulations across traditional and Reform congregations echoed some version of those rules stipulated by B'nai Jeshurun that "persons who shall have married out of the Jewish Faith . . . shall not be entitled to interment in a burying-place possession."[3] Even Temple Emanu-El, New York's most progressive synagogue, upheld those prohibitions in Salem Fields.[4] That all New York synagogues maintained such stark internal limits stood out as they established new cemeteries closer than ever before, in style and proximity, to their non-Jewish peers. Thus as Jewish grounds clustered together behind gates, fences, and roadways, they strove not only to set clear spatial boundaries from so many Christian rural cemeteries alongside them but to embody again the symbolic particularity that New York Jews vested in burial. Nevertheless, with those physical and metaphorical divisions carefully preserved, New York synagogues also celebrated their cemeteries as new foundational cornerstones of their lives in America, symbols of the "happy privilege to be citizens of a republic in which perfect equality of rights, civil and religious, is fully carried out."[5] For despite the number of universal ideals rural cemeteries eased into Jewish communal sensibilities, they also safeguarded particularity amid far wider and more exciting social openness.

Similar trends defined the twentieth century when the allure of professionalism, fine service, and skilled expertise fueled the development of New York's Jewish funeral industry. Despite aesthetic and ideological shifts, New York Jews held fast to certain limits. They long refused to outsource the most intimate aspects of funeral labor to professionals, preserving communal oversight nearly four decades after fellow Christian urbanites had already made the transition. Even then, from the most traditional to avowedly secular, and whether native-born or newly arrived, most Jews still frequented Jewish funeral homes and directors, committing to the ideal that only Jewish hands should tend the Jewish dead.

Even by the 1950s, when Jewish mobility reached new heights and extended beyond familiar urban enclaves to new suburban frontiers, the uncertainties that that integration raised for some led them to find some constancy in the continuity of a separate Jewish funeral realm. The period witnessed a host of studies, in which scholars fretted as well as celebrated Jews' growing socioeconomic advances. Most included Jews among other ethnic Europeans of immigrant origins, all seemingly melting into a new white middle class of coveted "unhyphenated Americanism."[6] As Jonathan Sarna has pointed out, works like Will Herberg's *Protestant, Catholic, Jew* downplayed ethnic divisions among European immigrant groups, and its "triple melting pot" elevated American Jews to define one-third of the very contours of a trifaith America despite their composing just over 3 percent of its population.[7] Likewise, as a host of demographic studies eagerly traced Jewish affluence and movement to white suburbia, it was also deeply concerned about Jewish "group survival in the open society," especially as new Jewish communities branched off from onetime urban, ethnic centers.[8] To many onlookers, the symbolic and socioeconomic advance of Jewish mobility at midcentury seemed akin to the deterioration of identity or strong communal bonds.

In this context, a sociologist like C. B. Sherman asserted in his study of American Jews' "ethnic individuality" in 1960, "the role of the cemetery in the formation of Jewish communal life in America cannot be overestimated." Sherman cast the cemetery as a consistent symbol of Jewish identity and preservation, especially given the voluntarism and integration that Jews then enjoyed. "The ghetto," he proclaimed, "accompanied the Jew who wanted to remain a Jew from cradle to grave . . . for though a Jew might live among Gentiles, he wanted to be buried among

Jews."⁹ Separation in death embodied one firm continuity, which Sherman threaded far back into America's Jewish past to the early eighteenth-century settlers in Boston and Philadelphia and, of course, those few Jewish merchants in New Amsterdam who "had hardly shaken foreign dust from their shoes when they began to concern themselves with establishing a Jewish cemetery."¹⁰

The power of that trope of "burying among Jews" despite "living among Gentiles" also informed the methods of several contemporary studies that aimed to better understand the makeup of Jewish suburban life. As a host of demographers attempted to identify their subjects from the blurring boundaries of the white American suburbs, they created what they called "the death records technique" and "the Yom Kippur technique." The former especially relied on the assumption that the majority of Jews would seek separate Jewish funeral provisions by drawing on local Jewish cemeteries and funeral records to identify Jewish families in a given community.¹¹ Like their American Jewish counterparts in each century before them, uneasy about Jewish mobility or its implications for communal continuity, observers of those challenges in the 1950s looked to Jewish deathways and cemeteries as grounding institutions, maintaining particularity and tradition amid so many fading divisions.

By navigating the modern problems of urban and industrial life and negotiating integration while preserving a sense of continuity, Jewish cemeteries and their managing institutions took on central importance in New York Jewish communal systems. Given the seriousness of family interest and the awe inspired by the fate of the soul, Jewish burial-providing groups and their policies had immense influence over living social realities. The degree to which family and financial ties permeated those policies also assured that they would impact daily life as well as strategies to plan for death. For most Jews, religious tradition or their people's proclivity to stress loving care over the dead and their rest in Jewish-owned soil served as the only incentives they needed to secure traditional provisions. For others, even if their eternal being had little influence on their affiliation, the personal stake they maintained in respectable funeral services, the taboo of deviating from Jewish spaces, and the near universal aim to protect their loved ones' well-being proved of equal if not greater importance.

Either way, Jewish institutions enjoyed significant influence through the burial and funeral needs they provided, especially as death represented one of the few communal needs for which Jews had to or desired to maintain collective ties in an otherwise voluntary society. At the same time, given the personal stake that most Jews had in these matters, husbands and wives, daughters and sons, fathers and mothers, siblings, and a host of other family members all maintained a vested interest to push the system over time. They did so even more as emotional, industrial, and commercial values over three centuries elevated family interests and their broader legitimacy. When affiliated Jews felt that their needs could be better met, they advocated for change and proved New York's Jewish burial enterprise to be an immensely fluid and dynamic institution despite the near-uncompromising pillar of separation that gave it much of its meaning. When Jews felt that the status quo fulfilled important social or ritual concerns, they also played an active part in its perpetuation over time. They contributed to its growth so that a thriving self-segregated Jewish funeral and cemetery economy stretched over long spates of time and, by the middle decades of the twentieth century, across the East Coast.

Jewish cemeteries in New York, and their associated institutions and accoutrements, served as immense engines of change while simultaneously preserving profound continuity. Each force enabled death and burial to promote grassroots agency, especially where individual will or family well-being were at odds. These realities marked Jewish cemetery spaces as far more complex sites of negotiated power, beyond the simple dynamics of top-down authority so often associated with them. They also underscored the capacity of American values linked to industry, urban growth, civic inclusion, and commerce to influence matters as introspective and intimate as Jewish death and burial, ultimately reshaping them in line with popular will. Where the masses sought change, they could act through death to achieve it. Where tradition met their needs, they took comfort in continuity.

Epilogue

"Who's going to sit shiva for me when I die, Mr. Sacks? My daughter won't. My son won't. Will you?"

Sacks turned the question into a joke. "I'll tell you what, Mrs. Goldberg. I'll make you a deal. I'll promise to sit shiva for you if you promise to sit shiva for me." Sacks has fulfilled his part of the bargain: he recites the prayer each year on the anniversary of her death.

—Jack Kugelmass, *The Miracle of Intervale Avenue*

New Age Approaches to Age-Old Hevrot

A decade after most mainstream denominations first took up calls in the 1960s to reform America's Jewish funeral industry, baby boomers of the counterculture continued that work for themselves. Among several aims in a chapter on death and burial in the widely popular *Jewish Catalog* (1973), compilers of the how-to guide hoped to resuscitate spiritualism and popular participation in death. They embarked on an effort to reorient the market by encouraging young women and men "to study what goes on in their own community when a death occurs, and to act wherever necessary to change funeral and burial practices so that they are more in keeping with Jewish tradition."[1] Although the book itself hoped to inspire an alternative approach to organized American Judaism, it echoed critiques that were familiar by then, deriding commercialism and even calling into question the very motives of Jewish funeral directors.

Reviving interest in the hevra kadisha surfaced once more as an obvious remedy for all of these problems. The *Catalog* valorized traditional burial societies as timeless Jewish institutions. Not without sugarcoating, it even claimed that communal honor and responsibility were their sole motivations. With profit supposedly anathema, hevrot kadisha seemed to offer ideal counterweights to "the power and influence" of their far-less-ancient industry foils.[2] Readers were not only prescribed to study Jewish funeral law but encouraged to find out if their communities maintained a hevra. If so, they should support it and perhaps even join. Along with other fence posts along the path to a meaningful Jewish life, death offered a fertile ground for the *Catalog*'s bigger mission "to move away from the prefabricated, spoon-fed, near-sighted Judaism" supposedly rampant among middle-class American Jews and to return to its humbler foundations and deeper communal ideals.[3]

Little had changed by the project's final installment, *The Third Jewish Catalog* (1980), save for the increased potential that editors saw in burial societies to work with other historic hevrot toward "the revitalized community that many of us envision for American Jewry."[4] Whether those dedicated to charity and loans (hevra gemilut hasadim), caring for and feeding the poor (hevra hakhnasat orchim and lehem la-reevim), visiting the sick (hevra bikor holim), providing dowries for poor brides (hevra hakhnasat kalah), tender care for the dead (hevra kadisha), or solace to those in mourning (hevra nihum avelim), all offered a model of interconnected support for modern American Jews to emulate. In so doing, they could realize "the reestablishment of the human sharing and mutual responsibility that was embodied in these hevrot." Poor working knowledge of burial societies, to say nothing of Jewish funeral law, posed the greatest challenge to that goal in 1980. Their relegation, where extant, to "function as subcontractors to the Jewish funeral homes in the area" did not help either.[5] Still, by offering a model to build Jewish burial societies and other old dedicated hevrot, the third *Catalog* hoped to strengthen collective Jewish renewal by providing women and men an incentive to act in their communities rather than relying on rabbinic or industry professionals. By the closing decades of the twentieth century, the simple wonder of performing that ultimate care over departed peers offered as much promise for renewal to modern American Jews as it did their forebears in the 1780s. Although Jews during the new republic's infancy saw the first Jewish burial societies as ripe institutions for fostering fraternalism among fellow Jews, by the 1970s, hevrot instead seemed the ideal vehicles for fostering Judaism among fellow Americans.

You Don't Die When You Have a Grave

As one generation came of age seeking communal bonds through death, another approaching its twilight found purpose in old funerary promises. Death is always in the background of *The Miracle of Intervale Avenue*, for instance, a poignant study of elderly Jews who, in the 1980s, refused to abandon the South Bronx neighborhood of their youth.[6] While the drive to remain may have given some a sense of purpose, so did the companionship they found in their Intervale congregation. The memory of friends who had predeceased them surfaces time and again in the book, as does the unspoken prospect that any one of the group could be next. Perhaps the whimsical exchange between Mr. Sacks and Mrs. Goldberg above draws its meaning less as a light-hearted joke than as a heartfelt promise kept. Others of the Intervale community would not leave commemoration to chance. Lena Zalben, then in her eighties, divided her pleasure between an apartment full of old photos and the visits from her nephew. She had helped raise him after her sister became an early widow, and although she traded much of her own life in making that sacrifice, she grew immeasurably close to each of them.[7] Lena delighted in his weekly phone calls and their trips to a New Jersey cemetery to visit her sister's grave. She found comfort in that memorial and in the sight of her own plot waiting patiently alongside it, which she had purchased for herself years earlier. Although it cost a hefty sum of $1,000, she had gradually paid it off month by month, knowing that her affairs would be settled. "I didn't bother nobody when I was alive," she proudly reminded. "They will only have to put me in the thing where I'm going. Did I do a foolish thing that I did? No. Why? You don't die when you have a grave."[8]

Onlookers throughout the 1980s found meaningful symbols in old immigrant cemeteries, spurring reflection on a moment of New York Jewish history, while also quietly marking its fast-approaching demise. Framing his early study of Jewish landsmanshaftn in New York, for instance, Michael Weisser chose regular meetings of remaining elderly members of the Boyerker Benevolent Society. They met each month, and like so many of their contemporaries, they bitterly fought over their cemeteries. Beyond the specifics of the debate, the unspoken issue remained one of legacy and memory because "the real underlying fear of the old immigrants . . . was that once deceased and removed from life, they would be forgotten by their children and grandchildren. . . . Only the Beth David Cemetery would remain as a visible symbol of the society's existence."[9] A contemporary write-up promoting a 1986 exhibit at the YIVO Institute for Jewish Research, "Hello Landsman: A History of New York's Jewish Mutual Aid Societies, 1880–1950," could not resist a similar note of generational nihilism. Although the Minsker Young Friends Association soldiered on with eighty-five active members, its weekly meetings also centered on burial plots. Underscoring the mortality of the group as much as its members, the piece ended with their aging secretary. He had joined decades earlier at his father's behest, but his own children preferred ambivalence: "They didn't say yes, and they didn't say no . . . other members got the same response. The children feel there is no need for this kind of organization anymore."[10] Cemeteries were an easy device to capture the passing of an aging New York Jewish cohort. At the same time, they were particularly appropriate, since the need they met had been so important to communal formation, even when their founders had a lifetime ahead of them. Tragically, however, for some, the lack of continuity fulfilled their worst fears.

No One Left to Sign the Papers

Over the coming decades, deteriorating cemeteries became the new symbol of that passing generation, and the public at large did not fail to shift its gaze. The chaos of overgrown graves and ill-kept records became the next most potent sites for public mourning and action. Just four years apart, the *New York Times* ran two different human-interest stories that opened on Jewish widows visiting their husbands' graves, aghast to find other women mistakenly buried next to them. In 2005, Richard D. Fishman, director of the New York State Division of Cemeteries, cited at least three or four similar complaints each year. By 2009, he claimed weekly complications from the dwindling membership of Jewish burial societies: "A person dies, and they can't get buried because there is no one left to sign the papers, or the guy in charge is 99 years old and in a nursing home."[11] Robin Kraus, manager of the Liquidation Bureau of the New York State Insurance Department's Office of Miscellaneous Estates, and her assistant, Alice Jenkins, dedicated themselves to alleviating some of that bureaucratic burden. Taking charge of near-defunct society records throughout the 2000s, they sorted "with practiced deftness through the thousands of ancient index cards, yellowing ledger books and rolled-up oilcloth maps entrusted to their care" to bring some order to the materials and fulfill groups' fleeting promises to the last identifiable members.[12] Perhaps ironically, although state negligence and woefully inadequate social welfare at the turn of the twentieth century had inspired the birth of so many immigrant associations, government intervention one hundred years later played an important role in serving surviving members, graced with that bittersweet fortune to have outlived their peers.

The Impossible Promise of Perpetual Care

Beyond those still in need of burial, the disarray surrounding many who predeceased them and the anger of the families still visiting their graves shone a light on Jewish cemeteries without communities or funds to maintain them. Bayside Cemetery in Ozone Park, Queens, epitomized that situation at the turn of the twenty-first century. Sprawling vegetation had overrun the grounds since at least the 1990s, with vines engulfing gates and gravestones. Mausoleum walls literally cracked as roots invaded their foundation. Although the crypts had survived earlier instances of vandalism or thefts of Tiffany windows, when left unattended, they could little counter the advance of the very earth all around them. That chaos inspired neighbors, church groups, and Jewish communal activists to give of their time in an attempt to clear up the cemetery. If the futility of tearing at weeds as new crops replaced them had not discouraged their work, the real threat of monuments toppling at the weight of overgrowth rendered those efforts more hazardous than humanitarian. Still, a shrinking pool of volunteers soldiered on. Anthony Pisciotta, a bridge and tunnel worker for the Metropolitan Transportation Authority, passed countless hours every Sunday for more than a decade preening, repairing monuments, and clearing what he could.[13]

Poor publicity against the cemetery's owner, Manhattan's fourth synagogue, Shaare Zedek, came to a head in 2008 when a class-action lawsuit alleged that the congregation had misused or mismanaged funds earmarked for perpetual care.[14] Few would have imagined that outcome when Shaare Zedek had first established Bayside in 1865. Indeed, the move likely seemed an investment on par with Emanu-El's vaunted Salem Fields. By the turn of the century, Shaare Zedek had even sold more than 90 percent of the cemetery's lots to burial societies and landsmanshaftn. It had no way of knowing that the large-scale demise of those groups would ravage the grounds to a near irreparable state within a century. Although many also bought perpetual care, Shaare Zedek's own postwar financial troubles raised concerns equally as pressing as the cemetery's upkeep. Ironically many of the same pressures that undercut old aid groups, like demographic change in Jewish neighborhoods and generational apathy, also jeopardized the viability of the Upper West Side congregation.

With limited resources of its own and pressure from the attorney general's office to address the growing blight, Shaare Zedek appealed to Jewish philanthropies for assistance in what it cast as a wider communal crisis. The United Jewish Appeal (UJA)-Federation of New York offered $145,000 for initial clean up and another grant of $80,000 toward what would become the Community Alliance for Jewish-Affiliated Cemeteries (CAJAC).[15] The plan offered a longer-term solution to coordinate the restoration of deteriorating Jewish cemeteries in the metropolitan area. Since 2009, CAJAC has extended its reach well beyond Queens and its ongoing work at Bayside to projects like Staten Island's Baron Hirsch Cemetery and others in Suffolk and Westchester Counties.[16] By 2017, following years of continued brokering with the attorney general's office and Shaare Zedek's decision to sell its Ninety-Third Street Manhattan property for real estate development, the congregation agreed to set aside some of those profits to further Bayside's rehabilitation and a fund of $8 million for the cemetery's future upkeep.[17]

New York Real Estate

Although nature and neglect had overtaken those old frontiers of Jewish burial in Queens, an influx of Jewish immigrants from the former Soviet Union drove a renaissance for one of Brooklyn's first rural cemeteries. Founded as an early nonsectarian cemetery in 1850, within seven years, Washington Cemetery was designated as a Jewish burying place. Its preponderance of Jewish burial societies, landsmanshaftn, and congregations of a bygone era located just four miles from Brighton Beach made it an incredibly appealing place to bury for that community's new Jewish residents. In fact, plots became so valuable that by 1988, one

Brooklyn Jewish funeral home faced indictment for illegally purchasing unused graves from old societies and reselling them to Russian Jewish immigrants.[18] Within twenty years, single lots in Washington Cemetery commanded a $12,000 premium.[19]

Demand only increased as Brooklyn's largest Jewish cemetery ran out of space. Tearing up and narrowing old roadways to make room for new burials, managers employed one last strategy, "squeezing coffins into every barren inch."[20] Black marble headstones with laser-etched portraits of the dead, in vogue among Brighton's Russian Jews, soon lined most paths. As coffins made their final journey through passages so narrow that they could just fit a golf cart before being laid to rest, surrounding etchings looked on to witness the arrival of new graves soon to join them. In some old lots, the black stones have come to rest interspersed among Jewish graves of the nineteenth century, filling any stray unused plots wherever available. In another historical parallel, many elderly or ailing Jews of the former Soviet Union also received final dignity from the Hebrew Free Burial Association. The group assured them a respectable transition from this world to the next, and through the dedicated Jewish rites and Jewish graves it provided, it could publicly assert their Jewish identity that many for so long had to hide.[21] Bookending that long century of Jewish arrival to America, old and new Jewish immigrants found common ground in the city in which they chose to build new lives and the earth they desired to honor them in death.

Owned and Operated by the Jewish Community

Just as state and philanthropic intervention set a new course for New York's Jewish cemeteries, similar impulses challenged the city's Jewish funeral industry. In 2000, a coalition of Jewish communal interests, social service agencies, and philanthropists purchased Plaza Memorial Chapel on Manhattan's Upper West Side after the attorney general brought an antimonopoly suit against a funeral conglomerate. The coalition aimed to bring down costs of New York Jewish funerals and, at least symbolically, to take on the juggernaut of America's wider funeral industry. Since the late 1960s, the Texas-based firm Service Corporation International (SCI) had been buying up small family-owned funeral chapels across the country to corner regional markets and dictate local

funeral costs. In 1971, SCI made its way to New York and began acquiring Jewish funeral homes. Just over two decades later, SCI owned five of
Manhattan's six Jewish funeral chapels and seven of the twenty located
in Brooklyn. If not for the antitrust case, the Texas firm would have
continued its consumption of Jewish funeral homes with far less state
oversight. Through subsequent popular initiatives, the episode also galvanized a return to some communal supervision over Jewish death and
dying in the city.

As if out to fulfill twentieth-century stereotypes of exploitative
American funeral directors, SCI's excessive costs led the city's Consumer Affairs Commission to request an investigation of monopolis-
tic tendencies. The inquiry found that SCI had greatly derailed market
competition. It had not only bought a host of Jewish funeral homes but
concealed common ownership by retaining their old and trusted names.
Although Brooklyn branches of Garlick, Kirshenbaum, or I. J. Morris
funeral homes had once competed for neighborhood Jewish business,
their consolidation allowed SCI to steadily raise prices, leaving consumers few other alternatives and a false perception of industry competition.

And raise costs it did. After acquiring Riverside in Manhattan, for
instance, SCI doubled funeral costs in the space of ten years. Within a
week of its purchase of Plaza Memorial Chapel, the firm surged casket
costs alone from $100 to $2,500. Funerals at SCI-owned Jewish parlors
in Manhattan exceeded those offered by independent parlors by at least
$1,000.[22] The firm had other strategies to influence the market. It took
advantage of old ties to synagogues, winning endorsements for its newly
acquired parlors as "official" or "recommended" funeral homes for congregants to use. It also signed agreements with former owners and employees of the Jewish parlors it acquired that banned them from going
to work for competing chapels or opening new ones for twenty years.[23]
Had an order like the Workmen's Circle still wielded its old national
influence, it might have stood poised to counter those moves. Instead,
Jewish communal agencies relied on the state, the market, and Jewish
communal coffers to attempt to return some choice to the industry.

Following months of wrangling and threats of an antitrust suit, the
attorney general's office won modest concessions. SCI sold three of its
parlors in Manhattan and Brooklyn, agreed to alert the state for a decade
if it purchased other Jewish funeral homes, and released former owners

and employees from their noncompetition agreements.²⁴ The settlement marked the first time a city government officially intervened in the corporate ownership of funeral homes.²⁵ It also spurred a new coalition of large Jewish groups like the UJA-Federation of New York to team with other communal agencies and philanthropists to found an experimental not-for-profit parlor, Plaza Jewish Community Chapel. Even veteran players like the Union of Orthodox Jewish Congregations (OU) took a cue from the SCI settlement to revive old campaigns for prepurchased, low-cost funerals compliant with Jewish law. If these parties could not beat the market, they would join it themselves to change it from the inside by creating more affordable alternatives than the SCI consolidation had created.

SCI's sale of Plaza Memorial Chapel, the one Manhattan firm it gave up, created an opportunity for allied social service agencies, communal groups, congregations, and well-meaning investors to try their hand at the twenty-first century's first Jewish funeral home not driven by revenue. Echoing familiar contrasts between family service and consumerism, donor and board of directors' president Alfred Engelberg promised that the venture "will be run to meet the needs of families and the bereaved rather than the needs of a profit-making business based in Houston."²⁶ Although competitors scoffed at Plaza's promise to reduce basic funeral costs by 20 percent, they likely did not account for the funds and goodwill of its coalition partners. Contributors like the Jewish Communal Fund and the UJA-Federation of New York furnished $1 million in grants to kick-start the project, while eight Jewish philanthropists offered long-term no-interest loans to see its work continue. Three years later, with a modest share of the market, Plaza continued its pledge to gradually lower prices by applying any revenue after it had paid off its loans to subsidize future customers' costs.²⁷

As Plaza Jewish Community Chapel emerged as a lower-cost alternative for Jewish funerals in Manhattan, the OU launched its Levaya program with similar aims for Brooklyn and Queens. Reviving an old experiment, the Orthodox group partnered with Parkside Memorial Chapels to offer funeral packages that not only strictly adhered to Jewish law but shaved at least $1,000 off of comparable funeral costs at other parlors. Even as Plaza brought its costs down to around $4,500—in contrast to $6,000 at nearby Riverside—the OU and Parkside negotiated fixed-rate funerals for a striking $2,795, including services at the chapel, with even slightly lower prices if families opted only for the graveside. These funerals included transportation costs, pine box coffins, purification rituals, and work by Sabbath-observant Jews who would closely follow all aspects of Jewish law. The package also arranged for ritual supervision by the Queens-based hevra kadisha of that borough's Vaad Harabonim (Rabbinical Council) and its counterparts in Flatbush, Brooklyn.[28]

The OU forged an independent path because of frustrations with the still comparably high costs at Plaza and its instances of nonadherence to Jewish law, like its willingness to offer cremation. Despite its long annoyance with commercial ills in New York's Jewish funeral industry, the OU nevertheless harnessed consumerism in its mission to make traditional Jewish funerals desirable and accessible to the wider public. As one incentive for Parkside's partnership, for instance, the OU stressed that subsidized funerals could offer the chapel good publicity. In addition to perceptions of community service, many attendees of OU-Parkside funerals would likely think of that chapel when facing funeral needs of their own. Acting independently, they would pay full price for its services. Even more to the point was the OU's savvy to buy in bulk in order to bring down overall costs for the traditional funerals it promoted. As Parkside CEO Edward Goldstein explained to the press, "Do you belong to Costco? If you want to buy in quantity, you're going to get it for less. The OU is buying in quantity."[29]

At the turn of the twenty-first century, echoes of the last three hundred years of New York Jewish end-of-life planning still rang quite clearly. In one form or another, Jews continued to search out community to secure a proper burial and to honor each other in death. The market still loomed large, as did cemetery real estate. In some pockets, scarcity of land commanded higher sums on empty graves than those interred around them could have ever imagined in their lifetimes. In other areas, scarcity of *landslayt* (immigrant peers) imperiled those very holdings. Family sentiment remained a powerful driver of events, whether it was related to comfort to aging Jews looking forward to anticipated reunions, outrage from their descendants over the state of their final resting places, or a ready cause to champion for those seeking to rein in the industry. State intervention and communal activism also worked to counter those trends, as did Jewish philanthropists whose roles in some of those efforts cannot help but conjure allusions to Jewish elites of former centuries who donated their wealth to first secure New York Jews the ability to bury apart. After centuries of consumer and financial innovations complicating Jewish death and dying in New York, perhaps those late twentieth-century episodes suggest a return—if not a widespread revival—of deeper communal and traditional priorities on the horizon.

ACKNOWLEDGMENTS

Although I often assumed that the best part of finishing this project would be giving up the need to think about death and burial on a daily basis, the chance to thank all those who contributed to its development is by far the greater highlight. Without rich archives and helpful librarians, there would be little to fill these pages. Collections housed among partner organizations at the Center for Jewish History (CJH) offered the bulk of material for this study. A generous Dr. Sophie Bookhalter Fellowship in Jewish Culture from the CJH and fellowships from the Graduate School of Arts and Sciences at New York University (NYU) allowed me years of close work with those collections. I am indebted to archivists like Randall Belinfante of the American Sephardi Federation; Tanya Elder of the American Jewish Historical Society; Michael Simonson of the Leo Baeck Institute; Gunnar Berg, Ettie Goldwasser, Leo Greenbaum, and Fruma Mohrer of the YIVO Institute for Jewish Research; and CJH reference librarians Melanie Meyers, Zachary Loeb, and Ilya Slavutskiy for their excellent and always friendly assistance. I owe special thanks to Estelle Guzik, who always patiently answered my questions and shared her genealogical expertise.

Elsewhere in the city, Eleanor Yadin of the New York Public Library's Dorot Jewish Division always responded quickly to my research needs and always extended encouragement and friendship. My thanks also extends to librarians in the Map Division and the Milstein Division of US History, Local History, and Genealogy. Warren Klein provided much help with the Jewish Theological Seminary Library archives and also offered useful information about Temple Emanu-El. Thanks also go to librarians at NYU's Elmer Holmes Bobst Library like Andrew Lee and Evelyn Ehrlich and to librarians at Brooklyn College like Beth Evans and Judith Wild for research and reference help. Finally, Steven Siegel helped with the Holy Society collection, then under his care at the library of the Ninety-Second Street Y. He taught me a great deal about Jewish genealogical research and always patiently entertained my questions on the minutia of Jewish cemetery real estate. Steve was also enormously generous with his time. One week, he even kept the library open late in a snowstorm just so I could finish taking notes before a fast-approaching conference out of state.

Good friends and colleagues are just as important as good archives. Karen Adler Abramson, Ariana Alexander, Shirly Bahar, Gordon Beeferman, Judah Bernstein, Clemence Boulouque, Jeremy Brown, Julio Capó, July Deluty, Lori D'Nicuola Dobson, Dan Dinero, Shayne Figueroa, Josh Furman, Sonia Gollance, Ryan Grubbs, Miriam Haier, Madeleine Goico Hardie, Peter Hamilton, Donna Herzog, Adam Jones and Karen Wheeler, Anna Koch, Markus Krah, Michelle Lee, Ellen Messer, Cory Elizabeth Nelson, Vanita Neelakanta, Emily Poorvin, Carmen Soliz, Jonathan Michael Square, Amy Sinclair, Hilit Surowitz-Israel, Dan Tsahor, Jennifer Young, Pat and Joe Walter, Amy Weiss, Shayna Weiss, Helen Woo, and Sarah Zarrow have all offered friendship and support in various ways. Many have endured countless hours discussing this topic, and all provided immeasurable insight and encouragement.

I am also grateful for the many mentors I have had the chance to work with over the years like Robert Cohn, Francesca Bregoli, Hasia Diner, David Engel, Gennady Estraikh, Kirsten Fermaglich, Linda Gordon, Martha Hodes, Marion Kaplan, Ellen Kellman, Alice Kessler-Harris, Andrew Needham, Vardit Ringvald, Eugene Sheppard, and Jonathan Sarna. Each has modeled careful scholarship, beautiful prose, and immense generosity, giving of their time and guidance. I feel especially lucky that along the way I have become able to call some friends as well as colleagues, and I hope I can live up to their examples.

Robert Cohn and Hasia Diner each deserve special recognition. Bob stands out as a perfect teacher and friend. He sparked my interest for learning early on when I studied with him at Lafayette College, and he continues to mentor and advise me to this day. The year I began my current position at Brooklyn College was the year Bob retired. "Legacy and all that," he pointed out. Bob has always been a ready source of encouragement, and I thank him for his continued friendship. Then, of course, there is Hasia. Few words can describe how much her direction has meant to me. As a mentor, her high standards and always constructive criticism helped sharpen my scholarship. Professionally, as with all of her students, she has always been extremely invested in my development and continues to be so. She extends opportunities at every turn and supports our cause beyond expectations. I will always remember the excitement that stayed with me for weeks after one of our first conversations during an early visit to NYU and the voicemail she left several months later, welcoming me to the program. It was a dream come true then, and just over a decade later, the chance to have gotten to know her and learn from her has surpassed all those early hopes.

In the years since, I have been fortunate to join the faculty of Brooklyn College. I cannot write enough about the kindness of my colleagues in the Judaic Studies Department—Sara Reguer, David Brodsky, Sharon Flatto, Robert Shapiro, and Beverly Bailis—as well as colleagues in other departments like Myles Bassell, Prudence Cumberbatch, George Cunningham, Louis Fishman, Lauren Mancia, Rona Miles, Brian Sowers, Karen Stern, and Jeanne Theoharis. They have all extended friendship and advice and made it a bit easier to settle in these first few years. To serve under a chair as fiercely loyal and supportive as Sara Reguer is also one of the great privileges that Brooklyn has given me. I thank David and Sharon too for their efforts to help deepen my understanding of Jewish funerary law and ritual. I have also learned a great deal from my students, whose questions and particular interests have helped provide nuance to and broaden my own thinking. Dr. Lawrence Tydings took particular interest in this project during a class he audited with me. Larry not only read several chapters but also volunteered and assisted with some concluding research. He never turned down a request, be it the genealogical legwork that I know he enjoyed or the pouring through reels of microfilm that I inflicted on him. I thank him for his help and encouragement.

At NYU Press, I would like to thank Jennifer Hammer and all of her colleagues who saw something of value in this work and helped immensely to develop it. Jennifer's eye for detail and insightful questions helped me refine the argument, strengthen the prose, and better realize the importance of many aspects of this story that I had long ago taken for granted. Her patience as I often struggled with deadlines has also meant more than she can know.

In a work that centers on family, I must, of course, thank my own. My parents, Dora Amanik and Oscar Amanik, and my brother, Phil

Amanik, have each given me so much to get to this point. I thank my mother especially. She always patiently listened as I worked through ideas, read every page that I sent her, and responded with encouraging and thoughtful feedback. She also knew that things would turn out well, "as only a mother can," and made sure to let me in on that secret when I was otherwise most doubtful. To my "New York families"—Beverly Bailis, Avi and Haskell Grosgold, and Bonnie and Seymour Bailis; and Sophia Gutherz, Marty Miller, Laura, Max, Seamus, and Clem, Alec Gutherz, Alyssa Keene, Celeste Conway, and Jeffrey McEachern—I can only say thank you as well. They have all opened up their homes, hearts, and lives to me, making New York a place where I could truly set down roots. Individually and collectively, they have all shown me how wonderful family can really be.

Finally, I dedicate this work to my grandparents, Frieda and Samuel Striks and Rita and David Amanik. Their experiences showed me from an early age the importance of history, motivating my commitment to preserve some part of it. On the day that my grandmother Frieda died, I rushed to her bedside to say good-bye and to muster the courage to tell her just how much of an inspiration she had been and would always continue to be to me. I have no way of knowing if she heard those words that morning, but I dedicate the ones in this book to her memory especially.

NOTES

INTRODUCTION

1 Ezekiel and Lichtenstein, *History of the Jews of Richmond*, 58–59; Bingham, *Mordecai*, 30 and 278. Samson's marriage is unclear. Although Bingham states that he "scandalized his family by marrying a Christian woman," earlier apologetic histories ignore or deny the marriage in damning certitude: "Unlike his father, he [Samson] had founded no family, for, quite unlike his Biblical namesake, he had married no wife" (Pool, *Portraits Etched in Stone*, 301).

2 For an excerpt of the Brooklyn Jewish Center cemetery promotion and the United Synagogue's broader marketing advice, see "Cemeteries," *Congregational Handbook*, May 1961, 1–5, United Synagogue of America Publications, I-485, box 1, folder, "Leaders Portfolio, 1957–1961 (Department of Synagogue Administration)."

3 Some examples include Seeman, *Death in the New World*, 241; "The Earliest Extant Minute Book of the Spanish and Portuguese Congregation Shearith Israel in New York, 1728–1786," *Publications of the American Jewish Historical Society (PAJHS)* 21 (1913): 67, 74–75; Marcus, *American Jewry*, 129, 184, and 186; Elzas, *Jews of South Carolina*, 152.

4 Quoted in Pool, *Portraits Etched in Stone*, 7.

5 For a detailed overview of historic issues of Jewish law involved as well as a recent example of their interpretation in American Jewish practice, see Rabbi Bergman, "A Matter of Grave Concern," 418–25.

6 For the varying motivations (including real and perceived threats to the dead) of African Americans, Muslim and Christian Arabs, Indians, Chinese, Jews, and Polish Catholics (to name a few cases), see Allan Amanik and Kami Fletcher, eds., *Till Death Do Us Part: American Ethnic Cemeteries as Borders Uncrossed* (Jackson: University Press of Mississippi, forthcoming 2020).

7 Foote, *Black and White Manhattan*, 141–42, 146; Swan, *New Amsterdam Gehenna*.

8 Roediger, "And Die in Dixie," 163–83; a sample will of Mordecai Gomez (1750) is quoted in Rock, *Haven of Liberty*, 55–56.

9 "History," Hebrew Free Burial Association, accessed January 7, 2019, www .hebrewfreeburial.org.

10 Amanik, "'All Will Be Fine,'" 102–4.

11 *Asmonean*, September 21, 1855, 177.

12 Clipping from unidentified Yiddish newspaper, October 16, 1928, Louis Diamond Collection, RG 1364, box 2, folder 7.

13 Glazer, *American Judaism*, 19; See also Grinstein, *Rise of the Jewish Community*, 18; Sherman, *Jew within American Society*, 155–57; Goren, "Traditional Institutions Transplanted," 65; Barkai, *Branching Out*, 99; Diner, *Jews of the United States*, 36; Sarna, *American Judaism*, 10; Seeman, *Death in the New World*, 240.

14 Swichkow and Gartner, *History of the Jews of Milwaukee*, 33–34; Wolf and Whiteman, *History of the Jews of Philadelphia*, 24; Diner, *Time for Gathering*, 94; Vorspan and Gartner, *History of the Jews of Los Angeles*, 20–21; Weissbach, *Jewish Life in Small-Town America*.

15 Gorer, "Pornography of Death," 49–52; Mitford, *American Way of Death*; Kübler-Ross, *On Death and Dying*; Bowman, *American Funeral*; Feifel, *Meaning of Death*; Glaser and Strauss, *Awareness of Dying*; Quint, *Nurse and the Dying Patient*; Sudnow, *Passing On*.

16 Farrell, *Inventing the American Way of Death*, 4; Habenstein and Lamers, *History of American Funeral Directing*; Sloane, *Last Great Necessity*; Laderman, *Sacred Remains*; Laderman, *Rest in Peace*.

17 Field, Hockey, and Small, *Death, Gender and Ethnicity*; Isenberg and Burstein, *Mortal Remains*; de Chaparro, *Death and Dying in New Mexico*, xvii.

18 Seeman, *Death in the New World*.

19 Schantz, *Awaiting the Heavenly Country*.

20 Faust, *This Republic of Suffering*, 268.

21 Smith, *To Serve the Living*.

22 Abel, *Inevitable Hour*.

CHAPTER 1

1 Pool, *Portraits Etched in Stone*, 92–93.

2 Noah L. Gelfand, "A Transatlantic Approach to Understanding the Formation of a Jewish Community in New Netherland and New York," *New York History* 89, no. 4 (2008): 376–77; Jonathan Israel, "Curaçao, Amsterdam, and the Rise of the Sephardi Trade System in the Caribbean, 1630–1700," in *The Jews in the Caribbean*, ed. Jane S. Gerber (Portland, OR: Littman Library of Jewish Civilization, 2014), 33–38.

3 Rock, *Haven of Liberty*, 10–17; Faber, *Time for Planting*, 33.

4 Quoted in Pool, *Portraits Etched in Stone*, 7; Rock, *Haven of Liberty*, 8.

5 Jacobs, *Colony of New Netherland*, 200–201.

6 Quoted in Pool, *Portraits Etched in Stone*, 7.

7 Inskeep, *Graveyard Shift*, 146–47; Jacobs, *Colony of New Netherland*, 234.

8 Church marriage and baptismal records from as early as 1639 list foreign Protestant bridegrooms and congregation members from across Europe. Goodfriend, "Foreigners in a Dutch Colonial City," 243–44.

9 Goodfriend, "Practicing Toleration," 101; and Goodfriend, "Foreigners in a Dutch Colonial City," 250–52.

10 See Kreider, *Lutheranism in Colonial New York*, 21–25; Maynard, *Huguenot Church of New York*, 11 and 74; Cox, *Quakerism in the City of New York*, 28.

11 In 1674, Hendrick Rooseboom, official gravedigger and *aanspreker* in Willemstadt [later Albany], complained that Lutherans buried independently and assigned their own gravedigger. Authorities accepted Rooseboom's protest and reiterated his exclusive oversight. Jacobs, *Colony of New Netherland*, 234.

12 Kreider, *Lutheranism in Colonial New York*, 29.

13 Augustine, "Catholic Cemeteries of New York," 370; O'Brien, *In Old New York*, 3.

14 Goodfriend, "Practicing Toleration," 105.

15 Oppenheim, "Jewish Burial Ground on New Bowery," 81; Pool, *Portraits Etched in Stone*, 11.

16 Hershkowitz, "Some Aspects of the New York Jewish Merchant," 10; Pencak, *Jews and Gentiles in Early America*, 2; Butler, *Becoming America*, 26; Rock, *Haven of Liberty*, 93.

17 Translated in Pool, *Portraits Etched in Stone*, 188.

18 Kohler, "Civil Status of the Jews," 101–4.

19 Pool, *Portraits Etched in Stone*, 13–15; "The Earliest Extant Minute Book of the Spanish and Portuguese Congregation Shearith Israel in New York, 1728–1786," *PAJHS* 21 (1913): 8.

20 On Jews listed among freemen, see Kohler, "Civil Status of the Jews," 101; on title issues see Oppenheim, "Jewish Burial Ground on New Bowery," 99–100.

21 See wills 17 and 31 in Hershkowitz, *Wills of Early New York Jews*, 51, 69, and 151. See also similar sentiments among Jewish women like Rachel Luis, quoted in Seeman, *Death in the New World*, 237; Nunez, Bueno, and Mordecai Gomez are quoted in Rock, *Haven of Liberty*, 55–56.

22 Pool, *Portraits Etched in Stone*, 14.

23 Hershkowitz, "Some Aspects of the New York Jewish Merchant," 10; Pencak, *Jews and Gentiles in Early America*, 2; Butler, *Becoming America*, 26; Rock, *Haven of Liberty*, 93.

24 Snyder, "Rethinking the Definition of 'Community,'" 9.

25 Pool, *Portraits Etched in Stone*, 87.

26 See, for instance, Snyder, "Rethinking the Definition of 'Community,'" 16–17; Judson, *Pennies for Heaven*, 50–51.

27 Snyder, "Rethinking the Definition of 'Community,'" 16–17.

28 See minutes entries for August 7, 1737, and April 16, 1747, in "The Earliest Extant Minute Book," 36–37 and 52; Judson, *Pennies for Heaven*, 20–22; Rock, *Haven of Liberty*, 50–51.

29 See entries for April 10, 1752, and September 14, 1757, in "The Earliest Extant Minute Book," 66–67 and 74–75.

30 See minutes for March 22, 1758, in ibid., 75–76.

31 Pool, *Portraits Etched in Stone*, 407; Bernice Brandmark, Study of Wills in New York City Collection, P-833, box 1, folder 3, "1800–1850 Statistical Charts Paper and Presentation."

32 Quoted in Daniels, "Colonial Jewry," 395.

33 On the case, see Faber, *Time for Planting*, 120; and Marcus, *American Jewry*, 123–24. New York leaders in Philadelphia included Isaac Moses, Benjamin Seixas, Jonas Phillips, Hayman Levy, Matthew Josephson, and Gershom Mendes Seixas. They played a hand in founding the city's congregation, Mikve Israel, and wrote its bylaws. Rock, *Haven of Liberty*, 85.

34 Pool, *Portraits Etched in Stone*, 325.

35 Since Shearith Israel trustees were unwilling to convert Foster, he requested that they at least write a letter of introduction to Amsterdam's Jewish community on his behalf that he might pursue a conversion there. See "Letter of James Foster to Trustees of KKSI," June 5, 5548 [1788], *PAJHS* 27 (1920): 44.

36 Marcus, *American Jewry*, 156–58, 160–61.

37 Faber, *Time for Planting*, 121.

38 Rock, *Haven of Liberty*, 62–63.

39 Ibid.

40 Stern, "Function of Genealogy," 95.

41 See entries for Asher Levy and Mary Thompson (1782) in the Trinity Churchyard and Parish registers of baptisms, marriages, and burials at "Genealogy: Digital Churchyards & Registers," Trinity Church, accessed November 27, 2017, www.trinitywallstreet.org; Grinstein, *Rise of the Jewish Community*, 382; Marcus, *United States Jewry*, 137–38; Rosenbloom, *Biographical Dictionary*, 58.

42 Although Hart and Brett separated soon after, Hart supported their son, Henry, for the rest of his life. Stern, "Function of Genealogy," 92, 94; Marcus, *United States Jewry*, 606.

43 Wolf and Whiteman, *History of the Jews of Philadelphia*, 128–31.

44 On the Levy Family, see the Find A Grave database and images by Dawn-Marie Williams (contributor 47540447), accessed November 28, 2017, www.findagrave.com: Samson Levy (August 19, 1722–March 22, 1781), memorial no. 89397906; Henrietta Levy (October 1768–September 13, 1780), memorial no. 89398436; Martha Lampley Levy (July 24, 1730–March 24, 1807), memorial no. 89398049; Rachel Levy (unknown–December 28, 1862), memorial no. 88381651; Moses Levy (unknown–May 9, 1826), memorial no. 89396448; and Arabella Levy Jones (1760–December 17, 1830), memorial no. 87122424. All are buried in Saint Peter's Episcopal Churchyard, Philadelphia, PA. For Polly's obituary, see *Pennsylvania Gazette*, August 24, 1774, 3.

45 Stern, *David Franks*.

46 Find a Grave database and images by T.V.F.T.H. (contributor 46496806), accessed June 5, 2019, www.findagrave.com: Jacob "Old Hays" Hays (May 13, 1772–June 20, 1850), memorial no. 78205427.

47 Ezekiel and Lichtenstein, *History of the Jews of Richmond*, 58–59; Bingham, *Mordecai*, 30 and 278; Pool, *Portraits Etched in Stone*, 301.

48 Grinstein, *Rise of the Jewish Community*, 375.

49 See Jane Nathan (biography 129) in Pool, *Portraits Etched in Stone*, 422–23.

50 Stern, "Function of Genealogy," 93.

51 See appendix 2, "Converts to Judaism through Marriage before 1840," in Stern, "Function of Genealogy," 92–93.

52 Wolf and Whiteman, *History of the Jews of Philadelphia*, 129 and 131; Reznikoff and Engelman, *Jews of Charleston*, 152.

53 Grinstein, *Rise of the Jewish Community*, 320–21.

54 Faber, *Time for Planting*, 93. The proportion increased over time. Whereas in the eighteenth century only 10 to 15 percent of Jews married out, by the period between 1776 and 1840, 201 of 699 marriages involving Jews in early America—or 28.7 percent—took place between Jews and non-Jews. R. Cohen, "Jewish Demography in the Eighteenth Century," 112; Stern, "Jewish Marriage and Intermarriage," 142–43.

55 Over a period from 1775 until 1824, 54.3 percent of young Jewish men and 41.5 percent of young Jewish women of marrying age remained single into adulthood. See table 6.7 in R. Cohen, "Jewish Demography in the Eighteenth Century," 108.

56 Pencak, *Jews and Gentiles* in Early America, 48.

57 Grinstein, *Rise of the Jewish Community*, 584.

58 Stern, *First American Jewish Families*, 139.

59 On Shearith Israel's resolution, see Pool, *Portraits Etched in Stone*, 88. On Mikve Israel, see minutes for September 3, 1792, and May 7, 1793, printed in Marcus, *American Jewry*, 185–87.

60 Quoted in Pool, *Portraits Etched in Stone*, 92.

61 Grinstein, *Rise of the Jewish Community*, 321.

62 This quote is from an 1829 letter of protest by congregants to Shearith Israel trustees upon news that the leaders were considering a request for families to be buried together, quoted in Pool, *Portraits Etched in Stone*, 87.

63 The congregation clustered Aron Haim Welcome (1806); Joseph d'Aguilar (1807) of Jamaica, who died a year later and was buried just after Welcome; and another "foreigner," Moses Capadocia (1809). See biographies in Pool, *Portraits Etched in Stone*, 302, 307, and 314; and Pool, "Chart of Burials in the Chatham Square Cemetery," in *Portraits Etched in Stone*, 183.

64 Clustered in the corner of the Twenty-First Street graveyard are four graves belonging to N. G. Grafton (February 24, 1831), Isaac Freitman (March 12, 1837), a "stranger drowned," and a Mr. A. Benjamin (October 29, 1832). See a diagram of the Twenty-First Street grounds in Pool, *Portraits Etched in Stone*, 136–37; Grafton and Freitman's dates of death coincide with references in minutes to suicides cited in Pool and Pool, *Old Faith*, 307. See also the corresponding entries in the listing of deaths on record at the congregation and their places of burial for Freitman, listed as suicide, and for John and Raphael Hart in chart 9, "Shearith Israel Death Records, 1800–50," Bernice Brandmark, Study of Wills in New York City Collection, P-833, box 1, folder 3, "Statistics and Paper." The Hart brothers committed suicide in their Nassau Street lodgings. See Rock, *Haven of Liberty*, 98.

65 Pool, *Portraits Etched in Stone*, 327–28.

66 Pool, *Portraits Etched in Stone*, 271; Oppenheim, "Jews Who Died of Yellow Fever," 108; Rock, *Haven of Liberty*, 97.

67 Pool, *Portraits Etched in Stone*, 120.

68 The grounds on Eleventh Street were actually the third that the congregation acquired. Briefly in 1802, it had established a new cemetery on Thirteenth Street, again for the purpose of burying "any in our congregation who may die of Pestilential disorders," but only one man, Wolfe Pollock, who died of yellow fever in 1803, was buried there. Shortly thereafter, the city opened the street for development, forcing Shearith Israel to abandon that land for a new yard. When the congregation purchased and dedicated a new piece of land on Eleventh Street in 1805, it moved Pollock's grave there (Pool, *Portraits Etched in Stone*, 122).

69 Ibid., 124.

70 Minutes for October 27, 1770, "Minute Book of the Spanish and Portuguese Congregation Shearith Israel in New York, 1760–1786," *PAJHS* 21 (1913): 108.

71 Gomez served as the president in 1757 and again in 1762. Hershkowitz, *Wills of Early New York Jews*, 129.

72 Pool, *Portraits Etched in Stone*, 84; "Minute Book of the Spanish and Portuguese Congregation Shearith Israel in New York, 1760–1786," *PAJHS* 21 (1913): 132.

73 Quoted in Pool, *Portraits Etched in Stone*, 85.

74 Quoted in ibid., 85.

75 Ibid., 86.

76 Mintz and Kellogg, *Domestic Revolutions*, 20–23, 45–46, 58; Eustace, *Passion Is the Gale*; Hemphill, *Siblings*, 5–8.

77 Hershkowitz, "Some Aspects of the New York Jewish Merchant," 10.

78 Quoted in Faber, *Time for Planting*, 46.

79 Quoted in Pool, *Portraits Etched in Stone*, 87.

80 Minutes for March 21, 1830, quoted in Pool and Pool, *Old Faith*, 278.

81 Pool, *Portraits Etched in Stone*, 137.

82 Pool and Pool, *Old Faith*, 309.

83 Mikve Israel's Spruce Street yard in Philadelphia, for instance, originated in Nathan Levy's purchase in order to bury a child in 1740 and was intended as a family lot (Faber, *Time for Planting*, 39). Similarly, Jews in Easton, PA, were buried in what was originally Michael Hart's family graveyard. James Oglethorpe had granted Savannah's first Jewish settlers a burial plot in 1733, but within decades, Mordecai Sheftall turned over his family's burial plot for communal use (Marcus, *United States Jewry*, 244–45).

84 The Sheftalls in Savannah, for instance, enjoyed private grounds at least as late as 1773, when they turned over the land to the community (Marcus, *United States Jewry*, 244). Philadelphia's Mikveh Israel passed a motion in 1813 dedicating a "strip of ground" around the graves of the prominent patriarch of the Gratz family, Michael Gratz, and his wife, which would be "reserved for the exclusive burial of members of that family." Quoted in Elmaleh and Samuel, *Jewish Cemetery*, 9.

85 Brick Presbyterian Church offered family vaults for sale as early as 1760, when it opened its new Beekman Street church. By 1817, at least thirteen family vaults existed. See Sloane, *Last Great Necessity*, 22–23; Goodfriend, "Social Dimensions," 260; Pool, *Portraits Etched in Stone*, 84.

86 Pool and Pool, *Old Faith*, 309.

87 Quoted in ibid.

88 Quoted in Rock, *Haven of Liberty*, 133.

89 Brandly Isaacs died February 16, 1825; her grandchildren included Joshua Hendriks (biography 69), Frances Henrietta Hendricks (biography 99), and Justina Brandly Hendriks (biography 130). Her husband, Joshua Isaacs (biography 75), died February 17, 1810. For information on all, see Pool, *Portraits Etched in Stone*, 424, 311, 378, 423, and 317, respectively.

90 For Moses Gomez (biography 132) and Benjamin Gomez (biography 135), see Pool, *Portraits Etched in Stone*, 425 and 432.

91 For Grace Nathan (biography 139), see ibid., 438–41.

92 Ibid., 426 and 437.

CHAPTER 2

1 Shearith Israel, "Hebra Hased Va Amet," *Centennial Anniversary Hebra Hased Va Amet of the Congregation Shearith Israel, March 23, 1902*, 1, Congregation Shearith Israel (New York) Records, undated, 1755–1996 (hereafter Congregation Shearith Israel Records), I-4, box 2, folder 1, "Items pertaining to the *Hebra Hased Va Amet*."

2 Trattner, *From Poor Law to Welfare State*, 36.

3 Grinstein, *Rise of the Jewish Community*, 104.

4 Wolf and Whiteman, *History of the Jews of Philadelphia*, 266.

5 Hershkowitz and Meyer, *Letters of the Franks Family*, 57.

6 Seeman, *Death in the New World*, 237.

7 Blau and Baron, *Jews of the United States*, 2:506–9.

8 Communication from Rebecca Gratz, Philadelphia, Pennsylvania, to Maria Gist Gratz, Lexington, Kentucky, July 23, 1826, Gratz Family of Philadelphia Papers, P-8, box 4, folder 5, "Rebecca Gratz (1781–1869) to Maria Gist Gratz (1797–1841), Letters 1825–31."

9 Seeman, *Death in the New World*, 236; Wolf and Whiteman, *History of the Jews of Philadelphia*, 266; Marcus, *Communal Sick-Care*.

10 On hebra members, see "From the Notebooks of Rev. J. J. Lyons Transcribed from Various Sources, Items Relating to Congregation Shearith Israel, New York," *PAJHS* 27 (1920): 253. For a list of trustees, see "From the 2nd Volume of Minute Books of the Congn: Shearith Israel in New York," *PAJHS* 21 (1913): 167–68. On the synagogue presidents, elders, and other officers, see Naphtali Phillips, "Sketch," *PAJHS* 21 (1913): 211–15.

11 Pool, *Portraits Etched in Stone*, 98.

12 Ibid., 87.

13 Quoted in ibid., 98 and 91.

14 Rock, *Haven of Liberty*, 89–90.

15 Jacques Judah Lyons, "Substance of Memorandum as to the Hebra Gemilut Hasa-dim," *PAJHS* 27 (1920): 254; Pool, *Portraits Etched in Stone*, 100.

16 Lyons, "Substance of Memorandum as to the Hebra Gemilut Hasadim," 254.

17 Ibid., 252.

18 Trattner, *From Poor Law to Welfare State*, 35.

19 Ibid., 31–36.

20 Soyer, *Jewish Immigrant Aid Associations*, 29–48.

21 Pool, *Portraits Etched in Stone*, 269.

22 Marcus, "Handsome Young Priest in the Black Gown," 415–17.

23 Quoted in "Summary of Account by Rev. J. J. Lyons concerning the 'Society Mattan Basether,'" *PAJHS* 27 (1920): 256.

24 Ibid.

25 On recorded deaths, see a chronological register compiled in Pool, *Portraits Etched in Stone*, 496–500. See also the original list in "Chronological Register," undated, Congregation Shearith Israel Records, I-4, box 2, folder 6, "Cemetery."

26 Grinstein, *Rise of the Jewish Community*, 105; Congregation Shearith Israel, *Constitution of the Congregation of [Shearith Israel] as Ratified by the Members Thereof, at a Meeting Held on the Twenty-Sixth Day of [Sivan] Corresponding with the 24th of June, 1805* (New York: G. and R. Waite, 1805), Article 8, p. 7.

27 Pool, *Portraits Etched in Stone*, 103–4.

28 Grinstein, *Rise of the Jewish Community*, 152.

29 Ibid., 106.

30 Ibid.

31 For the most recent treatment of Seixas and his Jeffersonian inclinations, see Rock, *Haven of Liberty*, 137–41. Quote appears on p. 137.

32 "Naphtali Phillips," *PAJHS* 21 (1913): 172–74.

33 Rosenbloom, "Naphtali Judah," in *Biographical Dictionary*, 80; Grinstein, *Rise of the Jewish Community*, 103 and 551n18.

34 Grinstein, *Rise of the Jewish Community*, 103.

35 See "A Bill Declaratory of Rights Pertaining to the Members of this Institution," article 1, in a handwritten *Constitution of Hebra Hased Va-Amet* (New York: s.n., 1812), Congregation Shearith Israel Records, I-4, box 2, folder 2, "Second Constitution of the Hebra Hased Va Amet."

36 See "A Bill Declaratory of Rights Pertaining to the Members of this Institution," article 5, ibid.

37 See "Rules and Regulations," articles 8 and 9, and "Fines," article 22, ibid.

38 Soyer, *Jewish Immigrant Aid Associations*, 18.

39 On membership and constitutional amendments, see articles 8 and 11, respectively, in handwritten *Constitution of Hebra Hased Va-Amet* (New York: s.n., 1812), Congregation Shearith Israel Records, I-4, box 2, folder 2, "Second Constitution of the Hebra Hased Va Amet."

40 Marcus, *American Jewry*, 150.

41 Rock, *Haven of Liberty*, 113–14.

42 Hebra Hased Va-Amet and Congregation Shearith Israel, *Compendium of the Order of the Burial Service.*

43 *The Form of Daily Prayers, According to the Custom of the Spanish and Portuguese Jews as Read in Their Synagogues and Used in Their Families* (New York: S. H. Jackson, at the Hebrew and English Printing Office, 1826).

44 Hebra Hased Va-Amet and Congregation Shearith Israel, "Of the *keri`ah*, Rending of Garments," *Compendium of the Order of the Burial Service*, 3.

45 Hebra Hased Va-Amet and Congregation Shearith Israel, "Of the Day on Which the Death Takes Place (and Previous to the Funeral) [Onan]," *Compendium of the Order of the Burial Service*, 4.

46 Ibid.

47 Hebra Hased Va-Amet and Congregation Shearith Israel, "Of Things Forbidden to Mourners," *Compendium of the Order of the Burial Service*, 8.

48 See Hebra Hased Va-Amet and Congregation Shearith Israel, "Rihitsath Hameth [Washing the Dead]," in the Hebrew portion of *Compendium of the Order of the Burial Service*, 5–10.

49 Isaac Jalfon, *Order of Ceremonies and Laws of the Society "Mikveh Israel": Or Institution for Preparing for Interment the Deceased Members of the Spanish and Portuguese Jews' Congregation, London* (London: S. Meldola, 1845), 14–24.

50 Appleby, "Thomas Jefferson," 156.

51 Grinstein, *Rise of the Jewish Community*, 314.

52 Pool, *Portraits Etched in Stone*, 95; Pool and Pool, *Old Faith*, 302.

53 The Author of Dreams and Their Interpretation, "Jewish Burial Rites," *Good Words* 11 (August 1870): 566.

54 Kaplan, *Making of the Jewish Middle Class*, 194.

55 Soyer, *Jewish Immigrant Aid Associations*, 21.

56 Hebra Hased Va-Amet, "To the Ladies of the Jewish Persuasion," March 15, 1830, Jacques Judah Lyons Collection, P-15, box 3, folder 190.

57 See committee report on the follow-up of the effort by Isaac B. Seixas, June 23, 1830, Jacques Judah Lyons Collection, P-15, box 3, folder 190.

58 Grinstein, *Rise of the Jewish Community*, 152 and 554n33. See also a brief description of the group in Pool and Pool, *Old Faith*, 366–67.

59 "Preamble," *Constitution and Bylaws of Hevrath Nashim Hased Vaamet: Ladies Benevolent Society of the Congregation Bnai Jeshurun, for Visiting the Sick, Comforting the Dying, and Burrying the Dead* (New York: M. Jackson, 1843), 5; "Lyons Collection—Manuscripts Memo of MSS and Articles Deposited in the Cornerstone of 19th St. Synagogue of KKSI 1859," Jacques Judah Lyons Collection, P-15, box 3, folder 220.

60 Ibid., article 1, p. 5.

61 Ibid., article 5, section 1, p. 9.

62 Ibid., article 5, section 3, p. 10.

63 Ibid., article 4, section 4, p. 8.

64 Ibid., article 5, sections 2 and 3, p. 10.

65 Polland and Soyer, *Emerging Metropolis*, 13; see also appendix 1, "The Jewish Population of New York City," in Grinstein, *Rise of the Jewish Community*, 469.

66 See appendix 2, "New York Synagogues Established Prior to 1860," in Grinstein, *Rise of the Jewish Community*, 472–74.

67 Goldstein, *Century of Judaism*, 78.

68 Quoted in Pool, *Portraits Etched in Stone*, 91.

69 Quoted in ibid.

70 S. Cohen, *Shaaray Tefila*, 5–9.

71 Benjamin, *Three Years in America*, 67–69; On Emanu-El, see Stern, *Rise and Progress of Reform Judaism*, 20.

72 Grinstein, *Rise of the Jewish Community*, 106.

73 Ibid., 107–8.

74 Polland and Soyer, *Emerging Metropolis*, 26–27; Grinstein, *Rise of the Jewish Community*, 106–7.

75 Society charter, April 30, 1844, quoted in Weingart and Marks, *Three-Quarters of a Century*, 5–6.

76 Polland and Soyer, *Emerging Metropolis*, 32–33.

77 Kaganoff, "Organized Jewish Welfare," 29.

78 Grinstein, *Rise of the Jewish Community*, 108–9.

79 Grusd, *B'nai B'rith*, 27; Moore, *B'nai B'rith*, 6–15.

80 Grinstein, *Rise of the Jewish Community*, 110; Polland and Soyer, *Emerging Metropolis*, 33–35.

81 "History of the Noah Benevolent, Widows' and Orphans' Association," *Golden Jubilee: History of the Noah Benevolent, Widows' and Orphans' Association* (New York: s.n., 1899), 7, Noah Benevolent Society Records, I-186, box 17, folder 2, "Noah B. S.-Anniversary Journals-(50th–125th)"; Grinstein, *Rise of the Jewish Community*, 112–15.

82 Polland and Soyer, *Emerging Metropolis*, 35.

83 "Burial of the Dead," *Jewish Messenger*, February 8, 1861, 44.

84 Moore, *B'nai B'rith*, 10.

CHAPTER 3

1 "Salem Fields Cemetery, Family Burial Lots," *Asmonean*, January 25, 1852, 124.

2 Preamble of handwritten rules and regulations for Beth Olom Cemetery in trustee minutes, December 18, 1852, Board of Trustees' Bound Minutes Volume, 1840–52, Congregation B'nai Jeshurun (New York) Records (hereafter B'nai Jeshurun Records).

3 "A Cemetery Broken Up," *New York Daily Tribune*, September 18, 1850, quoted in Schuyler, *New Urban Landscape*, 39.

4 Inskeep, *Graveyard Shift*, 3.

5   St. Patrick's Cathedral established Calvary Cemetery in 1846 as the first major cemetery beyond Manhattan. For institutional information, see "Welcome," Calvary Cemetery, accessed June 6, 2013, www.calvarycemeteryqueens.com. St. Paul's German Lutheran Church purchased 225 acres in 1852 in Middle Village, Queens, for ground first known as the Lutheran Cemetery. It later took the name All Faiths Cemetery; see its website, accessed June 6, 2013, http://allfaithscemetery .org. On the Evergreens, see Rousmaniere and Druse, *Green Oasis in Brooklyn*, and "The Evergreens Cemetery," Evergreens Cemetery, accessed June 6, 2013, www.theevergreenscemetery.com.

6   Cypress Hills Cemetery, *Cypress Hills Cemetery*, 6.

7   Schuyler, *New Urban Landscape*, 39.

8   The Methodist Episcopal Church began a two-year project in 1854 to disinter graves from its Allen Street churchyard and move them to a tract it purchased in Cypress Hills after the Common Council banned all city burials in 1852 (Inskeep, *Graveyard Shift*, 5–6).

9   *Cypress Hills Cemetery Catalogue of Proprietors*, 12.

10 Kraska, *History of Cypress Hills Cemetery*, 4.

11 Rousmaniere and Druse, *Green Oasis in Brooklyn*, 45.

12 Robert Lyon, "Rural Cemeteries," *Asmonean*, April 25, 1851, 4.

13 Ibid.; emphasis in original.

14 "The New York Hebrew Cemetery," *Asmonean*, May 16, 1851, 28; emphasis in original.

15 Robert Lyon, "The Unity of Judaism," *Asmonean*, November 8, 1849, 4, quoted in Reed, "Unity, Not Absorption," 93.

16 Robert Lyon, "Rural Cemeteries," *Asmonean*, April 25, 1851, 4.

17 Weingart and Marks, *Three-Quarters of a Century*, 5–6.

18 Felix M. Rosenstock, "Five Years of Progress, 1924–1929," *80th Anniversary Souvenir Journal: Banquet and Reception Noah Benevolent Society* (New York: s.n., 1929), 27–28, Noah Benevolent Society Records, I-186, box 17, bound volume anniversary journals; and "History of the Noah Benevolent, Widows' and Orphans' Association," *Golden Jubilee: History of the Noah Benevolent, Widows' and Orphans' Association* (New York: s.n., 1899), 7, Noah Benevolent Society Records, I-186, box 17, folder 2, "Noah B. S.-Anniversary Journals-(50th–125th)."

19 Rosenstock, "Five Years of Progress," 27, Noah Benevolent Society Records, I-186, box 17, bound volume anniversary journals.

20 Henry J. Hyman, "The Why and Wherefore of the Independent Order Free Sons of Israel," *Independent Order Free Sons of Israel, Diamond Jubilee 1849–1924* (New York: s.n., 1924), Independent Order Free Sons of Israel Collection, I-368, box 1, folder 1, "Independent Order of the Free Sons of Israel, Anniversary Journal (1849–1924)."

21 Other lodges of the Free Sons of Israel included Ruben Lodge 3, Aryeh Lodge 5, or Isaacher Lodge 7. "List of Lot Holders in the Cypress Hills Cemetery," *Cypress Hills Cemetery*, 69.

22 Sloane, *Last Great Necessity*, 75–83; Sachs, "American Arcadia," 213.

23 On churches, see Kraska, *History of Cypress Hills Cemetery*, 4; Independent Order of Odd Fellows (IOOF) lodges included Pilgrim and Sincerity lodges. See "List of Lot Holders in the Cypress Hills Cemetery," *Cypress Hills Cemetery Catalogue of Proprietors*, 69.

24 Kraska, *History of Cypress Hills Cemetery*, 4; and "List of Lot Holders in the Cypress Hills Cemetery," in *Cypress Hills Cemetery*, 69; Inskeep, *Graveyard Shift*, 39–40.

25 *Cypress Hills Cemetery*, 12.

26 Stern, *Rise and Progress of Reform Judaism*, 32.

27 Fernbach had also designed Central Synagogue's new house of worship in 1872 and was then at work on the massive Stern Brothers department store on Twenty-Third Street. See Polland and Soyer, *Emerging Metropolis*, 74–75, 207.

28 "Salem Fields Cemetery: Dedication Services at the Jewish Cemetery Yesterday," *New York Times*, September 3, 1877, 8.

29 Stern, *Rise and Progress of Reform Judaism*, 32.

30 "Family Burial Lots," *Asmonean*, December 12, 1851, 77. The ad appeared every week for the next year until May, when the introductory rate expired.

31 Preamble of handwritten rules and regulations for Beth Olom Cemetery in trustee minutes, December 15, 1852, B'nai Jeshurun Records, Board of Trustees' Bound Minutes Volume, 1840–54, Reprinted in "The Beth Olom Cemetery," *Asmonean*, May 6, 1853, 25.

32 See, for instance, "Deed for Cemetery Lot 807," April 1, 1853, Goldstein Family Papers, P-259. See also "Certificate No. 11, Section 20 Lot 1: To John Levy, June 1, 1854," B'nai Jeshurun Records, box 36, folder 6, "Beth Olom Cemetery Documents, 1851–1884."

33 Judson, *Pennies for Heaven*, 38–40.

34 "Salem Fields Cemetery, Family Burial Lots," *Asmonean*, January 25, 1852, 124.

35 See early Emanu-El rates in ibid.; article 4 of handwritten rules and regulations for Beth Olom Cemetery in trustee minutes, December 15, 1852, B'nai Jeshurun Records, Board of Trustees' Bound Minutes Volume, 1840–54; "Deed for Cemetery Lot 807," April 1, 1853, Goldstein Family Papers, P-259; "Memorandum of Agreement," April 12, 1860, Records of Brothers in Unity (Bruder Verein #1), RG 1634, box 5, folder 14, "Documents of Bruderverein, 1850s."

36 Grinstein, *Rise of the Jewish Community*, 317–18.

37 See the minutes entry dated May 4, 1851, on assigning a committee "to purchase ground for a beth haim [written in Hebrew script]" near Cypress Hills. Compare this to later entries including August 12 or November 29, 1851, that refer to those holdings as a *burial ground*. Later in the year, minute bookkeepers began to make a distinction, reserving traditional terms for the city graveyard and employing *cemetery* for the congregation's Long Island holdings. See, for instance, entries on December 8, 1852, or December 12, 1852. All entries in B'nai Jeshurun Records, Board of Trustees' Bound Minutes Volume, 1840–54.

38 See entries for May 4, 1851, on p. 15, and September 19, 1851, on p. 68, B'nai Jeshurun Records, Board of Trustees' Bound Minutes Volume, 1850–52 / Letter Book, 1825–51.

39 Article 2, handwritten rules and regulations for Beth Olom Cemetery in trustee minutes, December 15, 1852, B'nai Jeshurun Records, Board of Trustees' Bound Minutes Volume, 1840–54.

40 "Family Plots Again," *American Israelite*, July 25, 1856, 21.

41 Ibid.; original text of preamble also found in handwritten rules and regulations for Beth Olom Cemetery in trustee minutes, December 15, 1852, B'nai Jeshurun Records, Board of Trustees' Bound Minutes Volume, 1840–54.

42 "Family Plots Again," *American Israelite*, July 25, 1856, 21.

43 Ibid.

44 "The Beth Olom Cemetery," *Asmonean*, May 6, 1853, 25.

45 Ibid.

46 "Resolutions by the Trustees, April 27, 5612 [1852]," *Constitution of the Congregation Shearith Israel* (New York: T. B. Harrison, 1865), 22. Soble Rare Book Collection, Soble 17.

47 "Resolutions by the Trustees, April 27, 5612 [1852]," *Constitution of the Congregation Shearith Israel* (New York: T. B. Harrison, 1865), 23. Soble Rare Book Collection, Soble 17.

48 "The Beth Olom Cemetery," *Asmonean*, May 6, 1853, 25; article 5, section 11, handwritten rules and regulations for Beth Olom Cemetery in trustee minutes, December 15, 1852, B'nai Jeshurun Records, Board of Trustees' Bound Minutes Volume, 1840–54.

49 "Resolutions by the Trustees, April 27, 5612 [1852]," *Constitution of the Congregation Shearith Israel* (New York: T. B. Harrison, 1865), 22. Soble Rare Book Collection, Soble 17; article 5, section 1, handwritten rules and regulations for Beth Olom Cemetery in trustee minutes, December 15, 1852, B'nai Jeshurun Records, Board of Trustees' Bound Minutes Volume, 1840–54; and appendix 8, "On the Removal of Bodies, Care of the Cemeteries and Related Subjects," section C, "Sale of Private Cemetery Plots and Related Material from the Minutes of Anshe Chesed," reprinted in Grinstein, *Rise of the Jewish Community*, 500.

50 On the case in general, see appendix 8, "On the Removal of Bodies, Care of the Cemeteries and Related Subjects," section B, "Extracts from the Minutes of Congregation Anshe Chesed on the Dittenhoeffer Removal Case," reprinted in Grinstein, *Rise of the Jewish Community*, 499–500.

51 Dr. L. Merzbacher, "The Mystery of the Law," *Asmonean*, January 9, 1852, 110.

52 Simeon Abrahams, "The Mystery of the Law: Replies" *Asmonean*, January 16, 1852, 117.

53 Emanuel Goldstein, "The Mystery of the Law: Replies," *Asmonean*, January 16, 1852, 116.

54 A. Rice, "The Mystery of the Law: Replies," *Asmonean*, January 16, 1852, 116; emphasis in original.

55 Dr. L. Merzbacher, "The Mystery of the Law II," *Asmonean*, January 30, 1852, 132.

56 Ibid.

57 Inskeep, *Graveyard Shift*, 5–6, 25.

58 Barnett Abraham Elzas reply, quoted in Grinstein, *Rise of the Jewish Community*, 328.

59 See May 3, 1856, and May 30, 1858, entries in appendix 8, "On the Removal of Bodies, Care of the Cemeteries and Related Subjects," section A, "Excerpts from the Minutes of Congregation Anshe Chesed," reprinted in Grinstein, *Rise of the Jewish Community*, 497–98.

60 The paper reprinted the letter of permission from the city inspector's department to B'nai Jeshurun in *Asmonean*, April 1, 1853, 282. A copy of the petition to the Common Council (March 11, 1853) is entered in the minutes entry for April 18, 1853, B'nai Jeshurun Records, Board of Trustees' Bound Minutes Volume, 1840–54.

61 A Jew [pseud.], "Is the Tomb Inviolate? No. II," *Asmonean*, April 8, 1853, 293; and N. Noah, "The 32d St. Burying Ground," *Asmonean*, April 8, 1853, 293.

62 A Jew [pseud.], "Is the Tomb Inviolate?," *Asmonean*, April 1, 1853, 282; emphasis in original.

63 Trustees claimed that they only intended to rearrange some graves that had shifted over time. Nevertheless, they had already begun surveying the yard nearly five months before the scandal. Initial minutes regarding the survey even originally referenced "the old burial ground." Only later was the entry revised to read "the *vacant lot in* the old burial ground" (emphasis added). November 14, 1852, p. 81, B'nai Jeshurun Records, Board of Trustees' Bound Minutes Volume, 1850–52 / Letter Book, 1825–51.

64 Robert Lyon, *Asmonean*, April 15, 1853, 305.

65 Letter from the committee to the Reverend Dr. Raphall, April 3, 1853, copied in the minutes entry for April 10, 1853, B'nai Jeshurun Records, Board of Trustees' Bound Minutes Volume, 1840–54.

66 Communication from Morris J. Raphall to the Committee of Trustees of the Congregation B'nai Jeshurun, April 4, 1853, copied in the minutes entry for April 10, 1853, B'nai Jeshurun Records, Board of Trustees' Bound Minutes Volume, 1840–54; emphasis in original.

67 A. Rice, "The Mystery of the Law: Replies," *Asmonean*, January 16, 1852, 116–17.

68 Ben Brith [pseud.], letter to the editor, *Asmonean*, April 15, 1853, 305.

69 Max Lilienthal, "Cemeteries and Family Plots," *Israelite* (Cincinnati), July 18, 1856, 13.

70 "Our Cemetery," *Israelite*, October 8, 1858, 108.

71 Cemetery Committee report to the board, November 23, 5617 [1856], B'nai Jeshurun Records, Board of Trustees' Bound Minutes Volume, 1856–60.

72 "List of Names of Some of the Remains Disinterred from Oliver Street and Reburied in the 21st Street Cemetery," November 20 to December 31, 1855, Jacques Judah Lyons Collection, P-15, box 3, folder 192.

73 See the excerpt of the letter to *The Sun* reprinted in "Duty to the Dead," *Asmonean*, April 23, 1852, 4.

74 Peter Mactowros, "About Cremation," *Jewish Messenger*, March 13, 1874, 5.

75 "Jewish City Cemeteries," *Jewish Messenger*, July 2, 1875, 5.

76 Minutes entry, May 3, 1856, in appendix 8, "On the Removal of Bodies, Care of the Cemeteries and Related Subjects," section A, "Excerpts from the Minutes of Congregation Anshe Chesed," reprinted in Grinstein, *Rise of the Jewish Community*, 497–98.

77 The other grave belonged to a Mrs. Rosa Moss. See the Cemetery Committee report to the board, November 23, 5617 [1856], B'nai Jeshurun Records, Board of Trustees' Bound Minutes Volume, 1856–60.

78 Nathan's grave was among the first ten removed on the fourth day of the undertaking, November 25, 1855. See "List of Names," Jacques Judah Lyons Collection, P-15, box 3, folder 192.

79 "Removing the Dead," *Jewish Messenger*, March 26, 1875, 4.

80 It claimed the congregation simply intended to empty the land for profit and pleaded that other congregations not "follow their example of contempt for the departed." See "Disturbing the Dead," *Jewish Messenger* (New York), November 26, 1875, 4.

81 Although a member of Clinton Street successfully negotiated down the sum, the solution saved the ground only temporarily. See "Local News: An Up-Town Cemetery," *Jewish Messenger*, March 7, 1879, 2.

82 "Jewish Cemeteries II: The Oliver Street Cemetery," *Jewish Messenger*, July 9, 1875, 5.

83 "Removal of Bodies to Family Plots," *American Hebrew*, December 28, 1883, 78.

84 See "Instructions of the Rev. Dr. Raphall to the Committee of Trustees Appointed to Secure and Enclose the Burial Ground in 32nd St," copied in the minutes entry for April 27, 1853, B'nai Jeshurun Records, Board of Trustees' Bound Minutes Volume, 1840–54.

85 Robert Lyon, Lewis M. Morrison, B. I. Hart, A. Godfrey, and John Levy, "The Cemetery Question," *Asmonean*, August 29, 1856, 156–57.

86 Ibid.; emphasis added.

87 Grinstein, *Rise of the Jewish Community*, 318; article 4, section 3, "Extracts of the Statutes of Salem Fields Cemetery" on the back of "Deed of Cemetery Lot 807," April 1, 1853, Goldstein Family Papers, P-259.

88 Grinstein, *Rise of the Jewish Community*, 110; Grusd, *B'nai B'rith*, 41–42; Polland and Soyer, *Emerging Metropolis*, 35–36; Wilhelm, "Independent Order of True Sisters," 41.

89 Appendix 7, "New York Burial and Mutual Aid Societies," in Grinstein, *Rise of the Jewish Community*, 491–95. On the Bruder Verein, see also "Memorandum of Agreement," April 12, 1860, Records of Brothers in Unity (Bruder Verein #1), RG 1634, box 5, folder 14, "Documents of Bruderverein, 1850s."

90 "Salem Fields Cemetery: Dedication Services at the Jewish Cemetery Yesterday," *New York Times*, September 3, 1877, 3.

91 *Reprinted in an editorial by Robert Lyon, Asmonean,* October 31, 1851, 17.

92 "Jewish Cemeteries," *Jewish Messenger,* September 21, 1866, 4.

93 "The Cemetery Question," *Jewish Messenger,* February 22, 1878, 4.

94 "Buried Cheaply!," *American Israelite,* September 3, 1875, 4.

95 "Burial of the Dead," *Jewish Messenger,* February 8, 1861, 44; and "Burial of the Dead," *Jewish Messenger,* February 15, 1861, 52.

96 These included Philadelphia, Baltimore, Brooklyn, Rochester, Albany, Pittsburgh, Cincinnati, Providence, Louisville, Savannah, Charleston, Richmond, Buffalo, Detroit, St. Louis, Milwaukee, Atlanta, New Orleans, Memphis, and Cleveland. See Sachs, "American Arcadia," 213.

97 Mintz, *Prison of Expectations,* 13; Mintz and Kellogg, *Domestic Revolutions,* 44–45.

98 Sloane, *Last Great Necessity,* 79–84; Bender, "The 'Rural' Cemetery Movement," 203.

CHAPTER 4

1 "Buried Cheaply!," *American Israelite,* September 3, 1875, 4.

2 Society charter, April 30, 1844, quoted in Weingart and Marks, *Three-Quarters of a Century,* 6.

3 For a full range of groups and their stated objects, see a forty-six-reel microfilm collection of incorporation certificates composed of eighty-one folio volumes of Jewish societies founded between 1848 and 1920 in New York (County) Hall of Records Selected Incorporation Papers, 1848–1920, I-154.

4 These are only a few of the hundreds of similar groups that proliferated throughout the period. Even the archive reflects their rapid growth. Although one microfilm reel could cover a decade's worth of groups from 1848 to 1858, by the 1860s and 1870s, one reel covered only three or four years' worth of incorporation certificates. See reel 1, New York (County) Hall of Records Selected Incorporation Papers, 1848–1920, I-154.

5 Diner, *Time for Gathering,* 63.

6 Trattner, *From Poor Law to Welfare State,* 56–60.

7 Orloff, "Gender in Early U.S. Social Policy," 253–55.

8 On early B'nai B'rith benefits, see Grusd, *B'nai B'rith,* 27; On the Mendelssohn Society, see Weingart and Marks, *Three-Quarters of a Century,* 7.

9 Grusd, *B'nai B'rith,* 27.

10 Weingart and Marks, *Three-Quarters of a Century,* 7.

11 Article 4, "Committees," section 7, *By-Laws of Jonathan Lodge, No. 14, K.S.B.* (New York: A. G. Levy, 1871), 8–9, Kesher Shel Barzel Records 186?–1904, I-28, box 1, folder 2.

12 Felix M. Rosenstock, "The History of the Noah Benevolent Society— 1849–1934," *Ninetieth Anniversary 1849–1939* (New York: s.n., 1939), 18–20, Noah Benevolent Society Records, I-186, box 17, folder 2, "Anniversary Journals, 50th–125th."

13 See preamble and article 2, "Duties of a Lodge," sections 4 and 5, *Constitution and General Laws of the United States Grand Lodge Brith Abraham and Constitution and General Laws for the Government of District Grand Lodges and Subordinates* (Cincinnati: A. Donnelly, 1865), 26–27. Soble Rare Book Collection, Soble 357.

14 The group may have exempted local widows and orphans' funds earlier, but the earliest available constitution only dates to 1865. See article 11, "Revenue," section 1, *Constitution and General Laws of the United States Grand Lodge Brith Abraham and Constitution and General Laws for the Government of District Grand Lodges and Subordinates* (Cincinnati: A. Donnelly, 1865), 16.

15 On founding purposes, see Alexander Rosenbaum, "A Retrospect of Our Society's Past, Its Men and Events," in *Fifty Years of Useful Existence of the Erster Ungarischer Kranken und Unterstuetzungs Verein* (New York: s.n., 1915), 8; on allocation of funds, see article 15, "Duties and Rights of Members," section 1a, *Gesetze des Ersten Ungarischen Kranken und Unterstutzungs-Vereins* (New York: Druct von Jacob Kafta, 1908), 39, 1865 Mutual Benevolent Society Ungarische Kuv Collection, RG 1869, box 1, folder, "Gesetze Ungarische Kuv 1908," YIVO, Institute for Jewish Research, New York.

16 The preamble to the B'nai B'rith's 1843 constitution, for instance, only referenced the group's obligation to "providing for, protecting, and assisting the widow and orphan" of a member when it came to caring for family upon a man's death. Beyond mutual relief in illness, the group's 1860 and 1863 revisions again only committed to "[dry] the tears of the widow and orphan" and "to protect and assist widows and orphans," respectively. For excerpts of these constitutions, see Grusd, *B'nai B'rith*, 20, 47, and 62.

17 Weingart and Marks, *Three-Quarters of a Century*, 7.

18 Bush, *Our Widows and Orphans Endowments*, 3.

19 Henry J. Hyman, "The Why and Wherefore of the Independent Order Free Sons of Israel," *Independent Order Free Sons of Israel, Diamond Jubilee 1849–1924* (New York: s.n., 1924), Independent Order Free Sons of Israel Collection, I-368, box 1, folder 1, "Independent Order of the Free Sons of Israel, Anniversary Journal (1849–1924)."

20 Felix M. Rosenstock, "The History of the Noah Benevolent Society—1849–1934," *Ninetieth Anniversary 1849–1939* (New York: s.n., 1939), 25, Noah Benevolent Society Records, I-186, box 17, folder 2, "Anniversary Journals, 50th–125th."

21 Bush, *Our Widows and Orphans Endowments*, 5–28.

22 Grusd, *B'nai B'rith*, 79.

23 Weingart and Marks, *Three-Quarters of a Century*, 7.

24 Grusd, *B'nai B'rith*, 85–86.

25 See application questionnaires 1–53 of a membership initiation book containing application forms for potential candidates in the records of the Samaritan Society Collection, 1868–1961, RG 583, box 1.

26 Bush, *Our Widows and Orphans Endowments*, 231.

27 These findings come from a survey of members' declarations of endowment beneficiaries in the case of their death. Declarations list members' marital status, address, and declared beneficiary. See two bound volumes of declarations, "Declaration, Manhattan Lodge No. 156 November 21, 1871–December 6, 1880" and "Declaration, Manhattan Lodge No. 156 February 21, 1876–January 21, 1905" included in series 2, Manhattan Lodge No. 156, 1871–1918, in composite collection records of B'nai Brith Manhattan-Washington Lodge No. 19, 1871–1931, I-31, box 5. Since only a handful of declarations made after 1885 did not involve members altering earlier declarations, my survey did not include them in this analysis.

28 On propositions, see certificates filled out by a membership committee attesting to candidates' "character, standing, etc." This survey sampled 311 propositions between 1873 and 1898. Although in some cases the committee did not fill in a candidate's marital status, 143 single members came under review during that two-decade period compared to only 58 married applicants (of those able to be identified). See propositions in series 2, Manhattan Lodge 156, 1871–1918, in composite collection records of B'nai Brith Manhattan-Washington Lodge No. 19, 1871–1931, I-31, box 9, folder 1, "Propositions of Candidates and Reports, Manhattan Lodge No. 156, August 18, 1873–July 7, 1879," and folder 2, "Propositions, Manhattan Lodge No. 156 August 18, 1879–March 7, 1898."

29 Of sixty-three men who entered the group unmarried and later issued new declarations between 1871 and 1885, thirty-seven of them married later, and upon those marriages, all revoked their previous declarations to list their wives as heirs. See "Declaration, Manhattan Lodge No. 156 November 21, 1871–December 6, 1880" and "Declaration, Manhattan Lodge No. 156 February 21, 1876–January 21, 1905" included in series 2, Manhattan Lodge 156, 1871–1918, in composite collection records of B'nai Brith Manhattan-Washington Lodge No. 19, 1871–1931, I-31, box 5.

30 Article 4, "Benefits to Widows and Orphans," section 2, *Constitution and General Laws for Lodges of the Independent Order Free Sons of Israel* (New York: G. Van der Potendyk and W. Cahi, 1878), 17; see also article 3, division 1, "Endowment Fund," section 1, *Constitution of the Grand Lodge of the United States of the Independent Order Free Sons of Israel*, 1888, p. 10, in Independent Order Free Sons of Israel Collection, 1871–1984, I-368, box 1, folder 2, "Constitutions, 1878 and 1888."

31 Article 16, "Rules and Regulations in Case of Death," section 4, *Gesetze des Ersten Ungarischen Kranken und Unterstutzungs-Vereins* (New York: Druct von Jacob Kafta, 1908), 45–47, 1865 Mutual Benevolent Society Ungarische Kuv Collection, RG 1869, box 1, folder, "Gezetse 1908," YIVO.

32 Article 14, "Beneficiaries," section 12, in *Constitution and By-Laws of the Independent Order Brith Abraham* (New York: s.n., 1928), 36, Henry Clay Lodge 15, IOBA Collection, RG 784, box 2, folder, "Miscellaneous: Constitution."

33 See article 6, "Members and Their Admission," section 2, *Constitution and By-Laws of the Noah Benevolent Widows' and Orphans' Association* (New York: Rode

and Brand, 1889/1906), 16, Noah Benevolent Society Records, I-186, box 28. This constitution is a revised version for 1906 but includes printed pages from the 1889 version that constitution writers cut and pasted into a ledger with additional handwritten clauses to reflect the new policy for 1906. In the printed 1889 version, policy already required members to undergo a physician's exam.

34 Physician's certificate in series 4, Mount Sinai Lodge 270, 1878–1903, in composite collection records of B'nai B'rith Manhattan-Washington Lodge No. 19, I-31, box 13, folder 3, "Mount Sinai's Lodge, No. 270, Physician's Certificate, 1884."

35 "Applicant's Statements," Kolomear Friends Association Collection, RG 792, box 3, folders 16–19, "Kolomaer frends asosyeyshon, aplikatsyes." For other examples of increasing medical emphasis in groups at the time, see the medical questionnaires of the Chicago-based Independent Order Bickur Cholem Ukadishu, I-60, box 1, folder 4, "Medical Examiner Certificates," AJHS, NY.

36 Between 1887 and 1895, among twenty-five orders, average death rates per year rose from 7.17 to 10.04, sometimes even doubling. Beito, *From Mutual Aid to Welfare State*, 132.

37 G. L. Lowenthall, *Conveniton Independent Order Free Sons of Judah: Message G. L. Lowenthall, Grand Master* (New York: Jacob Kafka, 1904), 24–25, records of Independent Order Free Sons of Judah, I-369, box 1, folder 1, "Conventions (1904), Pamphlets, Reports, Grand Masters Address."

38 Sigmund Foror, *1904 Convention of the United States Grand Lodge Indep. Order Free Sons of Judah, Reports of the Grand Secretary, Finance Committee, Chairman of Endowment, and Chairman of Relief Committee* (New York: Jacob Kafka, 1904), 1–2, records of the Independent Order Free Sons of Judah, I-369, folder 1, "Conventions (1904), Pamphlets, Reports, Grand Masters Address."

39 Julius Harburger, "Message of the Grand Master," *Convention of the Grand Lodge of the United States, Independent Order Free Sons of Israel Atlantic City, May 1902* (New York: Oppenheimer, 1902), 24, Independent Order Free Sons of Israel Collection, 1871–1984, I-368, box 1, folder 4, "Independent Order Free Sons of Israel, Convention Proceedings (1902–1912)."

40 Shelvin, *History of the Independent Order*, 37.

41 Bush, *Our Widows and Orphans Endowments*, 265–66.

42 Weingart and Marks, *Three-Quarters of a Century*, 7.

43 Trattner, *From Poor Law to Welfare State*, 81.

44 Orloff, "The Political Origins," 45–59; Orloff, "Gender in Early U.S. Social Policy," 251–56; Skocpol, *Protecting Soldiers and Mothers*, 129–35.

45 Igra, *Wives without Husbands*, 32–35; Leff, "Consensus for Reform," 399; Skocpol, *Protecting Soldiers and Mothers*, 425.

46 In 1909, a White House Conference on Children elevated the issue, and in its aftermath, several states adopted mothers' aid legislation. In 1911, Illinois passed the first "Mothers' Aid Law," and thirty-nine states followed suit by 1919. See Nelson, "Origins of the Two-Channel Welfare State," 138–39. New York created a program to aid "dependent children of widowed mothers" in 1914, but again it did not

address the needs of intact families. See Soyer, *Jewish Immigrant Aid Associations*, 100; Orloff, "Gender in Early U.S. Social Policy," 251.

47 Nelson, "Origins of the Two-Channel Welfare State," 135–40; Skocpol, *Protecting Soldiers and Mothers*, 286–304.

48 Introductory note, excerpted and reprinted in the group's bylaws, *Constitution of the Kolomear Friends Association* (New York: Relter and Reiner, 1937), 4, Kolomear Friends Association Collection, RG 792, box 1, folder, "Kolomaer frends asosyeyshon, konstitutsye."

49 Conclusions of the group's application process come from a sampling of 250 candidates' applications between 1907 and 1956. The society's collection houses these forms in near alphabetical order by applicant across five folders. This study sampled roughly the first fifty forms in each folder. Of those surveyed, between 1907 and 1911, sixty-three single men and fifty-seven married men applied for membership. See "Applicant's Statements," Kolomear Friends Association Collection, RG 792, box 3, folders 16–19, "Kolomaer frends asosyeyshon, aplikatsyes."

50 Diner, *Jews of the United States*, 108; Kessner, "Jobs, Ghettoes and the Urban Economy," 228.

51 Samuel Joseph, *Jewish Immigration to the United States from 1881 to 1910* (New York: Columbia University, 1914), 140, 145, cited in Polland and Soyer, *Emerging Metropolis*, 122. See also Soyer, *Jewish Immigrant Aid Associations*, 100.

52 Article 2, "*Tsvek der khevre*," section 1, *Konstitutsyan der khevre kol yisroel anshey bronsvil* (New York: Maurice Ravnitzky, 1912), 2, Chevra Kol Yisroel Brownsville Collection, RG 1027, box 1, folder, "Constitutions."

53 On similar trends among Jewish and other European immigrant societies in Chicago during this period, see L. Cohen, *Making a New Deal*, 56–64.

54 Shelvin, *History of the Independent Order*, 60–61.

55 Article 9, "Sick Benefits," sections 3 and 4, *Constitution and By-Laws of the Noah Benevolent Widows' and Orphans' Association* (New York: Rode and Brand, 1889/1906), 24; see also article 9, "Rights and Benefits," sections 3–6, *Constitution and By-Laws of the Noah Benevolent Society* (New York: s.n., 1917), 15–16. Both in Noah Benevolent Society Records, I-186, box 28.

56 Article 7, "Initiation Fees and Dues," and article 8, "Division and Application of the Fund," in *Constitution and By-Laws of the Noah Benevolent Widows' and Orphans' Association* (1889/1906), 18–22, Noah Benevolent Society Records, I-186, box 28.

57 Article 1, "Name and Language," section 1, *Constitution and By-Laws of the Noah Benevolent Society* (New York: s.n., 1917), 5, Noah Benevolent Society Records, I-186, box 28.

58 Article 7, "Dues and Initiation Fee," section 4, and article 9, "Revenues and their Purpose," sections 1 and 2, in *By-Laws of Loyal Benevolent Society and Rules and Regulations of Burial Ground* (New York: s.n., 1932), 15 and 17, Loyal Benevolent Society Collection, RG 900, box 1, folder 1, "By-Laws."

59 Article 19, "Funerals and Cemetery," clause 6, *Constitution of the Kolomear Friends Association* (New York: Relter and Reiner, 1937), 20, Kolomear Friends

Association Records, RG 792, box 1, folder, "Kolomaer frends asosyeyshon, konstitutsye."

60 This information is based on an analysis of burial receipts, permit books, and a cemetery map of the society's cemetery holdings dating to the late 1930s but recording interments from the 1870s. See Holy Society Collection, box 1, folder 1:19, "Burial Permits, 1872–1914; 1927."

61 See order 66, March 13, 1923, in burial permits book, records of the Chevra Kadisha Beth Israel Collection, RG 865, box 3, folder, "Burial Permits, 1914–1965."

62 See the minutes entry for May 5, 1897, for a widow's request to reserve a grave next to her husband at the time of his death; see September 22, 1895, and March 12, 1896, entries for two instances of children seeking to bury their widowed mothers next to their fathers who had predeceased them. See the records of Congregation Kahal Adath Yeshurun with Anshe Lubitz [Eldridge Street Synagogue] (henceforth Kahal Adath Yeshurun), I-10, box 3, folder 2, "Minutes book 1890–97."

63 See "Plot C" of a cemetery map depicting the Ceres Union's holdings in section 2 of Mount Zion Cemetery, Ceres Union Collection, RG 919, box 4, folder 42a, "Ceres Cemetery Maps."

64 See order 12, November 5, 1916, and follow-up order 143, February 5, 1931, in burial permits book, records of the Chevra Kadisha Beth Israel Collection, RG 865, box 3, folder, "Burial Permits, 1914–1965."

65 See the minutes entry for April 23, 1919, p. 278, Henry Clay Lodge 15, IOBA Collection, RG 784, box 1, folder, "Farzamlungen, 1915–1919."

66 In 1891, Y. Heyzer paid a $25 fee to buy a grave for his deceased mother. In 1895, the congregation sold a grave to Mrs. Ita Heyman, mother-in-law of congregant Yitzhak Morris, as well as another to Merdkhe Rosenthal for his mother-in-law. See the minutes entries for December 23, 1891, May 5, 1895, and October 6, 1895, records of Kahal Adath Yeshurun, I-10, box 3, folder 2, "Minutes Book 1890–97."

67 Minutes entry for December 10, 1918, p. 259, Henry Clay Lodge 15, IOBA Collection, RG 784, box 1, folder, "Farzamlungen, 1915–1919."

68 See article 10, "Burial Plot," section 3, *Constitution and By Laws of the Noah Benevolent Widows' and Orphans' Association* (New York: s.n., 1889/1906), 34; and article 10, "Burial Plots," section 2, *Constitution and By-Laws of the Noah Benevolent Society* (New York: s.n., 1917), 19. Both are in the Noah Benevolent Society Records, I-186, box 28.

69 On Dinah Rodin, see the minutes entry for May 5, 1897. On the cases of adult children purchasing graves, see entries for September 22, 1895, and March 12, 1896, records of Kahal Adath Yeshurun, I-10, box 3, folder 2, "Minutes Book 1890–97."

70 Article 10, "Burial Plots," section 3, *Constitution and By-Laws of the Noah Benevolent Society* (New York: s.n., 1917), 18–19, Noah Benevolent Society Records, I-186, box 28.

71 For developments in the Noah Benevolent Society, see article 10, "Burial Plots," section 3, *Constitution and By-Laws of the Noah Benevolent Society* (New York:

s.n., 1917), 18–19; and article 13, "Burial Plots," section 6, *Constitution and By-Laws of the Noah Benevolent Society* (New York: s.n., 1936), 26–27, Noah Benevolent Society Records, I-186, box 28.

72 Weingart and Marks, *Three-Quarters of a Century*, 21.
73 See article 10, "Deaths," section 7, *Constitution, Plotzker Young Men's Independent Association* (New York: s.n., 1929), 21, Plotzker Young Men's Independent Association Collection, RG 785, box 1, folder, "Konstitutsye"; emphasis added.
74 Polland and Soyer, *Emerging Metropolis*, 107.
75 Soyer, *Jewish Immigrant Aid Associations*, 190; L. Cohen, *Making a New Deal*, 54.
76 L. Cohen, *Making a New Deal*, 64–65.
77 Shelvin, *History of the Independent Order*, 39.
78 Soyer, *Jewish Immigrant Aid Associations*, 157–61.
79 Wenger, *New York Jews and the Great Depression*, 145.
80 "Fifty Years of Ups and Downs," *Moses Family Society, Fiftieth Anniversary 1910–1960*, Moses Family Society Collection, RG 839, box 2, folder, "Anniversary Journals, Menus, Seating Arrangements."
81 See, for example, article 16, "Rules and Regulations in Case of Death," section 3, *Gesetze des Ersten Ungarischen Kranken und Unterstutzungs-Vereins* (New York: Druct von Jacob Kafta, 1908), 49, 1865 Mutual Benevolent Society Ungarische Kuv Collection, RG 1869, box 1, folder, "Gezetse 1908," YIVO; article 9, "C. Endowments," section 2, *Constitution and By Laws of the Noah Benevolent Widows' and Orphans' Association* (New York: s.n., 1889/1906), 28–30, Noah Benevolent Society Records, I-186, box 28.
82 Article 12, "Rights and Benefits," section 7, *Constitution and By-Laws of the Noah Benevolent Society* (New York: s.n., 1936), 26–27, Noah Benevolent Society Records, I-186, box 28.
83 See "Endowment to Beneficiary" and "Endowment to Member," *Constitution of the First Storoznetzer Bukowiner Sick and Benevolent Association* (New York: s.n., 1937), 23 and 26, First Independent Storoznetzer Bukowiner S & B Association Collection, RG 901, box 1, folder 1, "Constitution."
84 See communication from Mrs. Y. Tow to H. Lipner, August 18, 1932, Henry Clay Lodge 15, IOBA Collection, RG 784, box 2, folder, "Correspondence 1930–2"; and minutes entry, May 18, 1932, p. 73, Henry Clay Lodge 15, IOBA Collection, RG 784, cash ledger, box 1, folder 3, "Barikhtn vegn farshtorbene mitglider."
85 Communication from Mrs. M. Folkman to H. Lipner, June 25, 1935, Henry Clay Lodge 15, IOBA Collection, RG 784, box 2, folder, "Correspondence 1933–36."
86 Cash ledger entry, February 25, 1931, p. 11, Henry Clay Lodge 15, IOBA Collection, RG 784, box 1, folder 3, "Barikhtn vegn farshtorbene mitglider."
87 Communication from H. Lipner, secretary, to Mrs. M. Folkman, March 31, 1934, Henry Clay Lodge 15, IOBA Collection, RG 784, box 2, folder, "Correspondence 1933–36."
88 Weisser, *Brotherhood of Memory*, 222–23; Soyer, *Jewish Immigrant Aid Associations*, 201; Wenger, *New York Jews and the Great Depression*, 144–46.

89 See article 16, "Rules and Regulations in Case of Death," section 8, *Gesetze des Ersten Ungarischen Kranken und Unterstutzungs-Vereins* (New York: Druct von Jacob Kafta, 1908), 49, 1865 Mutual Benevolent Society Ungarische Kuv Collection, RG 1869, box 1, folder, "Gezetse 1908," YIVO.

90 Soyer, *Jewish Immigrant Aid Associations*, 86.

91 See article 15, "Disability Benefit Laws," *Constitution and By-Laws of the Independent Order Brith Abraham* (New York: s.n., 1928), 42, Henry Clay Lodge 15, IOBA Collection, RG 784, box 2, folder, "Miscellaneous: Constitution."

92 Article 7, "Initiation Fees," section 3, *Constitution, Plotzker Young Men's Independent Association* (New York: s.n., 1929), 16, Plotzker Young Men's Independent Association Collection, RG 785, box 1, folder, "konstitutsye."

93 By 1932, the Loyal Benevolent Society charged its widows $4.00, with the Henry Clay Lodge 15 charging them $5.90 each quarter. Article 7, "Dues and Initiation Fee," section 4, *By-Laws of Loyal Benevolent Society and Rules and Regulations of Burial Ground* (New York: s.n., 1932), 15, Loyal Benevolent Society Collection, RG 900, box 1, folder 1, "By-Laws"; and communication from H. Lipner to Mrs. M. Folkman, March 31, 1934, Henry Clay Lodge 15, IOBA Collection, RG 784, box 2, folder, "Correspondence 1933–36."

94 Article 7, "Dues and Initiation Fee," section 4, and article 9, "Revenues and their Purpose," sections 1 and 2, *By-Laws of Loyal Benevolent Society and Rules and Regulations of Burial Ground* (New York: s.n., 1932), 15 and 17, Loyal Benevolent Society Collection, RG 900, box 1, folder 1, "By-Laws."

95 Article 19, "Funerals and Cemetery," clause 6, *Constitution of the Kolomear Friends Association* (New York: Relter and Reiner, 1937), 20, Kolomear Friends Association Collection, RG 792, box 1, folder, "Kolomaer frends asosyeyshon, konstitutsye."

96 See article 8, section 1, *Constitution of the Kolbuszower Young Men's Benevolent Society* (New York: s.n., 1936), 15, Kolbuszower Young Men's Benevolent Society Collection, RG 957, box 1, folder 1, "Constitution Kolbuszower YMBS."

97 Article 13, "Burial Plots," section 4, *Constitution and By Laws of the Noah Benevolent Society* (New York: s.n., 1936), 29, Noah Benevolent Society Records, I-186, box 28.

98 Meeting minutes, May 23, 1926, p. 300, Minutes Book 1, Bizoner Chebra B'nai Shaul Collection, RG 934, box 1, folder 1, "Minutes, Bizoner Chebra Bnai/Beis Shule."

99 See article 9, "Benefits of Members in Cases of Sickness, Mourning and Death," section 3, *Constitution und Neben Celeke der Hevra Kadisha Wohlthatigheits—Verein* (New York: Druck von Adolph L. Goehl, 1907), 25, and article 8, "Benefits of Members in Case of Death," sections 1–7, *The Holy Society of the City of New York (Chevra Kadisha): Constitution and By-Laws* (New York: s.n., 1930), 17–20, Holy Society Collection, box 1, folder 1:3, "Constitution 1907, 1930."

100 Meeting minutes, November 25, 1931, p. 342, and February 28, 1932, p. 347, Minutes Book 1, Bizoner Chebra B'nai Shaul Collection, RG 934, box 1, folder 1, "Minutes, Bizoner Chebra Bnai/Beis Shule."

101 Article 10, clause 25, *Constitution of the Independent Orler Benevolent Society* (New York: s.n., 1937), 23, Independent Orler Benevolent Society Collection, RG 1023, box 1, folder 1, "Constitutions."

102 Article 10, "Burial Plots," section 3, *Constitution and By-Laws of the Noah Benevolent Society* (New York: s.n., 1917), 18–19, Noah Benevolent Society Records, I-186, box 28.

103 See, for instance, article 10, "Burial Plot," section 2, *Constitution and By-Laws of the Noah Benevolent Society* (New York: s.n., 1889/1906), 34; and article 13, "Burial Plots," section 4, *Constitution and By Laws of the Noah Benevolent Society* (New York: s.n., 1936), 29, Noah Benevolent Society Records, I-86, box 28; article 10, "Deaths," section 20, *Constitution, Plotzker Young Men's Independent Association* (New York: s.n., 1929), 24–25; Plotzker Young Men's Independent Association Collection, RG 785, box 1, folder, "konstitutsye"; and article 19, clause 7, "Funerals and Cemetery," *Constitution of the Kolomear Friends Association* (New York: Relter and Reiner, 1937), 20, Kolomear Friends Association Collection, RG 792, box 1, folder, "Kolomaer frends asosyeyshon, konstitutsye."

104 Article 8, "Benefits bay shterbe fele r"l," section 6, *Konstitutsyan der khevre kol yisroel anshey bronsvil* (New York: Maurice Ravnitzky, 1912), 10, Chevra Kol Yisroel Brownsville Collection, RG 1027, box 1, folder, "Constitutions."

105 Article 10, clause 27, *Constitution of the Independent Orler Benevolent Society* (New York: s.n., 1937), 24; and Article 10, clause 26, *Constitution of the Independent Orler Benevolent Society* (New York: s.n., 1957), 20, Independent Orler Benevolent Society Collection, RG 1023, box 1, folder 1, "Constitutions."

106 Article 20, clause 7, "Death Benefit," *Constitution of the Kolomear Friends Association* (New York: Relter and Reiner, 1937), 22, Kolomear Friends Association Collection, RG 792, box 1, folder, "Kolomaer frends asosyeyshon, konstitutsye."

107 See article 8, "Cemetery," section 20, *Constitution of the Kolbuszower Young Men's Benevolent Society* (New York: s.n., 1936), 19, Kolbuszower Young Men's Benevolent Society Collection, RG 957, box 1, folder 1, "Constitution Kolbuszower YMBS"; article 7, "Dues and Initiation Fee," sections 2 and 3, *By-Laws of Loyal Benevolent Society and Rules and Regulations of Burial Ground* (New York: s.n., 1932), 14–15, Loyal Benevolent Society Collection, RG 900, box 1, folder 1, "By-Laws"; or "Widower-Remarriage," *Constitution of the First Storoznetzer Bukowiner Sick and Benevolent Association* (New York: s.n., 1937), 22, First Independent Storoznetzer Bukowiner S & B Association Collection, RG 901, box 1, folder 1, "Constitution."

108 Weisser, *Brotherhood of Memory*, 162.

109 Communication from Mrs. M. Folkman to Mr. H. Lipner, April 13, 1934, Henry Clay Lodge 15, IOBA Collection, RG 784, box 2, folder, "Correspondence 1933–36."

110 See the card from Eva Feirtag to the Weinreb Benevolent Society, November 25, 1992, attached to dues payments recorded in the financial ledger, pp. 12–13, Weinreb Benevolent Society Collection, RG 1678, box 1, ledger book of records.

111 See letter from Sarah Kleinman to Jacob Gordon, 1985, Ershte Bolshowcer Sick Benevolent Society and Lodge 517, RG 872, box 2, folder, "Miscellaneous."

CHAPTER 5

1 "No Funeral Pomp: Some Characteristics of the East Side Hebrews," *New York Tribune*, November 17, 1895, 28.

2 See the sample ad in *News Bulletin of the Society for the Advancement of Judaism*, vol. 22, no. 1, September 11, 1942, Society for the Advancement of Judaism Records, I-70, box 1, folder 10, "Bulletins, 1942–1944."

3 Habenstein and Lamers, *History of American Funeral Directing*; Sloane, *Last Great Necessity*, 120, 174; Laderman, *Sacred Remains*; Smith, *To Serve the Living*, 32.

4 See advertisement for J. Winterbottom and Son, Funeral Directors, that claimed operation since 1849 in the April 1905 issue of *Shearith Israel Review* on p. 126, Congregation Shearith Israel Records, I-4, box 7, folder 1, "The Shearith Israel Review, 1905."

5 Article 2, section 1, *Constitution and Bylaws of Hevrath Nashim Hased vaamet: Ladies Benevolent Soceity of the Congregation Bnai Jeshurun, for Visiting the Sick, Comforting the Dying, and Burrying the Dead* (New York: M. Jackson, 1843), 5, Jacques Judah Lyons Collection, P-15, box 3, folder 220, "Lyons Collection—Manuscripts Memo of MSS & Articles Deposited in the Cornerstone of 19th St. Synagogue of KKSI 1859."

6 See *Asmonean*, September 21, 1855, 177, quoted in Goren, "Traditional Institutions Transplanted," 70.

7 On funeral utensils, see article 8, "Duties and Rights of the Officers," section 1, and article 13, "Deaths," section 2, *Constitution of the "Erster Galizisher Kranken- und Unterstuetzungs-Verein"* (New York: Hebrew Orphan Asylum, 1872), 12 and 24, Samaritan Society Collection, RG 583, box 1.

8 See, for instance, expense entries for November 1883, p. 22; April 13, 1884, p. 31; October 7, 1884, p. 39; January 18, 1885, p. 45; and November 13, 1885, p. 57, records of Kahal Adath Yeshurun, I-10, box 1, account book, 1883–87.

9 See article 4, "Duties of Officers," section 1, and article 5, "Committees and Their Duties," section 5, *Constitution and By-Laws of the Noah Benevolent Widows' and Orphans' Association* (New York: Rode and Brand, 1889/1906), 4 and 16, Noah Benevolent Society Records, I-186, box 28.

10 Article 23, "Messasskim," sections 2–11, *Constitution of the Congregation Kahal Adas Jeshurun with Anshe Lubtz* (New York: s.n., 1913), 26–28, records of Kahal Adath Yeshurun, I-10, box 2, folder 1.

11 On benefits, see article 8, "benefits bay shterbe fele r"l," sections 3 and 4, *Konstitutsyan der khevre kol yisroel anshey bronsvil* (New York: Maurice Ravnitzky, 1912), 8–9, Chevra Kol Yisroel Brownsville Collection, RG 1027, box 1, folder, "Constitutions"; and for undertaker charges, see entries covering 1929 and 1932 on pp. 204, 210, 380, and 382 in the financial ledger, 1926–32, Chevra Kol Yisroel

Brownsville Collection, RG 1027, box 1, folder, "Income and Expenses Ledger, April 1926–December 1932."

12 Laderman, *Sacred Remains*, 45; See also the bill of N. P. Whitney, undertaker, reprinted in Habenstein and Lamers, *History of American Funeral Directing*, 154.

13 See article 12, "Rights of the Brothers," sections 4 and 5, *Constitution of the "Erster Galizisher Kranken-und Unterstuetzungs-Verein"* (New York: Hebrew Orphan Asylum, 1872), 22–24, Samaritan Society Collection, RG 583, box 1.

14 Article 4, "Duties of Officers," section 7, *Constitution and By Laws of the Noah Benevolent Widows' and Orphans' Association* (New York: s.n., 1889/1906), 8. See also article 5, "Standing Committees and Budget," section 1, *Constitution and By-Laws of the Noah Benevolent Society* (New York: s.n., 1917), 11. Both appear in Noah Benevolent Society Records, I-186, box 28.

15 Article 9, "Benefits of Members in Cases of Sickness, Mourning and Death," section 1, *Constitution und Neben Celeke der Hevra Kadisha Wohlthatigheits—Verein* (New York: Druck von Adolph L. Goehl, 1907), 23, Holy Society Collection, box 1, folder 1:3, "Constitution 1907; 1930."

16 Article 8, "Benefits of Members in Case of Death," section 2, *The Holy Society of the City of New York (Chevra Kadisha): Constitution and By-Laws* (New York: s.n., 1930), 17, Holy Society Collection, box 1, folder 1:3, "Constitution 1907; 1930."

17 Schneider, *History of a Jewish Burial Society*, 124. Schneider's study keeps this society anonymous and does not supply its real name, calling it instead the "Peloni Almoni [John Doe] Benevolent Society of New York" and providing a brief overview of its history.

18 Meeting minutes, April 25, 1920, p. 217, Minutes Book 1, Bizoner Chebra B'nai Shaul Collection, RG 934, box 1, folder 1, "Minutes, Bizoner Chebra Bnai/Beis Shule." A year earlier, in 1919, the group also contracted with Meyers & Co. to price coffins and shrouds and to make regular arrangements for use of the parlor's hearse and carriage. See entries for August 24, 1919, p. 201, and October 26, 1919, p. 205, which also appear in Bizoner, Minutes Book 1.

19 Rosenthal advertised his services throughout the 1910s in the Jewish press. See, for example, Chas. Rosenthal, funeral director, *American Hebrew & Jewish Messenger*, April 20, 1917, 853.

20 "Articles of Agreement, Guzeit & Smith Funeral Chapel Inc.," Louis Diamond Collection, RG 1364, box 2, folder 2.

21 E. Bernheim and Sons ad in *Jewish Daily Forward*, May 6, 1931, 11; Sigmund Schwartz ad in *Morgen zhurnal*, March 16, 1922, 14.

22 "History," Riverside Memorial Chapel, accessed February 2, 2019, www .dignitymemorial.com.

23 Sample advertisements for Perlshteyn and Diamond in *Jewish Daily Forward*, September 1, 1929, 24.

24 See a bill from Gutterman as "undertaker and embalmer," a title he also frequently used in ads, in records of Kahal Adath Yeshurun, I-10, box 2, folder 1; and an example of the full page ad Garlick frequently purchased in *Souvenir Journal*,

30th Anniversary, Plotzker Young Men's Independent Association (New York: s.n., 1923), Plotzker Young Men's Independent Association Collection, RG 785, box 1, folder, "Ondenk zhurnaln 1918–1928."

25 "Fun a shehne levaye," newspaper clipping, press and date not preserved, Louis Diamond Collection, RG 1364, box 2, folder 7.

26 "Independent Burial Association Inc. for Jewish Burials Exclusively," *American Hebrew & Jewish Messenger*, March 21, 1913, 596.

27 See sample ads like "Riverside Cemetery: The Finest Exclusively Jewish Cemetery Near New York City," *American Hebrew & Jewish Messenger*, May 14, 1915, 44.

28 See ads for Diamond in the *Jewish Daily Forward*, September 1, 1929, 24; on individual cemeteries, see correspondence from Frank G. Lyons, president of Highland View Cemetery Corporation, to Louis Diamond, September 12, 1922; Louis Singer, secretary of Mount Carmel Cemetery Association to Louis Diamond, January 23, 1925; and Washington Cemetery Board of Trustees to Louis Diamond, April 3, 1928. All appear in the Louis Diamond Collection, RG 1364, box 1, folder 1.

29 *Jewish Daily Forward*, September 1, 1929, 24.

30 Goren, "Traditional Institutions Transplanted," 71.

31 Article 9, "Rights and Benefits," section 11, *Constitution and By-Laws of the Noah Benevolent Society* (New York: s.n., 1917), 18, Noah Benevolent Society Records, I-186, box 28. The same was true for the 1922, 1926, 1930, and 1936 constitutions.

32 June 26, 1921, p. 231, Minutes Book 1, Bizoner Chebra B'nai Shaul Collection, RG 934, box 1, folder 1, "Minutes, Bizoner Chebra Bnai/Beis Shule."

33 Among the group's expenditures for the month was an $88 payment marked "Meyers Undertaker Rosenberg Funeral." March 25, 1923, p. 258, Minutes Book 1, Bizoner Chebra B'nai Shaul Collection, RG 934, box 1, folder 1, "Minutes, Bizoner Chebra Bnai/Beis Shule."

34 May 24, 1925, pp. 293–94, Minutes Book 1; Bizoner Chebra B'nai Shaul Collection, RG 934, box 1, folder 1, "Minutes, Bizoner Chebra Bnai/Beis Shule."

35 Ritual observance would not permit her body to go unattended between death and burial, so the extra days led to extra fees for employing a watcher to sit with the body until it was laid to rest. In a previous era, members of the hevra would have overseen this task. For Mrs. Goldstein, see June 26, 1910, p. 41, Minutes Book 1, Bizoner Chebra B'nai Shaul Collection, RG 934, box 1, folder 1, "Minutes, Bizoner Chebra Bnai/Beis Shule."

36 On Silber, see Bizoner, March 25, 1910, p. 32, Minutes Book 1. For the discussion on the coverage of children, see June 26, 1910, p. 41, Minutes Book 1, Bizoner Chebra B'nai Shaul Collection, RG 934, box 1, folder 1, "Minutes, Bizoner Chebra Bnai/Beis Shule."

37 For representative charges of the period, see "Articles of Agreement, Guzeit & Smith Funeral Chapel Inc.," Louis Diamond Collection, RG 1364, box 2, folder 2.

38 Article 11, "Deaths," sections 2 and 3, *Certificate and By-Laws of the Ceres Union* (New York: s.n., 1921), 31–32, Ceres Union Collection, RG 919, box 1, folder 2, "Constitutions, 1921, 1926, Ceres Union."

39 See, for example, several expense entries for minyan payments dated March 4, 1901, p. 9, and instances of shiva gelt paid out, March 6, 1904, and April 3, 1904, p. 97, records of Kahal Adath Yeshurun, I-10, box 4, cash ledger, 1900–1904.

40 Article 21, "Benefits," sections 6, 7, and 12, *Constitution of the Congregation Kahal Adas Jeshurun with Anshe Lubtz* (New York: s.n., 1913), 23–24, records of Kahal Adath Yeshurun, I-10, box 2, folder 1.

41 Article 21, "Benefits," section 13, *Constitution of the Congregation Kahal Adas Jeshurun with Anshe Lubtz* (New York: s.n., 1913), 24, records of Kahal Adath Yeshurun, I-10, box 2, folder 1.

42 Soyer, *Jewish Immigrant Aid Associations*, 91.

43 See February 22, 1920, p. 213, and May 27, 1928, p. 323, both in Minutes Book 1, Bizoner Chebra B'nai Shaul Collection, RG 934, box 1, folder 1, "Minutes, Bizoner Chebra Bnai/Beis Shule."

44 Soyer, *Jewish Immigrant Aid Associations*, 93–94; Beito, *From Mutual Aid to Welfare State*, 116–25.

45 *Annual Report of the Attorney General of New York for the Year Ending December 31, 1929* (Albany: New York State Department of Law, 1930), 58.

46 "Funeral Inquiry Opens. Undertaker Tells of Threats by Jewish Association," *New York Times*, June 6, 1929, 21; and "Tells of Funeral Clash," *New York Times*, June 8, 1929, 6.

47 "Inquiry Dissolves Undertakers' Group," *New York Times*, June 28, 1929, 29.

48 See, for instance, ads at the ends of *Souvenir Journal, 30th Anniversary, Plotzker Young Men's Independent Association* (New York: s.n., 1923) and *Souvenir Journal, 40th Anniversary, Plotzker Young Men's Independent Association* (New York: s.n., 1933), Plotzker Young Men's Independent Association Collection, RG 785, box 1, folder, "Ondenk zhurnaln 1918–1928."

49 Undated clipping, Louis Diamond Collection, RG 1364, box 2, folder 2.

50 Communication from H. Kapfelman, president, and S. Kudritzen, secretary, of Dockshitzer Benevolent Society, to Louis Diamond, June 1, 1934, Louis Diamond Collection, RG 1364, box 1, folder 2.

51 January 9, 1924, p. 273, Minutes Book 1, Bizoner Chebra B'nai Shaul Collection, RG 934, box 1, folder 1, "Minutes, Bizoner Chebra Bnai/Beis Shule."

52 December 13, 1925, p. 297, Minutes Book 1, Bizoner Chebra B'nai Shaul Collection, RG 934, box 1, folder 1, "Minutes, Bizoner Chebra Bnai/Beis Shule."

53 Communication from Morris S. Kahn, secretary of the Congregation Beth Israel, to Louis Diamond, June 1, 1926, Louis Diamond Collection, RG 1364, box 1, folder 3.

54 "High Cost of Dying," *Ziben un tsvantsigster yehrlekher report fun dem semeteri department arbeter ring* [Twenty-seventh annual report of the Cemetery Department of the Workmen's Circle] (New York: s.n., 1934), 46–48.

55 Ibid., 46.

56 "Tsu di mitglider fun arbeyter ring un tsu di delegaten fun 23-ten yehrlikhen konferents fun semeteri department," *Dray un tsvantsigster yehrlikher report fun*

dem semeteri department arbeter ring [Twenty-third annual report of the Cemetery Department of the Workmen's Circle] (New York: s.n., 1930), 7.

57 Ibid.

58 Shelvin, *History of the Independent Order*, 22.

59 *News Bulletin*, vol. 24, no. 2, September 29, 1944, Society for the Advancement of Judaism Records, I-70, box 1, folder 11, "Bulletins, 1944–1950."

60 "Peace of Mind," *Brooklyn Jewish Center Review* 21, no. 20 (January 1940): 21.

61 Soyer, *Jewish Immigrant Aid Associations*, 197–205; Glazer, "American Jew," 138–39.

62 Soyer, *Jewish Immigrant Aid Associations*, 191.

63 Studies cited in Sarna, *American Judaism*, 282.

64 Ben Seligman and Alvin Chenkin, "Jewish Population of the United States, 1953," *American Jewish Year Book* 55 (1954): 10–11; Horowitz and Kaplan, *Jewish Population of the New York Area*, 21–25; Moore, "Jewish Migration," 107; Lederhendler, *New York Jews*, 148–52.

65 Sarna, *American Judaism*, 277; Diner, *Jews of the United States*, 288.

66 Wertheimer, *A People Divided*, 4; Zeitz, *White Ethnic New York*, 38.

67 Wertheimer, "Conservative Synagogue," 124.

68 Israel Community Center brochure, quoted in ibid., 126. On Rego Park and Forest Hills, see Moore, *At Home in America*, 234–41.

69 Wertheimer, "Conservative Synagogue," 125; Wertheimer, *A People Divided*, 5–6; Moore, *At Home in America*, 234; Sklare, *Conservative Judaism*, 256.

70 *So You Want New Members*, 8, United Synagogue of America Publications, I-485, box 1, folder, "Membership & Architecture Guides, 1955–1956."

71 "Cemeteries," *Congregational Handbook*, May 1961, 1, United Synagogue of America Publications, I-485, box 1, folder, "Leaders Portfolio, 1957–1961 (Department of Synagogue Administration)."

72 Communication from M. Bernstein to Mr. Albert Miner, December 5, 1951, Congregation B'nai Jeshurun Records, box 8, folder 10, "Correspondence with Al(bert) Minor."

73 Communication from Bernstein to Minor, February 6, 1952, Congregation B'nai Jeshurun Records, box 8, folder 10, "Correspondence with Al(bert) Minor."

74 "Our History," Parkside Memorial Chapels, accessed June 7, 2018, www.jewishfuneral.net.

75 Promotional items, Jewish Center of Williamsbridge Records, I-509, box 8, folder 7, "Calendars, Funeral Directors, Wallet-size 1953–1957, 1959, 1963–1964, 1966–1968, 1970, 1972, 1975, 1979–1990."

76 Roul Tunley, "Can You Afford to Die?," *Saturday Evening Post*, June 17, 1961, 24. See also "The Death Industry," *Time*, November 14, 1960, 65; "The High Cost of Dying," *Collier's*, May 19, 1961.

77 Mitford, *American Way of Death*. For analysis on the book's reception, see Laderman, *Rest in Peace*, xxi–xxxi and 83–100.

78 "More on Standards," *United Synagogue Review* 14, no. 1 (Spring 1961): 3.

79 Communication from Sidney Applbaum to Funeral Standards Committee, memorandum, "Funeral Standards," September 27, 1962, Union of Orthodox Jewish Congregations of America Records, I-66, box 1, folder 8.

80 Quoted in Dresner, *Jew in American Life*, 28.

81 "Excerpt from Report of Henry N. Rapaport, Chairman of the Committee on Congregational Standards to the Biennial Convention of the United Synagogue of America, November 18, 1963," Union of Orthodox Jewish Congregations of America Records, I-66, box 1, folder 9.

82 "Simple Funerals Sought by Jews," *New York Times*, November 19, 1963, 36; "Guide to Funeral Practices as Adopted by the Committee on Funeral Practices of the Synagogue Council of America to Be Presented on April 14, 1965," Synagogue Council of America Records, I-68, box 8, folder 13, "Funeral Practices Committee Correspondence and Press Releases, 1963–1965"; "Report of the Committee on Guide for Synagogue Decorum," *Central Conference of American Rabbis Seventy-Fifth Annual Convention* 74 (1965): 60–62.

83 Samuel Dresner, "Simplicity and Equality in Funerals," *United Synagogue Review* 14, no. 1 (Spring 1961): 8; "Standards for B'nai Mitzvah, Weddings and Funerals," *The Proceedings of the Biennial Convention* (New York: United Synagogue of America, 1962), 56; Dresner, *Jew in American Life*, 20–49. Representative pieces published under Dresner's editorship include Goldblum, "Matter of Life and Death," *Conservative Judaism* 15, no. 4 (1961): 28; and a 1962 issue of the journal that published in full all eighteen funeral regulations adopted by the Temple Beth El of Lancaster, PA. See *Conservative Judaism* 26, nos. 2–3 (Winter–Spring 1962): 69–70.

84 *Proceedings of the Rabbinical Assembly of America*, edited by Rabbi Jules Harlow (Philadelphia: Press of Maurice Jacobs, 1960), 302; Rabbi Samuel H. Dresner, "Standards for B'nai Mitzvah, Weddings and Funerals," *The Proceedings of the Biennial Convention, November 12–16, 1961* (New York: United Synagogue of America, 1962), 56; Henry N. Rapaport, "Plenary Session: Standards for Synagogue Practice," *Proceedings of the Golden Jubilee Convention, November 17–21, 1963* (New York: United Synagogue of America, 1963), 7–11.

85 United Synagogue of America, *Proceedings of the Biennial Convention, November 12–16, 1961* (New York: United Synagogue of America, 1962), 25–27.

86 United Synagogue of America, *The Proceedings of the Golden Jubilee Convention, November 17–21, 1963* (New York: United Synagogue of America, 1963), 7–13, 27–28.

87 "Jewish Family Living," *Proceedings 1964 Biennial Convention of the National Women's League United Synagogue of America* (Kiamesha Lake, NY: Shulsinger Bros., 1964), 75.

88 Funeral Standards Committee, memorandum, "Conference with Officers of Metropolitan Association of Jewish Funeral Directors," May 21, 1962, Union of Orthodox Jewish Congregations of America Records, I-66, box 1, folder 8.

89 Communication from Sidney Applbaum to Funeral Standards Committee, memorandum, "Funeral Standards," September 27, 1962, Union of Orthodox

Jewish Congregations of America Records, I-66, box 1, folder 8, "Correspondence Funeral Standards Committee, 1960–1968."

90 "Draft for Contract," in communication from Sidney Applbaum to Funeral Standards Committee, memorandum, "Funeral Standards," December 18, 1961, Union of Orthodox Jewish Congregations of America Records, I-66, box 1, folder 8, "Correspondence Funeral Standards Committee, 1960–1968."

91 Communication from Sidney Applbaum to Joint Funeral Standards Commission, memorandum, "Final Memorandum," October 7, 1963, p. 3, Union of Orthodox Jewish Congregations of America Records, I-66, box 1, folder 8, "Correspondence Funeral Standards Committee, 1960–1968."

92 Ibid.

93 Goldblum, "Matter of Life and Death," 27.

94 Ibid., 28.

95 Dresner, *Jew in American Life*, 37.

96 Mitchell Gordon, "The Funeral Furor, Top-Selling Book Spurs Expansion of Societies Promoting Simple Rites," *Wall Street Journal*, September 30, 1963; Sher, "Funeral Prearrangements," 415–79.

97 "Church Dictation of Funerals" and "Synagogues Are Seeking Control of Burials," *Casket and Sunnyside* 92, no. 3 (March 1962): 15, 80, 50, and 71.

98 Quote in ibid., 15; for an overview of Mitford and anticommunism, see Sharon Crook West and Joseph P. McKerns, "Death and Communists: The Funeral Industry's Attack on Jessica Mitford's *The American Way of Death*," *American Journalism* 26, no. 1 (2009): 31–53.

99 "Basics . . . ," *New York Times*, February 9, 1964, 89.

CONCLUSION

1 Pool and Pool, *Old Faith*, 309.

2 See entries for June 6, 1756, and July 7, 1756, in "The Earliest Extant Minute Book of the Spanish and Portuguese Congregation Shearith Israel in New York, 1728–1786," *PAJHS* 21 (1913): 72–73.

3 Article 5, clause 4, handwritten rules and regulations for Beth Olom Cemetery in trustee minutes, December 18, 1852, Board of Trustees' Bound Minutes Volume, 1840–52, B'nai Jeshurun Records.

4 Grinstein, *Rise of the Jewish Community*, 318.

5 "The Beth Olom Cemetery," *Asmonean*, May 6, 1853, 25.

6 Goldman, *Crucial Decade*, 128.

7 Herberg, *Protestant, Catholic, Jew*; Sarna, *American Judaism*, 275–76.

8 Sklare and Greenblum, *Jewish Identity on the Suburban Frontier*. Others included Albert Gordon, *Jews in Suburbia* (Boston: Beacon Press, 1959); Morris Freedman, "A New Jewish Community in Formation," *Commentary* (January 1955): 36–47; Geller, "How Jewish Is Jewish Suburbia," 318–30, along with regular essays in the *American Jewish Year Book*—each year detailing Jewish movement beyond New York City, beginning in early 1950s.

9 Sherman, *Jew within American Society*, 155.

10 Ibid., 155–56. Sherman also invoked global Jewish parallels that he asserted "appl[y] equally to the development of the Jewish community in the United States."

11 Horowitz and Kaplan, *Jewish Population of the New York Area*, 82–83; Demographers for the *American Jewish Year Book* also referenced use of Yom Kippur and death records techniques. See, for instance, "Socio-Economic Data: Jewish Population of the United States, 1953," *American Jewish Year Book* 55 (1954): 4–5; or "Socio-Economic Data: Jewish Population of the United States, 1954," *American Jewish Year Book* 56 (1955): 173–74.

EPILOGUE

1 Siegel, Strassfeld, and Strassfeld, *Jewish Catalog*, 172.

2 Ibid., 177.

3 Ibid., 9.

4 Strassfeld and Strassfeld, *Third Jewish Catalog*, 136.

5 Ibid., 138.

6 Kugelmass, *Miracle of Intervale Avenue*.

7 Ibid., 149.

8 Ibid., 152.

9 Weisser, *Brotherhood of Memory*, 38–39.

10 Joseph Berger, "Organizations That Aided Immigrant Jews Recalled in Exhibition," *New York Times*, January 20, 1986.

11 Stephanie Strom, "Taking Confusion to the Grave: Demise of Burial Societies Leads to Fights over Plots," *New York Times*, February 24, 2005; Paul Vitello, "With Demise of Jewish Burial Societies, Resting Places Are in Turmoil," *New York Times*, August 2, 2009.

12 Vitello, "With Demise of Jewish Burial Societies."

13 Scott Rapoport, "The Gentle Gentile: Local Catholic Man Volunteers His Time to Fix up Jewish Cemetery," CBSlocal.com, accessed July 23, 2018, https://newyork.cbslocal.com; Angi Gonzalez, "Volunteer Makes Sure Neglected Queens Cemetery Is Not Forgotten," NY1.com, accessed July 23, 2018, www.ny1.com; Ari Feldman, "Can a Catholic Guy save This 'Hellhole' Jewish Cemetery—(and Why Hasn't Its Own Synagogue)?," Forward.com, accessed July 23, 2018, https://forward.com.

14 Annie Wilner, "Weeds among the Graves and Dismay among the Survivors," *New York Times*, August 15, 2018, www.nytimes.com; Lee Landor, "Suit against Cemetery Is Revived," *Queens Chronicle*, August 28, 2008, www.qchron.com.

15 Landor, "Suit against Cemetery Is Revived."

16 "Our Work," CAJAC.us, accessed July 21, 2018, www.cajac.us.

17 Jim Hoffer, "Queens Cemetery Still in Disrepair despite Development Deal," abc7ny.com, June 29, 2018, https://abc7ny.com.

18 Marvin Howe, "Funeral Home in Brooklyn Indicted in Sale of Burial Plots," *New York Times*, July 27, 1988, B2.

19 Marc Santora, "Graveyard Gridlock," *New York Times*, August 15, 2010, RE 1.
20 Ibid.
21 "History," Hebrew Free Burial Association, accessed January 2, 2019, www .hebrewfreeburial.org.
22 Eric J. Greenberg, "City Blasts Funeral Giant: Report Calls for State Attorney General to Probe Possible Anti-Trust Violation against SCI," *New York Jewish Week*, February 12, 1999, 1.
23 Eric J. Greenberg, "State, SCI Settle Fight over Funeral Homes: Texas Firm Agrees to Sell Three Jewish Parlors in the City but Dismisses Monopoly Charges," *New York Jewish Week*, November 19, 1999, 10.
24 Ibid.
25 Greenberg, "City Blasts Funeral Giant," 1.
26 Eric J. Greenberg, "Community Enters the Funeral Business: Jewish Coalition Makes Landmark Purchase of Manhattan Chapel, Expects 20% Drop in Costs," *New York Jewish Week*, March 16, 2001, 8.
27 Julie Wiener, "Low-Cost Funerals Slowly Making Inroads: Alternatives to for-Profit Funeral Homes Emerge but Have Yet to Bury the Competition," *New York Jewish Week*, August 30, 2002, 8.
28 Eric J. Greenberg, "Funeral Deal to Lower Costs: Pact between OU and Parkside Chapels to Save Families up to $1000 on Burial Services," *New York Jewish Week*, September 10, 2000, 10.
29 Wiener, "Low-Cost Funerals," 8.

BIBLIOGRAPHY

ARCHIVAL COLLECTIONS

B'nai Brith Manhattan-Washington Lodge 19 Collection, American Jewish Historical Society (AJHS), New York.

Bernice Brandmark, Study of Wills in New York City Collection, AJHS, New York.

Bizoner Chebra B'nai Shaul Collection, YIVO Institute for Jewish Research (YIVO Institute), New York.

Ceres Union Collection, YIVO Institute, New York.

Chevra Kadisha Beth Israel Collection, YIVO Institute, New York.

Chevra Kol Yisroel Brownsville Collection, YIVO Institute, New York.

Churchyard and Parish Registers, Trinity Church Archives, New York.

Congregation B'nai Jeshurun (New York) Records, Jewish Theological Seminary Archives (JTS), New York.

Congregation Ezras Achim Bnei Pinsk Collection, YIVO Institute, New York.

Congregation Kahal Adath Yeshurun with Anshe Lubtz (New York) Records, AJHS, New York.

Congregation Shearith Israel (New York) Records, AJHS, New York.

David Kantrowitz Family Benevolent Association Collection, YIVO Institute, New York.

Ershte Bolshowcer Sick Benevolent Society and Lodge 517 Collection, YIVO Institute, New York.

First Independent Storoznetzer Bukowiner Sick and Benevolent (S & B) Association Collection, YIVO Institute, New York.

Goldstein Family Papers, AJHS, New York.

Gratz Family of Philadelphia Papers, AJHS, New York.

Henry Clay Lodge 15, Independent Order Brith Abraham (IOBA) Collection, YIVO Institute, New York.

Holy Society Collection, Ninety-Second Street Y Library, New York.

Independent Order Free Sons of Israel Collection, AJHS, New York.

Independent Order Free Sons of Judah Collection, AJHS, New York.

Independent Orler Benevolent Society Collection, YIVO Institute, New York.

Israel Cantor Family Society Collection, YIVO Institute, New York.

Jacques Judah Lyons Collection, AJHS, New York.

Jewish Center of Williamsbridge Records, AJHS, New York.

Kesher Shel Barzel Records, AJHS, New York.

Kolbuszower Young Men's Benevolent Society Collection, YIVO Institute, New York.
Kolomear Friends Association Collection, YIVO Institute, New York.
Lipsonian Kinsmen Collection, YIVO Institute, New York.
Louis Diamond Collection, YIVO Institute, New York.
Loyal Benevolent Society Collection, YIVO Institute, New York.
Moses Family Society Collection, YIVO Institute, New York.
New York (County) Hall of Records Selected Incorporation Papers, 1848–1920, AJHS, New York.
Noah Benevolent Society Records, AJHS, New York.
Plotzker Young Men's Independent Association Collection, YIVO Institute, New York.
Records of Brothers in Unity (Bruder Verein #1), YIVO Institute, New York.
Samaritan Society Collection, YIVO Institute, New York.
Society for the Advancement of Judaism Records, AJHS, New York.
Soll Family Circle Collection, YIVO Institute, New York.
Synagogue Council of America Records, AJHS, New York.
Temple Beth El (Birmingham, MI) Records, AJHS, New York.
Union of Orthodox Jewish Congregations of America Records, AJHS, New York.
United Children of Joseph Solomon Collection, YIVO Institute, New York.
United Synagogue of America Publications, AJHS, New York.
Weinreb Benevolent Society Collection, YIVO Institute, New York.

NEWSPAPERS AND PERIODICALS
American Hebrew
The American Israelite
American Jewish Year Book
The Asmonean
The Brooklyn Daily Eagle
Central Conference of American Rabbis Annual Convention
Conservative Judaism
Jewish Daily Forward
The Jewish Messenger (New York)
National Women's League United Synagogue of America, Biennial Convention Proceedings
The New York Times
The Pennsylvania Gazette
Publications of the American Jewish Historical Society (PAJHS)
Rabbinical Assembly, Proceedings
United Synagogue of America, Biennial Convention Proceedings
United Synagogue Review

PUBLISHED PRIMARY SOURCES
Bush, Isidor. *Our Widows and Orphans Endowments: A Study Dedicated to the Members of the I.O.B.B.* New York: P. Cowen, 1885.

Congregation Shearith Israel. *Constitution of the Congregation of [Shearith Israel] as Ratified by the Members Thereof, at a Meeting Held on the Twenty-Sixth Day of [Sivan] Corresponding with the 24th of June, 1805.* New York: G. and R. Waite, 1805. www.jewishlife.amdigital.co.uk.

———. *Constitution of the Congregation [Shearith Israel] as Ratified by the Members Thereof at a Meeting Held on the Twenty-Sixth Day of [Sivan] . . . Corresponding with the 24th of June, 1805.* New York: T. B. Harrison & Co., 1865. Viewed at the American Jewish Historical Society, Rosenbach Rare Book Collection, call number Rosenbach #S 157.

Cypress Hills Cemetery. *The Cypress Hills Cemetery.* New York: Printed for the Cemetery, 1858. Promotional catalog.

"The Earliest Extant Minutes of the Spanish and Portuguese Congregation Shearith Israel in New York, 1728–1786." *Publications of the American Jewish Historical Society* 21 (1913): 1–81.

"From the 2nd Volume of Minute Books of Congn: Shearith Israel in New York." *Publications of the American Jewish Historical Society* 21 (1913): 83–172.

General Society of Mechanics and Tradesmen of the City of New York. *The Charter and Bye-Laws of the General Society of Mechanics and Tradesmen of the City of New-York. Also—the Rules of Orders with a Catalogue of Members' Names.* New York: General Society of Mechanics and Tradesmen of the City of New York, 1798.

Hebra Hased Va-Amet and Congregation Shearith Israel. *Compendium of the Order of the Burial Service and Rules for the Mournings, &c. Compiled by Desire and Published on Account of the Hebra Hased Va-Amet of the k'k Sefardim Shearith Israel.* New York: S. H. Jackson, 1827.

Jalfon, Isaac. *Order of Ceremonies and Laws of the Society "Mikveh Israel": Or Institution for Preparing for Interment the Deceased Members of the Spanish and Portuguese Jews' Congregation, London.* London: S. Meldola, 1845.

Kesher shel barzel, Maccabae Loge, *Neben-gesetze der Maccabae Loge No. 22, A.J.O.K.S.B.* New York: Thomsen & Wolff, 1873. Viewed at the American Jewish Historical Society, Soble Rare Book Collection, call number Soble 423.

Stern, Myer. *The Rise and Progress of Reform Judaism, Embracing a History Made from the Official Records of Temple Emanu-El of New York, with a Description of Salem Field Cemetery, Its City of the Dead, with Illustrations of Its Vaults, Monuments, and Landscape Effects.* New York: M. Stern, 1895.

Weingart, Samuel, and Cecil A. Marks. *Three-Quarters of a Century: The History of the Mendelssohn Benevolent Society, 1841 to 1916.* New York: s.n., 1916.

The Workmen's Circle. *Dray un tsvantsigster yehrlikher report fun dem semeteri department arbeter ring.* New York: Arbeter Ring, 1930.

———. *Ziben un tsvantsigster yehrlikher report fun dem semeteri department arbeter ring.* New York: Arbeter Ring, 1934.

BOOKS, ARTICLES, AND WEBSITES

Abel, Emily K. *The Inevitable Hour: A History of Caring for Dying Patients in America*. Baltimore: Johns Hopkins University Press, 2013.

All Faiths Cemetery. "Our History." Accessed February 1, 2018. http://allfaithscemetery .org.

Amanik, Allan. "'All Will Be Fine, Jewish and Promptly Attended': Tradition and the Rise of New York Jewish Undertakers, 1890–1950." *Shofar* 35, no. 4 (2017): 91–109.

Appleby, Joyce. "Thomas Jefferson and the Psychology of Democracy." In *The Revolution of 1800: Democracy, Race, and the New Republic*, edited by James Horn, Jan Ellen Lewis, and Peter S. Onuf, 155–72. Charlottesville: University of Virginia Press, 2002.

Ariès, Philippe. *The Hour of Our Death*. Translated by Helen Weaver. New York: Alfred A. Knopf, 1981.

———. *Western Attitudes toward Death: From the Middle Ages to the Present*. Translated by Patricia Ranum. Baltimore: Johns Hopkins University Press, 1974.

Augustine, Michael. "The Catholic Cemeteries of New York." *Historical Records and Studies* 1, no. 2 (January 1900): 369–78.

Barkai, Avraham. *Branching Out: German-Jewish Immigration to the United States, 1820–1914*. New York: Holmes & Meier, 1994.

Barnett, R. D. "The Correspondence of the Mahamad of the Spanish and Portuguese Congregation of London during the Seventeenth and Eighteenth Centuries." *Transactions of the Jewish Historical Society of England* 20 (1959–61): 1–50.

Beito, David T. *From Mutual Aid to the Welfare State: Fraternal Societies and Social Services, 1890–1967*. Chapel Hill: University of North Carolina Press, 2000.

———. "'This Enormous Army': The Mutual-Aid Tradition of American Fraternal Societies Before the Twentieth Century." In *The Voluntary City: Choice, Community, and Civil Society*, edited by David T. Beito, Peter Gordon, and Alexander Tabarrok, 182–203. Ann Arbor: University of Michigan Press, 2002.

Bender, Thomas. "The 'Rural' Cemetery Movement: Urban Travail and the Appeal of Nature." *New England Quarterly* 47, no. 2 (June 1974): 196–211.

Beneke, Chris, and Christopher S. Grenda, eds. *The First Prejudice: Religious Tolerance and Intolerance in Early America*. Philadelphia: University of Pennsylvania Press, 2011.

Benjamin, Israel Joseph. *Three Years in America*. Translated by Charles Reznikoff. Philadelphia: Jewish Publication Society of America, 1956.

Bergman, Ben Zion. "A Matter of Grave Concern: A Question of Mixed Burial." In *Responsa, 1991–2000: The Committee on Jewish Law and Standards of the Conservative Movement*, edited by Kassel Abelson and David J. Fine, 418–25. New York: Rabbinical Assembly, 2002.

Bingham, Emily. *Mordecai: An Early American Family*. New York: Hill and Wang, 2003.

Birnbaum, Pierre, and Ira Katznelson, eds. *Paths of Emancipation: Jews, States, and Citizenship*. Princeton, NJ: Princeton University Press, 1995.

Blau, Joseph L., and Salo W. Baron. *The Jews of the United States: A Documentary History, 1790–1840.* 3 vols. New York: Columbia University Press, 1963.

Bowman, LeRoy. *The American Funeral: A Study in Guilt, Extravagance, and Sublimity.* Washington: Public Affairs Press, 1959.

Bullock, Steven C. *Revolutionary Brotherhood: Freemasonry and the Transformation of the American Social Order, 1730–1840.* Chapel Hill: University of North Carolina Press, 1996.

Butler, Jon. *Becoming America: The Revolution before 1776.* Cambridge: Harvard University Press, 2000.

Calvary Cemetery. "Welcome." Accessed June 6, 2013. www.calvarycemeteryqueens .com.

Cohen, Lizabeth. *Making a New Deal: Industrial Workers in Chicago, 1919–1939.* Cambridge, UK: Cambridge University Press, 1990.

Cohen, Robert. "Jewish Demography in the Eighteenth Century: A Study of London, the West Indies, and Early America." PhD diss., Brandeis University, 1976.

Cohen, Simon. *Shaaray Tefila: A History of Its Hundred Years, 1845–1945.* New York: Greenberg, 1945.

Cott, Nancy F. *Public Vows: A History of Marriage and the Nation.* Cambridge: Harvard University Press, 2000.

Cox, John. *Quakerism in the City of New York, 1657–1930.* New York: Priv. Print, 1930.

Daniels, Doris Groshen. "Colonial Jewry: Religion, Domestic and Social Relations." *American Jewish Historical Quarterly* 66, no. 3 (1977): 375–400.

Davis, Moshe. "The Synagogue in American Judaism: A Study of Congregation B'nai Jeshurun, New York City." In *Two Generations in Perspective: Notable Events and Trends, 1896–1956,* edited by Harry Schneiderman, 210–35. New York: Monde, 1957.

de Chaparro, Martina Will. *Death and Dying in New Mexico.* Albuquerque: University of New Mexico Press, 2007.

Diner, Hasia R. *The Jews of the United States, 1654 to 2000.* Berkeley: University of California Press, 2004.

———. *A Time for Gathering: The Second Migration, 1820–1880.* Jewish People in America 2. Baltimore: Johns Hopkins University Press, 1992.

Dresner, Samuel H. *The Jew in American Life.* New York: Crown, 1963.

Duer, Stephen C., and Allan B. Smith. *Cypress Hills Cemetery.* Charleston, SC: Arcadia, 2010.

Elmaleh, L. H., and J. Bunford Samuel. *The Jewish Cemetery: Ninth and Spruce Streets Philadelphia.* Philadelphia: s.n., 1962.

Elzas, Barnett Abraham. *The Jews of South Carolina: From the Earliest Times to the Present Day.* Philadelphia: J. B. Lippincott, 1905.

———. *The Old Jewish Cemeteries at Charleston, S.C.: A Transcript of the Inscriptions on Their Tombstones, 1762–1903.* Charleston, SC: Daggett, 1903.

Eustace, Nicole. *Passion Is the Gale: Emotion, Power, and the Coming of the American Revolution.* Chapel Hill: University of North Carolina Press, 2008. Published for the Omohundro Institute of Early American History and Culture, Williamsburg, Virginia.

Evergreens Cemetery. "About Us." Accessed June 6, 2013. www.theevergreenscemetery .com.

Ezekiel, Herbert T., and Gaston Lichtenstein. *The History of the Jews of Richmond, 1769–1917*. Richmond, VA: Herbert T. Ezekiel, 1917.

Faber, Eli. *A Time for Planting: The First Migration, 1654–1820*. Jewish People in America 1. Baltimore: Johns Hopkins University Press, 1992.

Farrell, James. "The Dying of Death: Historical Perspectives." *Death Education* 6, no. 2 (1982): 105–23.

———. *Inventing the American Way of Death, 1830–1920*. Philadelphia: Temple University Press, 1980.

Faust, Drew Gilpin. *This Republic of Suffering: Death and the American Civil War*. New York: Alfred A. Knopf, 2008.

Feifel, Herman, ed. *The Meaning of Death*. New York: McGraw-Hill, 1959.

Field, David, Jenny Hockey, and Neil Small, eds. *Death, Gender and Ethnicity*. London: Routledge, 1997.

Foote, Thelma Wills. *Black and White Manhattan: The History of Racial Formation in Colonial New York City*. New York: Oxford University Press, 2004.

Gaster, Moses. *Order of Ceremonies and Laws of the Society "Mikveh Israel": Or Institution for Preparing for Interment the Deceased Members of the Spanish and Portuguese Jews' Congregation, London*. London: The Society, 1899.

Gelfand, Noah L. "A Transatlantic Approach to Understanding the Formation of a Jewish Community in New Netherland and New York." *New York History* 89, no. 4 (2008): 375–95.

Geller, Victor B. "How Jewish Is Jewish Suburbia." *Tradition* (Spring 1960): 318–30.

Glaser, Barney G., and Anselm L. Strauss. *Awareness of Dying*. Chicago: Aldine, 1965.

Glazer, Nathan. "The American Jew and the Attainment of Middle-Class Rank: Some Trends and Explorations." In *The Jews: Social Patterns of an American Group*, edited by Marshall Sklare, 138–46. New York: Free Press, 1958.

———. *American Judaism*. Chicago: University of Chicago Press, 1957.

Glenn, Susan A. *Daughters of the Shtetl: Life and Labor in the Immigrant Generation*. Ithaca, NY: Cornell University Press, 1990.

Goldblum, Moshe. "A Matter of Life and Death." *Conservative Judaism* 15, no. 4 (1961): 26–29.

Goldman, Eric Frederick. *The Crucial Decade: America, 1945–1955*. New York: Alfred A. Knopf, 1956.

Goldman, Yosef, and Ari Kinsberg, eds. *Hebrew Printing in America 1735–1926: A History and Annotated Bibliography*. New York: 2006.

Goldstein, Eric L. *The Price of Whiteness: Jews, Race, and American Identity*. Princeton, NJ: Princeton University Press, 2006.

Goldstein, Israel. *A Century of Judaism in New York: B'nai Jeshurun, 1825–1925; New York's Oldest Ashkenazic Congregation*. New York: Congregation B'nai Jeshurun, 1930.

Goodfriend, Joyce D. *Before the Melting Pot: Society and Culture in Colonial New York City, 1664–1730*. Princeton, NJ: Princeton University Press, 1992.

———. "Foreigners in a Dutch Colonial City." *New York History* 90, no. 4 (2009): 241–69.

———. "Practicing Toleration in Dutch New Netherland." In *The First Prejudice: Religious Tolerance and Intolerance in Early America*, edited by Chris Beneke and Christopher S. Grenda, 98–122. Philadelphia: University of Pennsylvania Press, 2011.

———. "The Social Dimensions of Congregational Life in Colonial New York City." *William and Mary Quarterly* 46, no. 2 (1989): 252–78.

Gordon, Linda. *Women, the State, and Welfare*. Madison: University of Wisconsin Press, 1990.

Goren, Arthur A. "Traditional Institutions Transplanted: The Hevra Kadisha in Europe and America." In *The Jews of North America*, edited by Moses Rischin, 62–78. Detroit: Wayne University Press, 1987.

Gorer, Geoffrey. "The Pornography of Death." *Encounter* 5 (October 1955): 49–52.

Grinstein, Hyman Bogomolny. *The Rise of the Jewish Community of New York, 1654–1860*. Philadelphia: Jewish Publication Society of America, 1947.

Grusd, Edward E. *B'nai B'rith: The Story of a Covenant*. New York: Appleton-Century, 1966.

Gutterman Brothers Funeral Directors. "About Us." Accessed March 21, 2013. http://guttermanbrothers.com.

Habenstein, Robert W., and William M. Lamers. *The History of American Funeral Directing*. 2nd rev. ed. Milwaukee, WI: National Funeral Directors Association, 1981.

Hareven, Tamara K. "The History of the Family and the Complexity of Social Change." *American Historical Review* 96, no. 1 (February 1991): 95–124.

Harrington, Spencer P. M. "Bones and Bureaucrats." *Archaeology* 46, no. 2 (1993): 28–38.

Hebrew Free Burial Association. "History." Accessed January 7, 2019. www.hebrewfreeburial.org.

Hemphill, C. Dallett. *Siblings: Brothers and Sisters in American History*. Oxford: Oxford University Press, 2011.

Herberg, Will. *Protestant, Catholic, Jew: An Essay in American Religious Sociology*. Garden City, NY: Doubleday, 1955.

Hershkowitz, Leo. "Some Aspects of the New York Jewish Merchant and Community, 1654–1820." *American Jewish Historical Quarterly* 66, no. 1 (1976): 10–34.

———, ed. *Wills of Early New York Jews, 1704–1799*. New York: American Jewish Historical Society, 1967.

Hershkowitz, Leo, and Isidore S. Meyer, eds. *Letters of the Franks Family, 1733–1748*. Waltham, MA: American Jewish Historical Society, 1968.

Horowitz, C. Morris, and Lawrence J. Kaplan. *The Jewish Population of the New York Area, 1900–1975*. New York: Federation of Jewish Philanthropies of New York, 1959.

Igra, Anna R. *Wives without Husbands: Marriage, Desertion, and Welfare in New York, 1900–1935*. Chapel Hill: University of North Carolina Press, 2007.

Inskeep, Carolee R. *The Graveyard Shift: A Family Historian's Guide to New York City Cemeteries.* Orem, UT: Ancestry, 2000.

Isenberg, Nancy, and Andrew Burstein, eds. *Mortal Remains: Death in Early America.* Philadelphia: University of Pennsylvania Press, 2003.

Israel, Jonathan. "Curaçao, Amsterdam, and the Rise of the Sephardi Trade System in the Caribbean, 1630–1700." In *The Jews in the Caribbean*, edited by Jane S. Gerber, 29–43. Portland, OR: Littman Library of Jewish Civilization, 2014.

Jackson, Charles O., ed. *Passing: The Vision of Death in America.* Westport, CT: Greenwood Press, 1977.

Jacobs, Jaap. *The Colony of New Netherland: A Dutch Settlement in Seventeenth-Century America.* Ithaca, NY: Cornell University Press, 2009.

Jick, Leon A. *The Americanization of the Synagogue, 1820–1870.* Hanover, NH: University Press of New England, 1992. Published for Brandeis University Press.

Judson, Daniel. *Pennies for Heaven: The History of American Synagogues and Money.* Waltham, MA: Brandeis University Press, 2018.

Kaganoff, Nathan M. "Organized Jewish Welfare Activity in New York City (1848–1860)." *American Jewish Historical Quarterly* 56, no. 1 (1966): 27–61.

Kaplan, Marion A. *The Making of the Jewish Middle Class: Women, Family, and Identity in Imperial Germany.* New York: Oxford University Press, 1991.

Katznelson, Ira. "Jews on the Margins of American Liberalism." In *Paths of Emancipation: Jews, States, and Citizenship*, edited by Pierre Birnbaum and Ira Katznelson, 157–205. Princeton, NJ: Princeton University Press, 1995.

Kessler-Harris, Alice. *In Pursuit of Equity: Women, Men, and the Quest for Economic Citizenship in 20th-Century America.* New York: Oxford University Press, 2001.

Kessner, Thomas. "Jobs, Ghettoes and the Urban Economy, 1880–1935." *American Jewish History* 71, no. 2 (December 1981): 218–38.

Kliger, Hannah. *Jewish Hometown Associations and Family Circles in New York: The WPA Yiddish Writers' Group Study.* Bloomington: Indiana University Press, 1992.

Kohler, Max J. "Civil Status of the Jews in Colonial New York." *Publications of the American Jewish Historical Society* 6 (1897): 81–106.

Kraska, Kurt T. *The History of Cypress Hills Cemetery and Its Permanent Residents.* New York: Woodhaven Cultural and Historical Society, 1980.

Kreider, Harry Julius. *Lutheranism in Colonial New York.* New York: Arno Press, 1972.

Kübler-Ross, Elisabeth. *On Death and Dying.* New York: Macmillan, 1969.

Kugelmass, Jack. *The Miracle of Intervale Avenue.* New York: Schocken Books, 1986.

Laderman, Gary. *Rest in Peace: A Cultural History of Death and the Funeral Home in Twentieth-Century America.* New York: Oxford University Press, 2003.

———. *The Sacred Remains: American Attitudes toward Death, 1799–1883.* New Haven: Yale University Press, 1996.

Lederhendler, Eli. *New York Jews and the Decline of Urban Ethnicity, 1950–1970.* Syracuse, NY: Syracuse University Press, 2001.

Leff, Mark H. "The Mothers'-Pension Movement in the Progressive Era." *Social Service Review* 47, no. 3 (September 1973): 397–417.

Levi, David. *The Form of Prayers According to the Custom of the Spanish and Portuguese Jews: As Read in Their Synagogues and Used in Their Families*. London: W. Justins, 1789.

Marcus, Jacob Rader, ed. *American Jewry: Documents, Eighteenth Century*. Cincinnati: Hebrew Union College Press, 1959.

———. *Communal Sick-Care in the German Ghetto*. Cincinnati: Hebrew Union College Press, 1947.

———. "The Handsome Young Priest in the Black Gown: The Personal World of Gershom Seixas." *Hebrew Union College Annual* 40/41 (1969–70): 409–67.

———, ed. *The Jew in the American World: A Source Book*. Detroit: Wayne State University Press, 1996.

———. *To Count a People: American Jewish Population Data, 1585–1984*. Lanham, MD: University Press of America, 1990.

———. *United States Jewry, 1776–1985*. 4 vols. Detroit: Wayne State University Press, 1989.

May, Elaine Tyler. *Homeward Bound: American Families in the Cold War Era*. New York: Basic Books, 2008.

Maynard, John Albert F. *The Huguenot Church of New York: A History of the French Church of Saint Esprit*. New York: s.n., 1938.

Mendez, Samuel Rodriguez. *Seder tefilot ha-mo'adim: ke-minhag ḳ. ḳ. ha-Sefaradim*. Amsterdam: Be-vet uvi-defus Hirts ben Aleksander Ziskind Leyi me-'Emdin, 1726.

Michel, Sonya, and Seth Koven, eds. *Mothers of a New World: Maternalist Politics and the Origins of Welfare States*. New York: Routledge, 1993.

Mintz, Steven. *A Prison of Expectations: The Family in Victorian Culture*. New York: New York University Press, 1983.

Mintz, Steven, and Susan Kellogg. *Domestic Revolutions: A Social History of American Family Life*. New York: Free Press, 1988.

Mitford, Jessica. *The American Way of Death*. New York: Simon and Schuster, 1963.

Moore, Deborah Dash. *At Home in America: Second Generation New York Jews*. New York: Columbia University Press, 1981.

———. *B'nai B'rith and the Challenge of Ethnic Leadership*. Albany: State University of New York Press, 1981.

———. "Jewish Migration in Postwar America." In *Studies in Contemporary Jewry*, vol. 8, *A New Jewry? America since the Second World War*, edited by Peter Y. Medding, 102–17. New York: Oxford University Press, 1992.

Morley, John. *Death, Heaven, and the Victorians*. Pittsburgh, PA: University of Pittsburgh Press, 1971.

Nelson, Barbara J. "The Origins of the Two-Channel Welfare State: Workmen's Compensation and Mothers' Aid." In *Women, the State, and Welfare*, edited by Linda Gordon, 123–51. Madison: University of Wisconsin Press, 1990.

O'Brien, Michael Joseph. *In Old New York: The Irish Dead in Trinity and St. Paul's Churchyards*. New York: American Irish Historical Society, 1928.

Oppenheim, Samuel. "The Jewish Burial Ground on New Bowery, New York, Acquired in 1682, Not 1656." *Publications of the American Jewish Historical Society* 31 (1928): 77–103.

———. "Jews Who Died of Yellow Fever in the Epidemic in New York in 1798." *Publications of the American Jewish Historical Society* 25 (1917): 123.

Orloff, Ann Shola. "Gender in Early U.S. Social Policy." *Journal of Policy History* 3, no. 3 (1991): 249–81.

———. "The Political Origins of America's Belated Welfare State." In *The Politics of Social Policy in the United States*, edited by Margaret Weir, Ann Shola Orloff, and Theda Skocpol, 37–80. Princeton, NJ: Princeton University Press, 1988.

Parkside Memorial Chapel. "Our History." Accessed March 21, 2013. www.jewish funeral.net.

Pencak, William. "Anti-Semitism, Toleration, and Appreciation: The Changing Relations of Jews and Gentiles in Early America." In *The First Prejudice: Religious Tolerance and Intolerance in Early America*, edited by Chris Beneke and Christopher S. Grenda, 241–62. Philadelphia: University of Pennsylvania Press, 2011.

———. *Jews and Gentiles in Early America, 1654–1800*. Ann Arbor: University of Michigan Press, 2005.

Phillips, Rosalie S. "A Burial Place for the Jewish Nation Forever." *Publications of the American Jewish Historical Society* 18 (1909): 93–122.

Piccioto, James. *Sketches of Anglo-Jewish History*. London: Trubner, 1875.

Polland, Annie, and Daniel Soyer. *Emerging Metropolis: New York Jews in the Age of Immigration, 1840–1920*. New York: New York University Press, 2012.

Pool, David de Sola. *Portraits Etched in Stone: Early Jewish Settlers, 1682–1831*. New York: Columbia University Press, 1952.

Pool, David de Sola, and Tamar de Sola Pool. *An Old Faith in the New World: Portrait of Shearith Israel, 1654–1954*. New York: Columbia University Press, 1955.

Quint, Jeanne C. *The Nurse and the Dying Patient*. New York: Macmillan, 1967.

Reznikoff, Charles, and Uriah Zevi Engelman. *The Jews of Charleston: A History of an American Jewish Community*. Philadelphia: Jewish Publication Society of America, 1950.

Rischin, Moses, ed. *The Jews of North America*. Detroit: Wayne University Press, 1987.

Riverside Memorial Chapel. "History." Accessed April 2, 2013. www.riversidememorial chapel.com.

Rock, Howard B. *Haven of Liberty: New York Jews in the New World, 1654–1865*. New York: New York University Press, 2012.

Roediger, David R. "And Die in Dixie: Funerals, Death, and Heaven in the Slave Community 1700–1865." *Massachusetts Review* 22, no. 1 (1981): 163–83.

Rosenbloom, Joseph R. *A Biographical Dictionary of Early American Jews: Colonial Times through 1800*. Lexington: University of Kentucky Press, 1960.

Rousmaniere, John, and Kenneth Druse. *Green Oasis in Brooklyn: The Evergreens Cemetery, 1849–2008*. Kittery Point, ME: Seapoint Books, 2008.

Sachs, Aaron. "American Arcadia: Mount Auburn Cemetery and the Nineteenth-Century Landscape Tradition," *Environmental History* 15 (April 2010): 206–35.

Sarna, Jonathan D. *American Judaism: A History.* New Haven: Yale University Press, 2004.

Schantz, Mark S. *Awaiting the Heavenly Country: The Civil War and America's Culture of Death.* Ithaca, NY: Cornell University Press, 2008.

Schneider, Mareleyn. *History of a Jewish Burial Society: An Examination of Secularization.* Lewiston, NY: E. Mellen Press, 1991.

Schneiderman, Harry, ed. *Two Generations in Perspective: Notable Events and Trends, 1896–1956.* New York: Monde, 1957.

Schuyler, David. *The New Urban Landscape: The Redefinition of City Form in Nineteenth-Century America.* Baltimore: Johns Hopkins University Press, 1986.

Seeman, Erik R. *Death in the New World: Cross-Cultural Encounters, 1492–1800.* Philadelphia: University of Pennsylvania Press, 2010.

Shelvin, Bernard. *History of the Independent Order Brith Abraham, 1887–1937.* New York: IOBA, 1937.

Sher, Byron D. "Funeral Prearrangements: Mitigating the Undertaker's Bargaining Advantage." *Stanford Law Review* 15, no. 3 (May 1963): 415–79.

Sherman, Charles Bezalel. *The Jew within American Society: A Study in Ethnic Individuality.* Detroit: Wayne State University Press, 1960.

Siegel, Richard, Michael Strassfeld, and Sharon Strassfeld, eds. *The Jewish Catalog: A Do-It-Yourself Kit.* Philadelphia: Jewish Publication Society of America, 1973.

Sklare, Marshall. *Conservative Judaism: An American Religious Movement.* Glencoe, IL: Free Press, 1955.

———, ed. *The Jews: Social Patterns of an American Group.* New York: Free Press, 1958.

Sklare, Marshall, and Joseph Greenblum. *Jewish Identity on the Suburban Frontier: A Study of Group Survival in the Open Society.* New York: Basic Books, 1967.

Skocpol, Theda. *Protecting Soldiers and Mothers: The Political Origins of Social Policy in the United States.* Cambridge: Belknap Press, 1992.

Sloane, David Charles. *The Last Great Necessity: Cemeteries in American History.* Baltimore: Johns Hopkins University Press, 1991.

Smith, Suzanne E. *To Serve the Living: Funeral Directors and the African American Way of Death.* Cambridge: Belknap Press, 2010.

Snyder, Holly. "Rethinking the Definition of 'Community' for a Migratory Age, 1654–1830." In *Imagining the American Jewish Community,* edited by Jack Wertheimer, 3–27. Hanover, NH: University Press of New England / Waltham, MA: Brandeis University Press, 2007.

Soyer, Daniel. *Jewish Immigrant Associations and American Identity in New York, 1880–1939.* Cambridge: Harvard University Press, 1997.

Stannard, David E., ed. *Death in America.* Philadelphia: University of Pennsylvania Press, 1975.

———. *The Puritan Way of Death: A Study in Religion Culture and Social Change.* New York: Oxford University Press, 1977.

Stern, Malcolm. *First American Jewish Families: 600 Genealogies, 1654–1977*. Cincinnati: American Jewish Archives, 1978.

———. "The Function of Genealogy in American Jewish History." In *Essays in American Jewish History to Commemorate the Tenth Anniversary of the Founding of the American Jewish Archives under the Direction of Jacob Rader Marcus*, 69–98. Cincinnati: American Jewish Archives, 1958.

———. "Jewish Marriage and Intermarriage in the Federal Period (1776–1840)." *American Jewish Archives Journal* 19, no. 2 (1967): 142–43.

———. "A Successful Caribbean Restoration: The Nevis Story." *American Jewish Historical Quarterly* 61, no. 1 (1971): 19–32.

Stern, Mark Abbott. *David Franks: Colonial Merchant*. University Park: Pennsylvania State University Press, 2010.

Strassfeld, Sharon, and Michael Strassfeld. *The Third Jewish Catalog: Creating Community*. Philadelphia: Jewish Publication Society of America, 1980.

Straus Reed, Barbara. "Unity, Not Absorption: Robert Lyon and the *Asmonean*, the Origins of the First English-Language Jewish Weekly in the United States." *American Journalism* 7, no. 2 (1990): 77–95.

Sudnow, David. *Passing On: The Social Organization of Dying*. Englewood Cliffs, NJ: Prentice-Hall, 1967.

Swan, Robert J. *New Amsterdam Gehenna: Segregated Death in New York City, 1630–1801*. Brooklyn: Noir Verite Press, 2006.

Swichkow, Louis J., and Lloyd P. Gartner. *The History of the Jews of Milwaukee*. Philadelphia: Jewish Publication Society of America, 1963.

Tobias, Thomas J. "The Cemetery We Rededicate." *American Jewish Historical Quarterly* 53, no. 4 (1964): 352–70.

Tom, Zoe. "Isaac Louzada." Find a Grave. Accessed May 31, 2013. www.findagrave.com.

Trattner, Walter I. *From Poor Law to Welfare State: A History of Social Welfare in America*. New York: Free Press, 1984.

T.V.F.T.H. "Jacob Hays." Find a Grave. Accessed May 31, 2013. www.findagrave.com.

Vorspan, Max, and Lloyd P. Gartner. *History of the Jews of Los Angeles*. San Marino: Huntington Library, 1970.

Weir, Margaret, Ann Shola Orloff, and Theda Skocpol, eds. *The Politics of Social Policy in the United States*. Princeton, NJ: Princeton University Press, 1988.

Weissbach, Lee Shai. *Jewish Life in Small-Town America: A History*. New Haven: Yale University Press, 2005.

Weisser, Michael R. *Brotherhood of Memory: Jewish Landsmanshaftn in the New World*. New York: Basic Books, 1985.

Wenger, Beth S. *New York Jews and the Great Depression: Uncertain Promise*. Syracuse, NY: Syracuse University Press, 1999.

Wertheimer, Jack. "The Conservative Synagogue." In *The American Synagogue: A Sanctuary Transformed*, edited by Jack Wertheimer, 111–52. New York: Cambridge University Press, 1987.

———, ed. *Imagining the American Jewish Community*. Hanover, NH: University Press of New England / Waltham, MA: Brandeis University Press, 2007.

———. *A People Divided: Judaism in Contemporary America*. New York: Basic Books, 1993.

West, Sharon Crook, and Joseph P. McKerns. "Death and Communists: The Funeral Industry's Attack on Jessica Mitford's *The American Way of Death*." *American Journalism* 26, no. 1 (Winter 2009): 31–53.

Wilentz, Sean. *Chants Democratic: New York City and the Rise of the American Working Class, 1788–1850*. New York: Oxford University Press, 1984.

Wilhelm, Cornelia. "The Independent Order of True Sisters: Friendship, Fraternity, and a Model of Modernity for Nineteenth-Century American Jewish Womanhood." *American Jewish Archives Journal* 54, no. 1 (2002): 37–63.

Williams, Dawn-Marie. "Arabella Levy Jones." Find a Grave. Accessed May 31, 2013. www.findagrave.com.

———. "Henrietta Levy." Find a Grave. Accessed May 31, 2013. www.findagrave.com.

———. "Martha Lampley Levy." Find a Grave. Accessed May 31, 2013. www.findagrave.com.

———. "Moses Levy." Find a Grave. Accessed May 31, 2013. www.findagrave.com.

———. "Rachel Levy." Find a Grave. Accessed May 31, 2013. www.findagrave.com.

———. "Samson Levy." Find a Grave. Accessed May 31, 2013. www.findagrave.com.

Wolf, Edwin, and Maxwell Whiteman. *The History of the Jews of Philadelphia from Colonial Times to the Age of Jackson*. Philadelphia: Jewish Publication Society of America, 1957.

Zeitz, Joshua M. *White Ethnic New York: Jews, Catholics, and the Shaping of Postwar Politics*. Chapel Hill: University of North Carolina Press, 2007.

INDEX

Adath Jeshurun, 132, 133, 150, 158

African Americans, 5, 12, 79, 85

African Methodist Episcopal Zion Church, New York City, 79

Ahawes Chesed. *See* Central Synagogue

Allen Street Methodist Episcopal Church, New York City, 97

Americanism, 74

American Israelite, 90

American Revolution, 17, 39, 49, 59

American Way of Death, The (Mitford), 170, 177

Anglicans, 21

Anshe Chesed, New York City, 69, 70, 94, 97–98, 101–2

antitrust law, 159, 196

Appleby, Joyce, 64

Asmonean, 81–82, 87, 91, 99

baptism, 17, 29–30, 31, 32

Baron Hirsch Cemetery, Staten Island, New York City, 194

Bayside Cemetery, Queens, New York City, 193–94

benevolent societies, 8, 48, 54, 55, 70, 174

bereavement. *See* mourning; shiva

Beth Abram Society, 84

Beth Olom Cemetery, Brooklyn, New York City, 102, 103; family lots and, 76, 89, 91, 97, 104

Bible, on family burial, 90

Bizoner Chebra B'nai Shaul, 140, 141, 152, 156–57, 158, 161–62

Blumenthal, Aaron, 172

B'nai B'rith: death endowment amounts, 120–21, 222n27; expansion of, 72, 106; founding of, 49, 72; funeral benefits and, 117; members' health and, 124; membership increase, 121; widow and orphan policies, 117, 125–26, 144, 221n16

B'nai Jeshurun, New York City, 68–69, 87–88, 103, 168, 185; burial society, 58, 66, 70; founding of, 24–25; reburial controversy, 97, 98–99, 101, 218n63; rural cemeteries and, 76, 82, 85, 89, 91, 92; women and, 66–67. *See also* Beth Olom Cemetery

Bolshowcer Sick and Benevolent Society, 143–44

Boyerker Benevolent Society, 191

Bretschneider, A., 155

Brick Presbyterian Church, New York City, 97, 211n85

Brooklyn, New York City, 76, 150, 194–95

Brooklyn Jewish Center, New York City, 1–2, 164

Brothers of Charity, 107

Bruder Verein (Union of Brothers), 107

Bueno de Mesquita, Benjamin, 22, 35

Bueno de Mesquita, Joseph, 22–23

burial: Christian, of baptized children, 31; Christian, of Jewish converts, 28, 31; chronological, 16, 17, 27, 35, 38, 41, 87, 91–92, 131; of converted spouses, 32, 105; of disease victims, 36–37, 43; of nonlocal Jews, 27, 35–36; as priority, 74; reliance on societies for, 74; reliance on synagogues for, 25;

graveyards. *See* burial grounds; cemeteries
Great Depression, 135, 136–37
Gutterman, Abraham, 146, 153, 230–31n24
Guzeit and Smith Funeral Chapel, New
York City, 152

Hart, Bernard, 59
headstones, 141, 163; security, 135–36, 139
Hebra Gemilut Hasadim (Society for
Dispensing Acts of Kindness), 48, 50,
52–54; disbanding of, 53, 56; legacy of,
55
Hebra Gemilut Hesed. *See* Hebrew Mutual
Benefit Society
Hebra Gemilut Hesed shel Emeth, 69
Hebra Gomle Hesed, 69
Hebrah Ahavath Achim (Society for
Brotherly Love), 69
Hebra Hased Va-Amet (Society for Acts of
True Kindness), 50, 55, 58–65; democracy
of, 60; founding of, 47, 57; organization
of, 60; women and, 66
Hebra Neshe Gomle Hesed, 69
Hebrew Free Burial Association, 195
Hebrew Free Burial Society, 5
Hebrew Mutual Benefit Society, 58, 69, 70–71
hebrot. *See* Jewish burial societies
heirs, designation of, 121–22
"Hello Landsman: A History of New
York's Jewish Mutual Aid Societies,
1880–1950" (YIVO Institute), 192
Henriques, Jacob Cohen, 19
Henry Clay Lodge 15, 132–33, 136–37
Henry Street, New York City, 100
Henry Street Synagogue, New York City, 103
Herberg, Will, 186
Hester Street, New York City, 146, 149
Hevrath Nashim Hased Vaamet (Ladies
Benevolent Society), 66–67
hevrot kadisha. *See* Jewish burial societies
Holche Zedek (Attendants of Justice), 107
Holy Society, 131, 140, 152
hospitals, death in, 148

immigrants, 49, 54, 82–83, 184, 186, 194–
95; demographics of, 128; founding of
burial societies, 71; German, 71; Jewish,
68, 74; marriage and, 116; organizations
established by, 82
immigration, 49, 55, 66; family, 128; mass,
10, 74
Independent Burial Association, 154–55
Independent Order Brith Abraham
(IOBA), 132, 134–35, 163; benefit
policies, 122, 125, 129; women members
of, 137–38
Independent Order Free Sons of Israel,
84, 106, 125; death endowment
amounts, 120, 122; founding of, 49,
72–73
Independent Order Free Sons of Judah,
124–25
Independent Order of Odd Fellows, 73, 84
industrial change, 8, 10, 111, 113, 126–27,
144, 145
intermarriage, 16, 17, 28–34, 206n8, 209n54
interment. *See* burial
interment rights, 16, 17, 130; denial of, 27;
punitive policies, 27, 34
IOBA. *See* Independent Order Brith
Abraham
Israel Community Center of Levittown,
New York, 167

Jefferson, Thomas, 64
Jeffersonianism, 59, 64
Jew in American Life, The (Dresner), 172–73
Jewish burial grounds, 36–38, 73, 77, 100;
community and, 27, 35; deterioration of,
97–98, 100–102; independent, 68–69,
71. *See also* cemeteries; *individual burial
grounds*
Jewish burial societies, 4, 8–9, 10,
49–51, 58–72, 131–34, 149–51;
autonomous, 70, 72; decline of, 151–54;
egalitarianism and, 46, 58; founding
of, 5, 47, 48–49, 68, 69–72;

ABOUT THE AUTHOR

Allan Amanik is Assistant Professor in the Judaic Studies Department at Brooklyn College, CUNY.